Y0-BPT-428

DOG-COLLAR DEMOCRACY

By the same author

Opinions, Publics and Pressure Groups (with Graeme C. Moodie)
Evidence and Explanation in Social Science

DOG-COLLAR DEMOCRACY

The Industrial Christian Fellowship,
1919–1929

Gerald Studdert-Kennedy

© Gerald Studdert-Kennedy 1982

All rights reserved. No part of this publication may be
reproduced or transmitted, in any form or by any means,
without permission

First published 1982 by
THE MACMILLAN PRESS LTD
London and Basingstoke
Companies and representatives
throughout the world

ISBN 0 333 29190 5

Typeset and printed in Great Britain by
Computacomp (UK) Ltd, Fort William
and printed in Hong Kong

To those who put up with it,
JUDITH, NICHOLAS AND MATTHEW

Contents

PART TWO

List of Plates

List of Cartoons

List of Tables

Acknowledgements

This study could not have been written without the assistance of a Nuffield Foundation Small Grant in 1977. It has been sustained since then by a succession of supplementary benefits from the Faculty of Commerce and Social Science at Birmingham. I am most grateful for this support, which has enabled me to take advantage of the generosity of a number of individuals. From the Industrial Christian Fellowship itself, still working from St Katherine Cree in the City of London, I have received most generous assistance. This is in no sense an official history of the ICF and has nothing to say about the organisation inherited in recent years by its Directors, the Rev. Nicholas Brown, and his successor the Rev. Hereward Cooke. It is written, too, from a point of view they do not share. I would be sorry after all they have done to help it along, if they found it tendentious rather than provocative. I thank also Miss K. E. Campbell, who has been organising the valuable material in the ICF Library. Mrs Lionel Hichens, CBE, JP, allowed me to borrow a substantial collection of cuttings, to read correspondence, copy photographs and draw on a vivid fund of recollections. I look back on visits to North Aston Hall with particular pleasure. I am grateful too for the hospitality of Sir John Barnes, whose personal recollections, though hardly extending as far back as those of Mrs Hichens, who was placed, as a small child, on the knee of her kinsman William Gladstone, gave me a lively impression of some of the church figures referred to here. I have used material he was kind enough to lend me, relating to his father's work as Trustee of the ICF.

I have spoken with many people who knew or heard my uncle, the Rev. G. A. Studdert Kennedy, Messenger of the ICF, most notably with my late father, the Rev. H. G. Studdert-Kennedy. Mr Fred Ambler, formerly Mayor of Pudsey, placed his recollections in a particularly interesting context, and made a number of inquiries on my behalf. My cousin, the Rev. Christopher Studdert Kennedy, put me on the right track at a number of points. He is not looking for an exhibition of family piety from me, and I hope he will share my belief that this account does something to place his father's extraordinary ministry in the complexities of its time, despite an evaluation which will be unacceptable at important points to many church people.

I am grateful to the Dean and Chapter of Durham Cathedral for allowing me to read the relevant sections from Bishop Henson's manuscript *Diaries*, to Professor O. Chadwick for making them physically available to me in Cambridge, and to the Librarian at Lambeth Palace for permission to consult material in Archbishop Davidson's Papers. The Rev. D. B. Dougall and Lt Col. G. C. E. Crew of the Royal Army Chaplains' Department at Bagshot have been most helpful. I have made special demands on a number of librarians, Father Arkell at the Community of the Resurrection, Mr D. Muspratt at the Working Men's College, and librarians at the Imperial War Museum, the TUC, Transport House, Birmingham City Library and Lichfield Public Library. Mr R. S. Swift of the Department of Geography at Birmingham has given me patient technical assistance with illustrations.

Dr Park Honan of the Department of English at Birmingham, and Professor Philip Brockbank, Director of the Shakespeare Institute and once my greatly valued supervisor at Cambridge, at a couple of points provided guidance on detail from which I derived a more general advantage. Old membership lists have sprung to life in the hands of Dr B. S. Benedikz, Sub-Librarian (Special Collections) at the University of Birmingham and Consultant Librarian to the Dean and Chapter at Lichfield. Dr Tony Fielding of the Faculty of Commerce gave advice on a modest statistical analysis.

Professor Rob Hinings, who has pursued the idea of organisation from church to local government, Dr Tony Wright of the Birmingham Extra-Mural Department, who has thrown light for me on the political thought of the period, and Denise Newton, a sociologist among theologians at Birmingham, criticised early drafts of the first chapters and gave me the confidence to proceed. I am grateful also for the fertile contradictions between the reports of three anonymous reviewers of that material. My colleague in the Political Science Department, Andrew Orridge, read a complete draft at a late stage, gave detailed attention to clumsy writing and suggested a drastic reorganisation which has greatly improved the final version.

I have exploited shamelessly the patience and scholarship of Dr Richard Garside and Dr Peter Cain of the Economic History Department at Birmingham. Their criticisms of sections of the study came in the most generous form, a succession of hints, reminders and suggestions, touching on many aspects of the social history of the period. It would not occur to them to embarrass me by advertising the extent of my indebtedness; I hope I will not embarrass them by what I have made of it.

W. G. S.-K.

Part One

1 Introduction

The Industrial Christian Fellowship was formed shortly after the end of the Great War. It still exists, though it can hardly be recognised as the organisation of the interwar years. Interpretations of the Church's mission in the world of industry have changed since then as part of an adjustment to institutional decline and the general process of secularisation, and subsequent developments have been expressed through other agencies. But if the ICF is an obscure organisation today, it was in its early years the vehicle for a very ambitious form of evangelism. It became controversial and well-known, attracting support from politicians in all three parties, from leading trade unionists and captains of industry, and from the intermediate world of industrial arbitration and social reform. Its crusades secured the attention of large numbers of ordinary people across the country, whose church connections were marginal or non-existent. It could field effective speakers, the most important of whom, the Rev. G. A. Studdert Kennedy, 'Woodbine Willie' as he came to be known during his period as an army chaplain in the war, had a national reputation which was enhanced over the last decade of his ministry, as the main speaker, the 'Messenger' for the organisation.

No study of this movement has so far been written. There are obvious reasons for this neglect. Documentary evidence is limited. Like many other church organisations, the ICF has shed the bulk of its records along the way, and a thorough study of the organisation as such is out of the question. From the point of view of the church historian one can see that it is in a sense marginal. It reflected developments initiated elsewhere, in its interdenominationalism, for instance, and in its association with the 1924 Birmingham Conference on Politics, Economics and Citizenship (COPEC), set up by William Temple, then Bishop of Manchester. Its attempts to carry a Christian message to the industrial masses may seem with hindsight to have been a gallant but fruitless stand against forces that were reconstructing politics 'on a virtually secular basis as a debate about economic redistribution by Conservatives and the new Labour

Party'.[1] Any consequences for the Anglican Church are difficult to identify. In the perspectives of political historians, the well-publicised activities with which it was associated at the time of the General Strike have appeared as merely symptomatic of a well-intentioned but inept concern. According to Baldwin's biographers, 'the story is not of detailed interest' and 'Baldwin was extremely irritated'.[2] Apart from a small number of interventions in the field of practical politics, such as a deputation on unemployment, received by Clynes on behalf of the Prime Minister in March 1924, the normal activities of the organisation were diffuse, verbal and propagandistic, and the consequences of such symbolic activity in a densely crowded political arena are impossible to measure. The claim that the ICF contributed significantly to a climate of public opinion, loosely identifiable as the 'MacBaldwinism' of the period, can only be tentatively made.

The ICF, nevertheless, was the most active and effectively organised group of Christians seeking to influence the political and industrial climate after the war, and there is ample evidence of the widespread attention it received. This provides the main justification for this study.

Formally, the *Industrial Christian Fellowship* was an amalgamation of the *Christian Social Union*, an organisation of socially concerned churchmen founded by a committee under the leadership of Henry Scott Holland in 1889,[3] and the *Navvy Mission Society*, an evangelical body founded in 1877, which maintained missioners on construction sites around the country. Changing patterns of employment had been affecting the latter for some years, but the ICF took over and developed its grass-roots organisation, modified and considerably developed its activist organisation. The CSU connection entailed a complex of affiliations which historians have not yet fully explored, and on which an account of the organisation might throw some light. The old cliché about the Church of England as the Tory Party at prayer, an association whose strength and gradual erosion over the last fifty years has been roughly measured by political scientists,[4] calls for some qualification. An analysis of the membership and support of the ICF brings into focus an association between elements in the Church of England and certain interests in Edwardian and post-war Liberalism. The connection was of long standing, but emerges in a new configuration of interests in the post-war setting. From the CSU, which was moribund well before 1920, the ICF inherited former members, many of them Liberals[5] with practical experience in the settlement movement and the promotion of reforming legislation.

Occasional references to the ICF in historical studies identify it too easily, however, as a post-war extension and adaptation of the old CSU. This is to ignore the traumatic implications of the war. The ICF coalition represented a fresh combination of interests and was affected by a number of new and urgent preoccupations, particularly in connection with the threat of radical political activity and the reconstruction of a national political economy. It brought together people with extensive experience in the management of labour before and during the war, an unbalanced representation from the political parties, and above all some leading nonconformists from the Labour movement. There were continuities with the CSU but, as Jones has shown in his distinguished study, the reformist vitality of the parent organisation had long since evolved into the uneventful respectability of a 'socialism for bishops', a rhetorical permeation of the Anglican establishment. The war, however, generated specific impulses which reactivated concern for a social gospel in oddly assorted groups, lay and clerical, and the most important of these were brought together in the new structure.

Any historical study of the relationship between specifically religious categories and other systems of values raises problems of definition and description. But here the loose structure of a voluntary organisation, comprising groups of activists and supporters that were not homogeneous in several important respects, compounds the obvious theoretical difficulties. How is one going to distinguish the 'religious' from the 'political' and in what sense will it be possible to claim that one of these categories is determining or influencing another? The hectic discussions provoked by Dr Edward Norman's Reith Lectures[6] showed very clearly how alternative general definitions of 'politics' and 'religion' place people in incompatible frames of reference and frustrate rational dialogue. Dr Norman's restrictive definition of the scope of Christian belief, for example, leads directly to his judgement on the political activities of the socially concerned churchmen who joined clerics like Bishop Charles Gore and Henry Scott Holland in the CSU. What Norman sees in this movement is not a rediscovery by the late Victorian Church of obligations incumbent on Christian believers, so much as an expression of class moralism and guilt, an essentially political, ameliorative assessment of social conditions, an early case, in fact, of politicisation.[7] Alternative definitions lead to contrasting conclusions, whilst leaving one with much the same sense of having been exposed to a polemic, in each case a fundamentally political one, which oversimplifies the nature of the relationships involved. Mayor's sharply contrasting claims for the positive influence of Christianity on the Labour movement can be set beside Norman's argument in this connection.[8]

The difficulties have been identified more carefully in the course of Robert Moore's detailed study of four Durham villages.

The apparently simple study of Methodism proved, in the event, to be much more difficult than we at first expected. The main reason for this was that it was difficult to separate out Methodism as a discrete social phenomenon. Methodism is not theology, nor an organisation, but a way of life, a code of ethics which are often unstated and only implicit in people's behaviour. This is particularly problematic when on the surface there are quite obvious characteristics of Methodism, like the familiar chapels and hymn singing in the valley. The problem is compounded by Methodism co-existing with social and economic philosophies which are also highly ethical, and known to have been penetrated by Non-conformist thought in their development.[9]

In other words, there are complex reciprocities and combinations between different types of value and interest to be considered, and these will not be uniform across the social structure. Moore is acknowledging that it is the 'particularity of the impact of religious systems upon social systems (and upon personality systems) which renders general assessments of the value of religion in either moral or functional terms impossible.'[10] But he implies that within the framework of an intensive field study by a sociologist or anthropologist it is possible to identify and distinguish different aspects of a specific situation and to discriminate one kind of influence upon collective choice from another.

However, an ephemeral voluntary organisation is not a community. The constraints on members are looser and the survival of the organisation and the pursuit of a limited number of broadly shared objectives can be maintained by mobilising more diverse values and perceptions. It is particularly striking that the ICF brought together, and by and large kept together, a heterogeneous coalition, and that the chemistry that compounded elements of religious belief, social theory, political economy and ethical commonplace operated unevenly across the organisation. Not only is it difficult to see the religious component as a discrete phenomenon, but it appears in very different forms from one group of activists and supporters to another. For some the problem of sustaining a religion was central. Geertz's definition neatly identifies the central preoccupation of the ICF Messenger, Studdert Kennedy.

> . . . a *religion* is:
> (1) a system of symbols which acts to (2) establish powerful, pervasive, and long-lasting moods and motivations in men by (3) formulating conceptions of a general order of existence and (4) clothing these conceptions with such an aura of factuality that (5) the moods and motivations seem uniquely realistic.[11]

Even in the Messenger's case, however, the religious beliefs are entangled with others, with which they have no necessary connection, whilst elsewhere in the organisation the same set of symbols and categories enters into other combinations, so that we can trace significant shifts in meaning. Thus the titular concept of Fellowship, along with other categories with a central position in new liberal discourse, such as Personality, Character and Community, emerges as an ambiguous abstraction, construed in a variety of ways, which it was perhaps necessary to proclaim but leave unexamined if the organisation was to hang together.

The structure of the book is dictated by these considerations. Chapter 2 and the first part of Chapter 3 describe the more important elements in the coalition and the broad terms in which they identified an acute social crisis in the post-war period. In a preliminary way, this introduces the main material and ideological interests and, hopefully without too much untidy allusion, indicates the variety of social links between the various groups of supporters. The bulk of Chapter 3, with Chapters 4 and 5, is concerned with the Rev. G. A. Studdert Kennedy, the 'Messenger' of the ICF, and with the sources on which he most heavily relied. There is no attempt at biographical completeness. He is in fact an unrewarding subject for biography, and his effectiveness as an orator may have derived largely from his total identification with his public performance and an unself-conscious expenditure of energy on his ministry. His was not by any means the only ICF voice, but it was without doubt the best known, the most popular and accessible. His books were widely read and his speeches were extensively reported. It is necessary, first of all, to account for his personal credibility as a source of interpretation and exhortation, by describing his wartime reputation and distinctive rhetorical talents. We can then, before turning to the activities of the ICF over the decade, examine the content of his message. Since he was a facile and intuitive adaptor of other people's ideas, it is not always possible to identify his sources precisely. The ideological perspective he propagated can, however, be described by identifying the themes he picked up and emphasised, and those he ignored, from the work of more considerable social theorists. An assortment of ideas from, among the clerics, William Temple and Charles Gore, but also from William Cunningham the conservative economic historian, and from lay authorities like the psychologist William McDougall, W. H. Mallock the right-wing apologist and, more indirectly, L. T. Hobhouse, to name the more obvious, was filtered through to many people in simplistic and sometimes garbled form in the writing and preaching of the ICF Messenger. The ideas he absorbed combine in a rather stable view of the world, in which we can distinguish a fervent religious commitment from a conservative social philosophy. His emphasis placed him to the right of the more radical liberals of the pre-war CSU, such as Gore and Scott Holland, whose admirers were often compelled to protect them from accusations of being 'socialistic',[12] and even further from the avowedly 'socialistic' parsons who are so consistently denigrated in the *Diaries* of the conservative Bishop Hensley Henson of Durham. It is a curious symptom of the inchoate state of the repertoire of arguments surrounding such notions as social reform, social gospel, socialism and social concern at the time, that Studdert Kennedy, who would certainly have been identified by Henson as one of Gore's men, an intellectually confused subversive, in fact adopted a political and social interpretation of the gospel rather close to that of the conservative Bishop of Durham.

Gore, who resigned the Bishopric of Oxford in 1919, to become a lecturer in theology at King's College, London, was perhaps the best known contributor to *Lux Mundi*, a volume of essays which had appeared, like the CSU, in 1889 and which was a seminal attempt to 'put the [Anglo-] Catholic faith into its right relation to modern intellectual and moral problems'.[13] A conservative in theology, his uncompromising interpretation of the social implications of the gospel[14] tended to alarm the conservative in politics. He was a leading figure in the earlier and more radical period of the CSU, and a powerful exponent at church conferences, on committees and in a substantial output of books and articles, of a fundamental reconstruction of the Church's function in society. He lent his name to the ICF in the last decade of his life, and participated in its more radical moments, in particular the ambiguous attempt by some ICF and allied churchmen to intervene during the General Strike of 1926, an initiative on which church historians have passed diametrically opposed judgements.[15] Studdert Kennedy greatly admired him, for reasons which will be discussed in Chapter 4, but did not draw the same practical and political conclusions from a common faith. Henson refers to 'Woodbine Willie' with contempt,[16] but he did not read the preacher's books and the judgement seems to have been based in part on a blanket condemnation of the broad drift in the Church with which, through the CSU/ICF and his personal links with Gore and Temple, he was identified, and in part on a dis-taste for his emotionalism and his intellectual limitations as a preacher.

Whatever the justice of such a response, the ICF *Messenger's* synthesis of guiding insights will have to be considered on its own terms, not, of course, in order to pass judgement on the truth or otherwise of the religious beliefs themselves, but in an attempt to recognise what Geertz identifies as a major methodological problem in writing scientifically about religion, by trying to ensure 'that the social and psychological implications of particular religious beliefs can emerge in a clear and neutral light'.[17]

Admiration for the ICF Messenger was by no means universal in the Church of England, and Chapter 6 attempts to identify general characteristics associated with a positive response to the ICF and its Messenger within the Church. An aggregate analysis of several groups of parsons, ICF supporters and others, it suggests that the conservative and élitist bias of the organisation's message is reflected in the social composition of its clerical support.

That completes Part One of the book, an account of the organisation's historical background, its structure and social composition and its ideology. Part Two is concerned with the activities, during this decade, of the organisation itself and with the public activities of its leading lay figures in areas of central concern to the organisation. Chapter 7 deals with the management of the ICF and its important external connections, but concentrates on the impressive Crusades and mass meetings of the decade. Chapter 8 is primarily concerned with the leading ICF laymen in relation to major incidents and trends in industrial relations in the post-war decade. The ICF was supported by people who were involved in a reconstruction of liberal social theory, whose constructive influence on the subsequent performance of both Labour and Conservative parties, Freeden has argued,[18] has been underrated. They placed a conservative gloss, however, on this perspective, an emphasis which reflects material, institutional and ideological interests with a stake in the organisation.

There seem to be good reasons for limiting this study to the first decade after the war. In several senses 1929 was a watershed. The full development of the economic crisis was about to take place, and the year also marked an important change in national politics. William Temple, a major influence on Studdert Kennedy, lost his political innocence by the end of the decade and began to develop the greater political realism of his later years.[19] By 1929, the year of Studdert Kennedy's death at the age of forty-six, the social gospel of the *Industrial Christian Fellowship*, in the form given it by its most articulate spokesmen, had served its turn. If it made a politically significant contribution to a public consciousness, it was during the first decade of its existence.

2 The Foundation of the Industrial Christian Fellowship

SOCIALISM AND SOCIAL CONCERN

On 22 February 1924, the *Church Times* published a letter from the Honourable and Reverend James Adderley:

> Sir,
>   The Dean of St Paul's tells the editor of the *New Leader* that, with exceptions, the Christian Socialists are a 'scurvy lot'. It would be interesting to know the names of the 'exceptions' in the Dean's mind. Would they include in the past such names as Maurice, Kingsley, Tom Hughes, Westcott, Scott Holland, Shuttleworth, Stubbs, Marson, Stanton and Dolling? In the present, Gore, Temple, Frere, Fry, Moore Ede, Headlam, Donaldson and Studdert Kennedy? I hope so. But then, who are the 'scurvy lot'?

Dean Inge could afford to leave this question open, for an astonishing variety of clergymen and laymen had found justification for describing themselves as Christian Socialists. The sharp edge of his disfavour was directed against those whose social radicalism led them into the 'radical mistake [of seeking] in the Gospel for legislation, instead of principles'.[1] Dr Norman has argued that Inge, with Henson and Bishop A. C. Headlam in a tiny minority within the leadership of the Church, was right to attack the tone of social criticism fashionable in the upper reaches of the hierarchy at the time, and also that in doing so he was in tune with the public mood, which was impatient with clerical interference.[2] Endorsements of specific legislative proposals in the name of the Gospels, and indeed the terms in which apparent evils in the contemporary social order were identified by concerned clerics, were frequently half-baked and ignorant. There was an unholy confusion about the social relevance of the Gospel. Of course, not all those who described themselves as Christian Socialists, in the past or the present, were necessarily addicted to proposing specific remedies. The label covers degrees of concern and indignation that could find expression in very general terms. The *Lux Mundi* principles on which the *Christian Social Union* was founded in 1889 by Gore and Scott Holland claimed 'for the Christian Law the *ultimate* authority to rule social questions' (italics added), called for *study* of how the moral truths and principles of Christianity might be applied to the social and economic difficulties of the present time, and for the presentation of Christ 'in practical life as the living Master and King, the enemy of wrong and selfishness, the power of righteousness and love'.[3] These principles could be attended to as a philosophy of life, a personal ideal that is the antithesis of Individualism, and from which social consequences will inevitably flow to the extent that the ideal is shared. This is how Bishop Westcott of Durham (d. 1901), the first President of the CSU, described by Binyon as Maurice's successor as the prophet of Christian Socialism, himself defined Socialism.[4] His own practical application of his ideals as mediator in the coal strike of 1892 went rather against his personal grain. At Westcott's normal level of philosophical generality, the ideal provides no clear bearings in the political sense that infuriated Inge. Many Christian Socialists, however, were prepared to move in that direction, on occasion with extravagant daring. In 1906 Bishop Gore told the Church Congress that the time had come to return to social conditions nearer to Christ's intention, 'if it may be without violence or revolution, but if not, then anyhow to return'.[5] Others, like Gertrude Tuckwell (Sir Charles Dilke's niece and daughter of the Rev. W. Tuckwell, a radical member of the CSU,[6] a Wykehamist and Fellow of New College) got involved effectively in promoting social legislation to improve conditions of work, in her case particularly for women. There were others still, like the Rev. William Cunningham, passed over for the Cambridge Chair of Economics in favour of Marshall in 1885, who regarded themselves as disciples of Maurice, but who moved in a different direction again, towards a thoroughly conservative, but not for that reason socially insensitive, view of political economy. In fairness to Inge, we might note that it did not occur to Adderley to include Cunningham in his list of Christian Socialists. Cunningham was certainly not a scurvy fellow from Inge's point of view, but then, in addition to being a 'Christian Socialist' in a Maurician tradition, he had vigorously attacked 'socialism' in its secular formulations.

Ross McKibbin has put forward the view that socialism was not in point of fact important in the Labour Party in this period.[7] But in the wake of his study labour historians have pointed out that the question of socialism at this time is thoroughly elusive, and that we get a distorted picture of the ideological flux of the period if with hindsight we impose the precise categories of theoretical discussion.[8]

Beliefs and values were fluid and variegated, and consequently difficult for contemporaries to hold in sharp focus. All sorts of people laid claim to the socialist label. MacDonald did so during his autocratic management of the first labour government, at a time when he was losing contact with the industrial wing of the movement. But the content of the Labour Socialism of such figures as MacDonald and Snowden was not consistent with the socialism of the ILP and the *Daily Herald*. In fact it was part of the same amalgam of moralism and nineteenth-century evolutionism as was represented in the Christian Socialist tradition. In both movements we encounter a similar ambivalence towards working-class militancy, on the one hand, and towards the institutions of capitalist society, on the other. At the same time there were commentators and theorists, whose arguments are hard to distinguish from those put forward under this banner, who no less energetically repudiated the socialist tag. Ideological developments and organisational loyalties did not neatly coincide.[9] Politicians, no less than parsons, could lose themselves, and others, in the woolliness of the available categories.[10] There were, nonetheless, substantial ideological differences, within which there were significantly different emphases, though these could be obscured by rhetorical invocations and by straightforward confusion. The present study is concerned with a part of this ill-defined spectrum.

Adderley's letter is a pertinent symptom of confusion on the part of many churchmen. He was himself a distinguished Christian Socialist, with a reputation for the practical implementation of his beliefs, like the Rev. Lewis Donaldson, leader of the march of Leicester unemployed in 1905, who was also a post-war member of the ICF, though a more restless one.[11] In 1889, the year of *Lux Mundi*, the seminal essays of Gore's 'holy party', Adderley worked for the dockers in the Great Dock Strike, and was warmly commended by Ben Tillett for doing so.[12] He also wrote prolifically for the cause and must be identified as a radical in the broad spectrum of Christian Socialism, a Headlamite who joined the CSU but admitted that he 'never felt very happy' in it.[13] The 'sacramental socialist' Steward Headlam, founder of the tiny Guild of St Matthew, which had preceded the CSU, made sardonic references to the respectable and 'distinguished gentlemen' of the early CSU.[14] The letter quoted here was not the first occasion on which Adderley had taken issue with Inge. In 1912 he had taken him up on the question of whether the pig makes the sty or the sty the pig, complaining of Inge's crude formulation of the problem of environment, and concluding that the 'gloomy Dean', as he was widely known, must spread joy and not gloom among his admirers, since he absolved them of any obligation to act on social conditions. This was in the *Church Socialist*, the journal of the *Church Socialist League*, a northern Labourist group founded in 1906, to which he belonged.[15]

Adderley continued with the *Industrial Christian Fellowship*, when it was formed at the end of the War by the amalgamation of the CSU and the *Navvy Mission Society*, and was an active member, writing for it, encouraging its spokesmen, appearing on its crusades and attending the biennial Council Meetings with great regularity from 1925. But writing at the end of the decade, D. A. Wagner describes the ICF as even more catholic than the CSU, and able to draw support from many quarters because in fact it proclaimed 'no fixed economic theories which might alarm the more diffident'.[16] A major reason for Adderley's support, despite his uneasiness about CSU limpness, was the contact with working people outside the Church, which the ICF acquired, in principle, through its incorporation of the Navvy Mission. For the sake of something so unique in the history of Christian Socialism, he was presumably prepared to swallow a good deal of academic moderation. However, his support for the ICF, and the inclusion of Studdert Kennedy in his list of great Christian Socialists is more remarkable than might appear at first sight.

Throughout the decade Studdert Kennedy was the 'Messenger' of the ICF. It had many other spokesmen, of course, but none of them could match his attractions on the platform. When he died in 1929, Adderley like many others felt that the ICF had lost its most expressive and powerful voice. But to describe him as a socialist, even, given the latitude the term has acquired, a Christian Socialist is to stretch things considerably further than one would think possible for a man with Adderley's record. In December 1924, Adderley concluded a series entitled 'The Man and his Message', in the ICF journal *The Torch*, with an appreciation of Studdert Kennedy. The series offers to trace the course of the Christian Social Movement from the days of Charles Kingsley, and the point is made that a number of important figures have been excluded for reasons of space, including Donaldson and William Temple, who had been a member of the Labour Party. It is an ambivalent piece. Giving Studdert Kennedy about a quarter of the space at his disposal, he celebrates in generous but uneasily general terms the remarkable eloquence of the preacher's invitation to the individual to stake his life on God and Christ. He concedes that 'his exact place in the history of the Christian Social Movement is difficult to name beyond what I have already suggested', his ability to convey 'the very elements of Christianity itself'. But as Messenger Studdert Kennedy offered the crowds more than this, and it is misleading to place him in this tradition. One is tempted, though it is unkind, because Adderley was by 1929 near retirement, to see a poetic justice in what happened when Adderley succeeded Studdert Kennedy as rector of St

Edmund the King, Lombard Street, a City living without normal parish duties. The congregation which had packed the church on Sundays when the rector rather than his curate was preaching, marshalled by a policeman at the door,[17] disappeared overnight. It was not to hear the flamboyant presentation of a fashionable clerical radicalism that people flocked to the heart of the City of London.

Adderley was not alone in assimilating Studdert Kennedy to the tradition Dean Inge found so disreputable. People less aware than he of the cross-currents in a thoroughly blurred theoretical arena could do so with some excuse. The ICF was, after all, the CSU in new guise, and 'Woodbine Willie', already a national figure because of his wartime reputation, had identified himself with it more or less from the time he stepped out of uniform. The myth of his social radicalism has persisted, partly for the interesting reason that it was not effectively disputed at the time, and partly because little of any consequence has been written on the ICF over this period, or about Studdert Kennedy's relationship with the organisation. Maurice Reckitt, it is true, wrote critically, though briefly, in 1932 of the gap between the ICF rhetoric and its conclusions,[18] but Wagner[19] gives the ICF four pages, based on the organisation's published material and, one would guess, talk with the Rev. P. T. R. Kirk, its capable Director, who was never in any doubt about how he wanted the organisation to be seen. This summary description is the basis for a number of subsequent references. Roger Lloyd, who joined the ICF Council in 1925, has nothing of substance to add to it.[20] W. Purcell's chapter on the decade, written some thirty years after Studdert Kennedy's death, at every turn reflects his recent discussions with Kirk. In any case, he makes no attempt at an historical analysis.[21]

The myth is perpetuated at a totally different level in Dr Norman's major and controversial survey, despite a brief but more realistic and differentiated account in one of his recent sources.[22] In the course of describing the increasingly articulate, and increasingly respectable, content of the criticisms of the social order being propounded by the CSU bishops, most clearly by the young William Temple, he observes that

The message got down to the popular preachers, too. G. A. Studdert Kennedy had first been drawn to a compassionate desire to improve conditions of life among the poor when he was Vicar of St Paul's Worcester—a working-class parish—just before the Great War. After his remarkable period as an Army Chaplain he became one of the great preachers of the post-war years, and a missioner with the Industrial Christian Fellowship. He too absorbed the familiar arguments. 'History', he wrote in 1919, 'is the tale of how the truth of Co-operation has fought the falsehood of strife and competition all down the ages.'[23]

It is certainly true that the preacher echoed many of the standard formulae of Christian social concern, but it is not the case that he provided a popular transcript of the familiar arguments on which Dr Norman has his eye. Co-operation, like other abstract and unimpeachable goods, was invoked on all sides. We shall see that Studdert Kennedy deployed these categories with a consistent emphasis which had significant political implications.

He did not of course pretend to theoretical rigour and thoroughness, and in fact his arguments are full of surface contradictions and evidence roughly treated, but the general orientation, expressed in ways that many thousands of people found memorable and exhilarating, articulated prejudices and aspirations held by those who attended to him and those who supported his ministry through the organisation. There were radicals like Adderley who admired him as a Christian witness but, perhaps because they lacked the resource of a critical theory, were not inclined to consider the implications of what he actually said. The centre of gravity of the organisation was not, however, provided by the more radical tradition, while there is a clear connection between the rhetoric of the preacher and attitudes held by other elements dominant in the movement.

FORMAL ANTECEDENTS AND THE NEW ICF COALITION

The CSU had run out of steam by 1910. Gore was already very restless with it by 1906, nudging socialists at Mirfield, the community of priests which had moved with him from Radley to Yorkshire in 1898, towards the northern *Church Socialist League*.[24] In 1908 he orchestrated a 'socialist field day' at the Lambeth Conference, round the theme of penitence for the guilt of the Victorian Church in its acquiesence in the social evils of industrial society, which crush the weak and deprive them of the possibility of spiritual life. This, Norman's study indicates, was both a standard and a thoroughly unhistorical form of self-indulgence among Christian Socialists. But, despite the climax at Lambeth, the CSU itself had to be reorganised two years later and soon after that Gore resigned. Early in 1920, the shell of the organisation amalgamated with the *Navvy Mission Society* to form the *Industrial Christian Fellowship*.

The ICF inherited a stock of books and pamphlets, and some members who maintained continuities, in particular with the CSU's interest in practical support for specific limited projects of social

reform. But the organisation that emerged in the post-war decade
was quite unlike what had existed previously, in terms of structure
and control, in terms of the interests represented in it and in terms of
its activities. Some existing resources were rapidly redirected, and
others were developed and used for fresh purposes.

The most significant organisational developments resulted from
the incorporation of the Navvy Mission. This merger, in addition,
introduced an important paternalistic and evangelical element into
the ICF. A detailed account of the Mission in its prime, well over by
the end of the War, would be out of place here. There is a brief but
vivid account in a chapter of Coleman's book on the navvies.[25] It was
founded in 1877 and run in its heyday by Mrs Elizabeth Garnett
(d. 1921), a formidable lady whose high-minded and patronising
concern for her rugged clientele could express itself in practically
effective ways. Her *Quarterly Letter to Navvies* was issued for thirty years.
In it, along with the diverting and often highly personal indictments
of wickedness and sin, there was news and information for navvies
on the tramp, from the different work sites.

The Society built up a staff of lay workers, or missioners, who
would generally be posted to a particular site for the duration of the
construction work. Employers frequently welcomed and supported
them as an encouragement to discipline and good habits. The
contradictions of paternalist welfare work first affected the Society in
the decade before the Great War, as railway work declined and the
navvy had to compete for employment with local labourers on local
authority work. Mrs Garnett protested on the navvy's behalf, but
with the result that her missioners found it harder to get access to the
sites.[26] The contradictions also emerged in connection with trade
union activity on the eve of the war, and in another form after the
war in the ICF. This last point will be picked up in a later chapter,
but here it is necessary to say something about the nature of the
missionary organisation of the Society, which survived the war and
was refashioned after it.

The missioners were very modestly remunerated and of limited
education. The ideal was a plain-speaking, fervent and energetic
man, who would exert himself on matters of individual welfare, and
miss no opening for evangelical activity with a group or a vulnerable
individual. Inevitably, he would harp on the virtues that might
promote a decent survival in a demoralising and frequently
dangerous occupation—abstinence, continence, honesty and thrift—
the virtues also of an industrious and effective work force. Moral
issues presented themselves to him in terms of individual successes
and failures, conversions and lapses. The social relations which
determined the lives of his labourers were outside his frame of
reference, or at least he would find it difficult to interpret a challenge

to them. Depending on the circumstances, he would be liable to see a challenge to management as a violation of the values he was engaged to represent. There is evidence that some missioners were not inclined to back away from the implications of such a situation. Thus Brother Taylor reports to his struggling union from the strike at the Gladstone Docks in Liverpool in 1913:

> I noticed that Mr Avery, the local representative of the Navvy Mission, was very busy among it all, and I am able to state without fear of contradiction that Avery came out from the dock that morning and told the men outside that 26 men had gone in. As a matter of fact we were able to prove that in spite of all the forces at work against us, not more than 7 had gone in. After doing his best to encourage the men to throw up the sponge, he (Avery), in the expectation that his advice would be taken, and that all the strikers would go in that day, then hurried away and spread the report abroad that Gladstone Dock strike was settled, that the men had been promised that their demands would be granted, that half the men had gone in by breakfast time and the remainder had gone in at dinner time; he advised all hands who had cleared away from Gladstone Docks to return at once, and actually assisted men get their back time and cards, and brought them or sent them back to the Gladstone Docks on the Monday. As proof of this I am in possession of a signed statement made by one of the men whom Avery induced to return to the dock ... The black-guard, the Navvy Missioner ... acted disgracefully towards us, and it is upon these people that the blame lies.[27]

Whether or not Taylor is strictly accurate in his frustration, he is clearly identifying an opponent of aggressive trade union activity.

The missioner David Smith of Birmingham, on the other hand, is reported to have responded with far more discretion to a strike over recognition against the Master Builders Association in Birmingham. That strike, too, was a failure, but J. W. Gardner ('The Old Man'), wrote in the Annual Report of the Union for 1913–14 that:

> There is one thing I must do—I must give credit where such is due. Therefore I must thank Mr D. Smith, the Navvy Mission man, for the noble service he rendered to the movement in looking up distress cases, and relieving them with the funds collected. It was a work of great trial and he did it well, and in so doing relieved the committee of great responsibilities.

Both Avery and Smith continued to work for the ICF after the war, though Avery does not seem to have taken particularly well to the

new administration. In October 1920, he asked for an increase in
salary, on the grounds that he was not receiving a living wage, and
resorted to a private go-slow when the Finance Committee declined
to deal with individual cases. He made his point, in the end. In
November 1925, supported by a letter from the Bishop of Liverpool,
he finally secured a rise to £3-10-0 a week, 'provided that he was
willing to fall into line with the other rules and regulations of the
Fellowship regarding reading, and to take more trouble with his
weekly reports'. Smith, along with others, also pressed for more
money, but without being tempted into the working man's sin of
'ca'canny', as Avery's classical form of industrial action was
identified in the idiom of the day.

These allusions crop up in a partial and fragmentary record, and
there is no way of knowing whether one man was more
representative than the other. But the strike incidents do illustrate at
the level of prosaic industrial conflict an aspect of the dilemma of
Christian social involvement over which some of the divines had
wrestled. Smith, 'Navvy' Smith as he was known in Birmingham,
had more tact than Avery, but neither then nor later could he
conceive of the working man's problems in terms of militant
collective action. The grass-roots activists acquired by the ICF were
not going to stir anyone's interests in that direction. On the contrary,
the patrician and middle-class officers of the Navvy Mission might
perhaps protest and expostulate with their peers, but the missioners'
activities were conditioned by a deeply rooted acquiescence in the
ordained configuration of society. They cannot in fact have been
challenged very often. The navvies were extraordinarily difficult to
unionise, and it was inevitable that their own union leadership
should have been on the conservative side.

However, they mobilised enthusiastically when it came to the war.
The Union's General Secretary, John Ward, 'The Navvy's MP', raised
a Battalion for pioneer work at the front. 'Navvy' Smith was reported
to have recruited upwards of a thousand navvies, and was put in
uniform and attached as recruiting officer to the 30th Battalion of the
Gloucestershire Regiment. He had hopes of following them to
France as their 'Chaplain'.[28] A number of the missioners did follow.
Six out of thirty-four, with Avery among them, were at the front in
1918. They were to receive glowing commendations for their
contributions to discipline and morale from commanding officers,
and from Major General Sir G. K. Scott-Moncrieff, Director of
Fortifications and Works at the War Office from 1911–18.[29] Scott-
Moncrieff died in 1924, but was on the Council of the ICF and
attended meetings for the first year of its existence.

John Ward was to command a Pioneer Battalion in Siberia. The
Hull Times of 16 October 1920 published an article by him on 'The

compensations of labour: contentment and peace of mind'. Mrs Garnett would have approved, as she would have approved of the more elevated work ethic expounded by Studdert Kennedy. We have no means of telling what Brother Taylor or 'The Old Man' would have made of it.

Some officers of the *Navvy Mission Society* moved into the ICF and gravitated to routine but important duties with which they were familiar. They were particularly important on the Candidates Committee which selected missioners. The records on individual candidates show that they appreciated the new element in the missioner's role, in a less restricted relationship with workers and a new industrial battlefield. 'Large experience of the Labour movement', 'interested in Trade Union movement and Labour Party but places spiritual side first of all', 'able to reply to hecklers and answer questions', 'left socialist party on account of materialism', 'good organiser'—all identified particularly desirable qualities. But they were also looking for the familiar evangelical outlook, for the man of 'superior education', but preferably not superior enough to tempt him to try for the Ministry, and for appropriate experience. This they encountered most frequently in ex-officers of the Church Army, though in one case in the work of a well-educated candidate on 'confidential and hazardous duties for the Home Office in Dublin'. H. P. Pease, Unionist MP for Darlington, President of the Church Army from 1917, created Lord Daryngton in 1923, joined the ICF Executive in that year. He was also an important layman on other grounds, for twenty-five years either Chairman or Vice-Chairman of the House of Laity.

Given the criteria of selection, the committee was clearly hard put to field an impressive team, and was constantly asking for more money to attract better material. It would be wrong to represent the permanent force of grass-roots missioners—ex-sergeant majors and store-room clerks, electrical engineers, the occasional factory worker and labourer, and a number of earnest men of unspecified skills with the war behind them and uncertain prospects—as a highly disciplined and effective one. But it was the old hands like Smith who trained the probationers, and there were groups of missioners, certainly in Birmingham, Rugby and Manchester, and apparently in Liverpool, that had local reputations. The more effective among them moved across the country on the massive crusades of the decade, bearing witness to the Church's attempt to repudiate and transcend irrelevant differences of class.

Other recruits to the ICF Executive and Council from the Navvy Mission were less in tune with the new organisation and did not get involved in committee work. A number of them left shortly after the war. With the exception of the Hon. Gertrude Kinnaird, they were all engineers in the tradition of works management established by the great contractors Brassey and Peto, concerned with the welfare of their men and sending evangelists among them. Gertrude Kinnaird's strongly evangelical father, the 11th Baron Arthur Fitzgerald, was Honorary Colonel of the Tay Division RE, and connected with the Submarine Miners from 1893. The others were all distinguished members of the Institute of Chartered Engineers. Sir Whately Eliot (d. 1927) was associated particularly with dock and harbour works, and had won the George Stephenson medal and the Trevithick Premium. He had been on the Navvy Mission Council. Sir Cyril Kirkpatrick (d. 1957) had done important work on bridges, docks and water supply. Many years later he was responsible with others for constructing thirty-three concrete caissons for the Second World War Mulberry Harbours. W. Terrey became General Manager of the Sheffield Corporation and was concerned particularly with reservoir construction. Round the turn of the century he urged the Council to make a considerable investment in the welfare of the men and their families at the Langsett works, including a hospital, a resident medical officer, a Mission Room and a library. In 1901 he mediated in a pay dispute, and pressed a claim by plumbers employed by the Water Department. In the event the Corporation paid the increase to their own men, bringing the wage up to 9½d per hour, a decision for which the Corporation was roundly abused by the employers. The privately employed men stayed out.[30] Sir John Dewrance (d. 1937), the son of a railway pioneer, was a naval engineer and winner of the Watt Medal and Trevithick Premium. He was a Director of Babcock and Wilcox from 1899–1937.

All these engineers were typical of the enlightened employers who had supported the old society. They felt an obligation to promote welfare and godliness on particular sites for which they were responsible, an emphasis which changed under the ICF, though there were still some missioners on the sites. Dewrance's resignation from the ICF Council in 1921 is, however, of particular significance. In 1915, Babcock and Wilcox undertook the erection of two shell factories at Renfrew[31] and Dewrance was familiar with the wartime developments in management and administration in this area. Others in a similar position emerged from the war with marked corporatist leanings, and several of these were actively associated with the ICF. But Dewrance was heavily involved in the development of the Kent Coalfields, a speculative and competitive area notable for rough business practices.[32] He represented interests that were desperately anxious to fend off nationalisation, and as Chairman of Kent Coal Concessions, he made the classic case for individualistic *laissez-faire* to the Sankey Commission.

Pioneer work is the very opposite of a mature industry. It is of an exploratory and intensely speculative character. Its success, in the present state of development of the coal industry, wholly and fundamentally depends on the special knowledge and courage of the adventurers, their readiness to risk always, and frequently to lose capital and face vicissitudes, often in the face of discouragement and scepticism from experts in the industry.[33]

The ICF ran a strong line on the greed and social irresponsibility of the coal-owners. Dewrance became the post-war President of the Engineering Employers Federation, a reactionary force in industrial relations.[34]

The Navvy Mission people constituted the only formally distinguishable group in the new ICF coalition. But the new Council was a substantial body, running up to three hundred members under the Constitution, four-fifths of them being members of the Church of England. Each Diocese or Bishop could elect two members, and the Branch Secretaries could elect two from each Diocese, but the bulk of the membership was appointed through co-optation, in which the full-time Director was particularly influential, operating through the powerful Executive. The Executive included the officers, twenty members elected by Council, four appointed by the 'Social and Industrial Committee' of the Church Assembly, and another ten co-opted by the group already constituted. Again, four-fifths of this body had to be members of the Church of England. For the purposes of this study, the members of Council and Executive can be sorted into a number of related and frequently overlapping groups. Not all of them played a particularly active or significant role in the ICF. The Rev. P. T. R. Kirk, who was a vigorous Director, brought a number of potential critics inside the organisation and tried to persuade as wide a spread of interests as possible that they had a stake in it. We will find some of them attempting to influence policy and attacking performance, but without much success. At this point it is only necessary to identify the most important groups of individuals. Others will emerge in due course in different connections, but the significant groups seem to be: a collection of industrialists and industrial lawyers; an element that can be identified at this point simply as Asquithian, people associated with the non-coalition and anti-Lloyd George fraction of the Liberal Party; some professional reformers connected with Gertrude Tuckwell, who has been referred to already; a group from the Trade Unions and the Labour Party; and the parsons. These divisions cut across old CSU membership, which does not define a distinctive group, and this for a reason that dominates every aspect of the organisation throughout the period, namely the war itself. Pre-war affiliations are quite insignificant beside the diverse impact of the war on these different groups.

For the most part, the ICF Executive and Council came from a stratum of society a degree below the layer of eminence and influence with which the political historian is normally concerned. Michael Bentley's study distills a shifting climate of opinion from an analysis of a compact, intensely interactive élite.[35] It might be crudely distinguished as the intelligentsia of the political dinner parties of the Capital. Several of the characters in the present study have noticeable walk-on parts in that drama. They step in from the wings, representatives of diffuse, attentive, somewhat informed networks in the outside world. As far as Bentley is concerned, the action is where his leading characters congregate and interact. But this is not a hermetically sealed world, and we are concerned here with the leakage and dispersion, so to speak, of some of the ideological processes he identifies, through the medium of intervening figures, the stars of conferences and rotary club luncheons, shareholders' meetings, Brotherhood gatherings and crusades. The threads of such an analysis disperse into a complex network in which causes and effects are not to be clearly distinguished. But we have to assume, nevertheless, that there are processes of determining significance to be identified here too. Some of the ICF people, for example Donald Maclean, MP, Lionel Hichens, Director of Cammell Laird, and C. G. Ammon, C. W. Bowerman, F. Hughes, H. H. Elvin, E. L. Poulton and F. Hodges from the trade unions, filled positions in institutions and organisations that one way or another affected the behaviour of large numbers of people.

For most of these people, their own investment of time in the ICF was relatively marginal. It was one of a number of organisations they supported and on occasion spoke for. But even if some of them actually did little beyond lending a name to add lustre to the annual report, they risked identification with an organisation that was very active and of considerable interest to the press. They were therefore individually representative of particular interests and sections of opinion and collectively representative of immensely confused processes that were taking place at other levels and in other areas of the society. Some of these interests, in particular the movements behind increasing rationalisation in industry and the extension of the welfare systems, to which a number of ICF people made significant contributions, have had important developments.

Before distinguishing the different groups, it would be as well to make a general point about the churchmanship and religious commitment of those concerned. All of them drew on religious sanctions both to sustain a general social philosophy and to justify specific applications of that social philosophy in management, law, trade union activity and the administration of welfare. But in each case, inevitably, there were other operative criteria of a complex nature. To put matters crudely, the religious sanctions are intelligible as elements in an ideology, for a number of reasons which will be explored in the body of this study. These have to do with the substantive content of the beliefs concerned, the inflections given them by people in different groups, and the various material and institutional interests at stake. But at no point does the evidence suggest that the structure of religious beliefs is factitious or applied in a manipulative sense. On the contrary, we are concerned with true believers, within the organisation itself, as well as with specific beliefs and attitudes which had a strong life outside the organisation among people who lacked any but the crudest framework of theological ideas.

The remainder of this chapter identifies the other main groups and sketches in their more relevant characteristics. It is concerned primarily with the lay members of the ICF Executive and Council, as leading figures in the society the churchmen sought to influence, but it concludes with a brief account of the parsons, who are given a more systematic treatment in Chapter 6. Since the intention here is simply to set the scene within the organisation, we can proceed in each case by identifying central figures in some detail and associates and satellites more briefly.

Lionel Hichens, Chairman of Cammell Laird since 1910, was the most many-sided and active of the group of businessmen. He was one of the three ICF Trustees throughout the period. He had presided over the recovery of his firm in the pre-war years, and in 1915 was sent by Lloyd George, the Minister of Munitions, to reorganise the Canadian output. His mission was a diplomatic and managerial success. The new Imperial Munitions Board, which was designed by Hichens and replaced the Shell Committee, was a significant achievement of the Lloyd George administration, subsequently spending £250 million in the course of the war. His approach to the job illustrates a consistently pragmatic concern with rational management. Inclined, as a matter of principle, to design an evolutionary development of the organisational structure, which would avoid discontinuities and their uncertain consequences, he was forced by a bottleneck in supply and by the prohibitive costs of delay to negotiate a drastic rationalisation, which should, as he reported to the Ministry, have taken place four or five months earlier. His brief had been to establish an 'essentially non-military and non-political organisation', and he achieved this by decentralising the executive into five departments, which could administer production in the light of rational criteria relating to procurement, cost and quality.[36]

There had been accusations of corruption against the Chairman of the Shell Committee, who, with Colonel David Carnegie, constituted its overcentralised Executive. The accusations were disposed of, Hichens noting that they came usually from unsuccessful applicants for contracts, and the new structure greatly reduced the possibility of political pressure. Carnegie was to continue as head of the new Technical Department. He had been in the Westminister branch of the CSU before the war, and reappears after it on the ICF Council, publishing a somewhat hysterical echo of Hichens' line on industrial relations[37] and contesting Canterbury as a Liberal in 1924, 1927 and 1929. There were a number of clerics in his family.

Hichens emerges from the account of these negotiations as a clear-headed exponent of managerial rationality, identifying objectives, sorting out priorities in the light of a realistic appraisal of constraints, and engineering compliance with a pragmatic solution. This is how he emerges with consistency throughout the decade, and it is worth looking at the roots of this capacity for controlled enthusiasm in his earlier experience. Something is accounted for by the fact that he was educated at Winchester and went on to New College in 1893. He has absorbed the values of the Victorian professional class in a distinctive variant, which emphasised the self-effacing competence, attention to detail and sense of duty characteristic of those imperial administrators, in particular, whose careers achieved solid distinction rather than outstanding success.[38] In 1889 he enlisted in a cyclist section organised by the Inns of Court for South Africa, where he distinguished himself under the command of the Canadian Colonel Sam Hughes, subsequently as it happens organiser of the Canadian Shell Committee, and ended up as a member of Milner's *kindergarten*, with an appointment as Town Treasurer of Johannesburg, a post which was not, of course, on Milner's own staff. Again, he served with great distinction, and the brief memorial which was printed after his death notes his characteristic refusal, in 1907, 'to accept the financial compensation offered by the Colonial Office for the termination of his official duties'.[39]

Milner's band of young men, most of them Oxford graduates, was then and later a self-consciously cohesive group. Hichens was one of the elect, whose membership was recognised by all the others.[40] He maintained close contact with them and joined in the activities that centred on the *Round Table*, when the others returned from South Africa after the campaign for South African unification.[41] As a group they were to 'exert an extraordinary influence on British politics, all bearing the imprint of the master'.[42] Hichens certainly acknowledged the imprint on himself, but there are reasons for not associating him automatically with the hard core of the group. He defied the group line briefly at one point in South Africa, and though, with Lionel Curtis, he drafted material for the *Round Table* scheme for devolution within the Imperial system, he was always doubtful about the practicability of 'home rule all round', siding with Amery in opposition to Brand and Oliver.[43] In this connection his links with the tendency within the Liberal Party represented by C. F. G. Masterman are important. Masterman, himself the more readable of Frederick Denison Maurice's biographers, married one of the daughters of General Sir Neville Lyttleton, Kitchener's successor in South Africa. Herbert Gladstone was her cousin. She had an acute interest in the political personalities of the day and was to write an important biography of her husband.[44] Her sister Hermione married Lionel Hichens. It is no less important that Hichens was an ironmaster with a special stake in international trade. His views on the costs of labour and the control of international trade, for instance, were influenced by an appreciation of short-run, as well as more general theoretical considerations and he did not preach a Milnerite line on tariff reform or inflation. However, the imprint of Milner was profoundly important in a number of respects that have a bearing on his lengthy identification with the ICF.

In his frequent public pronouncements he only occasionally took up the Milnerite theme of Empire, but that again reflects the emphasis of his concerns as an industrialist. South Africa had not been his only imperial experience. Before putting the finances of Johannesburg in order, he had spent nine months in the Ministry of Finance in Cairo under Cromer, and in 1907 he went on the Royal Commission on Decentralisation to India, under the chairmanship of Charles Hobhouse. The final report, which he took a great part in writing, was highly critical of the Indian Civil Service, and this reflects the conflict between the Imperial Government and the ICS, on the one hand, and the new Radical Government at Westminster, on the other.[45] Hichens himself saw the issues very much in terms of competence and rational structure. What he does develop as a publicist is the domestic corollary to the Imperial theme, summed up by Milner in his notion of a 'nobler socialism':

> There is a nobler socialism [than the socialism of class struggle] which so far from springing from 'envy, hatred, and all uncharitableness' is born of genuine sympathy and a lofty and wise conception of what is meant by national life. It realises the fact that we are not merely so many millions of individuals, each struggling for himself, with the State to act as policeman, but literally one body-politic, that the different classes and sections of the community are members of that body, and that when one member suffers all the members suffer. From this point of view the attempt to raise the well-being and efficiency of the more

backward of our people—for this is what it all comes to—is not philanthropy; it is business.[46]

Semmel makes the point that 'Milner's "nobler socialism" was in conception little different from the "collectivism" of the Fabians who considered the South African proconsul most worthy of their praise'. And as the Fabians demonstrated clearly enough, a political interpretation of such a collectivist vision entailed judgements about the means available to achieve it. Milner was unambiguous about them. There is, first of all, the problem of an ignorant democracy; secondly, a meaningless partisan struggle between ins and outs; thirdly, an executive structure in which quality is swamped by numbers; and, finally, a tradition of irrational and unscientific decision-making.[47] These judgements were shared and acted on by Hichens, though he expressed them without Milner's truculence, as one would expect from a man who had never himself experienced anything corresponding to the frustrations of the 'political Ishmaelite', as the master once styled himself.

The experience of the war did to a great extent transform these constraints, and Hichens emerged from the war deeply impressed by the potentialities of collective action, when there is a shared goal to pursue, and where this motive power is rationally directed. As an active Chairman of the Central Council of the Association of Controlled Firms, he had detailed and extensive experience of wartime planning and labour relations,[48] but unlike many fellow managers in engineering and heavy industry, was not inclined to take an hysterical view of the gravity of the threat of labour conflict. He was an optimist who believed that time was on his side, as processes of technological development generated demands for rationalisation in the light of obvious collective goals. The key elements in his perspective are set out in his Watt Anniversary Lecture of 1918.[49] We find him emphasising the theme of organised association, and the increasingly complete, but freely entered, subordination of the individual to the community. Within this process we are in a system based on a rational appreciation of economics, and this imposes certain logically necessary and limiting requirements, relating to the distribution of profits, the State's control over the reward of labour, and the scope of the political element. We cannot, in reason, pursue attractive chimeras, such as the democratisation of industry. But we are, on the other hand, committed to a scientific exploration of production possibilities, through labour relations, new machinery, organisation, the avoidance of waste, and an undogmatic and utilitarian approach to the question of economies of scale. It is an argument that somehow misses the grand touch one finds in Milner. Indeed it has a

1 Lionel Hichens (*Leeds Mercury*)

disconcertingly deflating quality to it. The large theme of the organic society slips without warning into a detailed discussion of tax measures and depreciation allowances.

Milner's forces were well represented in the Lloyd George Government at the end of 1916. But from that year, as Scally points out, there took place a remarkable convergence of views both inside and outside the government offices.[50] It included, at one level, 'the longtime proponents of massive state intervention, such as the Milnerites, the Fabians, and the Lloyd George reformers on the one hand, and on the other patriotic hardliners of all political descriptions, including a growing percentage of the trades union movement and the Liberal Party'. The war, and more specifically the success of Lloyd George's Ministry of Munitions, had gone a long way towards the realisation of 'the "National Reconstruction" of the coalition plan, of the Fabian's "National Minimum" and the "Organisation of the Labour Market" spelled out by Masterman and Beveridge to the Chancellor in 1909', and the emerging broad perspective in national management looked to the efficacy of state interference, operated by a bureaucracy of dedicated and politically independent experts. The obverse of this was a tacit contempt for democratic institutions. At another level the perspective included, or might be made to include, a diffuse popular sentiment, an elusive element which many had assumed to exist and some (Chamberlain, Rosebery, Milner, the Fabians and Lloyd George) had sought to enlist. Haldane identified it as the 'Centre', and Beatrice Webb in terms of the 'non-political voter ... the moderate politician; the capitalist or proletarian man who desires little social change and the Empire maintained'. Beveridge believed it could be reached to provide popular approval for government controls.[51] Thus this new wartime consensus housed a disparate collection of interests. Nearly all of them were later well represented in the ICF, which means that the political content of the consensus remains a point of reference when introducing groups other than the businessmen.

Other important figures from business, who participated in this general drift, though without any direct connection with Milner, also identified with the ICF. Two of them, Sir Benjamin Sands Johnson and Sir Robert Lowden Connell, worked in Liverpool and may well have been introduced to the ICF by Hichens. Both were leading Liberals and contested parliamentary seats. Johnson had been Alderman and Mayor of Bootle. He ran a large firm of dyers and cleaners, and was called on to become Chairman of the Directing Board of the No. 2 National Filling and Amatol Factories, and Director General of the Army Clothing Department, in succession to Lord Rothermere, in December 1917, and was Director General of National Factories in 1919. He had been a stolid but energetic party organiser of some importance before the war, as Chairman of the North West Liberal Federation.[52] Connell was a big shipowner. In 1917 he became Chairman of the War Office Contracts Committee, and Deputy Controller of Army Salvage later that year. Finally, passing over a number of businessmen who were not themselves part of Lloyd George's businessman's administration, Owen Hugh Smith ran the office responsible for Limitation of Profits, one of five divisions managed by Beveridge under Lloyd George in 1915, and was responsible for Controlled Establishments in the following year, a post that kept him in regular contact with Hichens.

The group of lawyers should be extended to include a number of people who had exercised judicial functions on Board of Trade courts of referees and other tribunals. For example, Sir Charles Bright, FRSE and MICE, who was involved in radio telegraphy and the air industry, served as a Board of Trade arbitrator. There were others with legal training, like Holford Knight, an early supporter of the movement to open the Bar to women, who are more important for their political activities in a narrower sense. One or two, like E. C. P. Lascelles, figure both as lawyers and among the reformers. Lascelles was called to the Bar in 1911, and was Chairman of Trade Board and other tribunals, a deputy umpire under unemployment insurance Acts and a member of the Royal Commission on unemployment insurance. He also produced a number of publications in the course of the twenties in collaboration with others associated with Toynbee Hall. But the most significant figures among the lawyers were Sir Henry Slesser and Sir Lynden Macassey, both of whom did a great deal of work under the Munitions Acts.

Slesser's reputation is in one sense distracting. He was a leading Anglo-Catholic and a medievalist with it, and joined the Labour Party, which he regarded simply as 'a vast federation of trade unionists and co-operators with but a small proportion of avowed socialists added thereto', on his own terms. His campaign for Leeds Central in 1922 was run 'very much on religious lines, appealing to the early fathers and St Thomas of Aquin for support of our condemnation of plutocracy'.[53] He turned to Gore for spiritual advice, contributed to *The Return of Christendom* (1922, with a Preface by Gore), and joined the *League of the Kingdom of God*, under the Rev. P. E. T. Widdrington and the Rev. Paul Stacy, when that group left the *Church Socialist League* in 1923.

... we came to see that our objective was not the promotion of Socialism, but the advent of the Will of God as expressed in His Kingdom on Earth. A society pledged to forward this purpose, sacramental in doctrine, composed solely of communicants, seemed far nearer to our desires than one pledged to Socialism, in

part supported by modernists and persons only Sub-Christian in
belief.[54]

The move was in line with Gore's tentative design for a Church with
fewer but better Christians. But Slesser's identification with it also
indicates a degree of insulation between his life as a churchman and
his life as a public figure. Certainly the ICF offered very little scope
for any leavening penetration by members of the new League.
Slesser's presence in the ICF as a distinguished lawyer with an
important position inside the Labour Party carried more weight.

His role inside the Party was a thoroughly professional one. He was
standing Counsel to the Party from 1912, and represented Poplar and
Bethnal Green in their disputes with the Ministry of Health. In 1921
there appeared his *The Law in Relation to Trade Unions* and three years
later *Industrial Law*, written in conjunction with A. Henderson Jr, son
of the politician and a former pupil who had joined him in
chambers. Arthur Henderson himself, a regular speaker on ICF
platforms, was a hero and a friend of long standing, and Slesser's
comments on him locate the lawyer in the Party of the period.

> Of all the many public men I have known, I have no hesitation in
> saying that Henderson was one of the noblest. His sacrifices of
> place in order to support MacDonald, whom he believed to be
> better equipped for leadership, is almost without parallel in
> political abnegation. His character was essentially English. He had
> a strong dislike of flummery, but also was possessed of deep
> religious convictions.[55]

Slesser came into conflict with MacDonald on a number of occasions.

Macassey's Anglican connections were altogether more subdued,
and more pastoral than theological. He had a brother who worked in
poor parishes in the Diocese of London for a quarter of a century. He
himself was in practice as a barrister in the Middle Temple in 1899,
King's Counsel in 1912. The war brought him into prominence as a
labour lawyer through his direct involvement in the major disputes
on the Clyde in 1916, where he was sent by Lloyd George, together
with Lord Balfour of Burleigh, to enquire into the Fairfield strike in
October of 1915. He is presented in Gallacher's account as a
contemptible mouthpiece of the forces of oppression.

> How these fellows kept themselves afloat on the tumultuous sea of
> war was a wonder to all mankind. Eliza never jumped the ice-floes
> with anything like the agility with which they jumped from one
> Commission to another.[56]

But he served Lloyd George well on that occasion[57] and later in the course of introducing dilution, the substitution of unskilled labour for skilled, on the Clyde. Wrigley writes that

> On the Tyne dilution was introduced with little disturbance, but on the Clyde the commissioners (Lynden Macassey, Sir Thomas Munro and Isaac Mitchell) had a stormy time. But the fact that Lynden Macassey and his colleagues followed a slow and delicate procedure (slower than the Government initially intended) without doubt lessened the resulting unrest.[58]

Macassey was able to persuade the men that the scheme of dilution was not intended to reduce the employers' cost of output, but to increase output, and he set up a procedure for immediate conciliation. His scheme progressed because David Kirkwood, the shop steward from Parkhead, was induced to accept negotiation on a factory-by-factory basis, a breach of the Clyde Workers' Committee position of no dealings with the Commissioners. After Kirkwood's concession, which naturally enraged Gallacher, 'the whole front started cracking up'.[59] We will be returning in due course to Macassey's involvement in these events. He was from 1914–19 Director of Shipyard Labour, and a member of the War Cabinet committees on labour, 1917–18, and women in industry, 1918–19.

Slesser and Macassey represent a perspective that was both philosophically clear and practically elaborated in law and precedent. Naturally enough, both were intransigent opponents of any kind of direct action. 'Perhaps the greatest menace to ordered constitutional government is the Labour Party's acceptance of the method of direct action for enforcement of its policy upon an unconforming minority',[60] wrote Macassey in 1922, and Slesser agreed with him, making the point in another context in his autobiography.

> I attribute the campaign of disorder then waged by women to obtain the franchise (their repudiation of lawful methods was the strongest and perhaps the only reason why they should not have been accorded the vote) to the same incipient distrust of the use of the reason and consequent sympathy with disorder which I have mentioned.[61]

Law is the embodiment of political reason and there is no justifiable appeal outside it.

This presupposes two essential attributes of law, which it is one function of the legal profession to advance and protect. One is the technical attribute of internal coherence, practical viability because of the absence of avoidable contradictions. This professional criterion brought the industrial lawyers quite regularly into conflict with the politicians, both in parliament and in the unions, who were by definition on these occasions instruments of unreason, forcing irrelevant and destructive preferences on to justiciable issues. Lord Askwith wrote in 1920, with Westminster primarily in mind, that 'the interference of politicians in labour disputes, much as many of them hankered to come in, was deleterious, and could be exposed far more strongly than I have mildly indicated'.[62] It is notorious that he was not always so mild. Slesser and Macassey express the same resentment and suspicion of the politicians, for the same reasons: the technical weakness of many of the Acts they passed, and the political undercutting of the judicial function. But in addition to this technical and positive definition of legal rationality there is the philosophically conservative one which sees the law as the expression of an evolved totality of social relationships. It emerges therefore out of a multitude of objective limitations and constraints.

> Experience constantly reveals that human nature is not indefinitely plastic; that its fundamental elements and instincts are apparently as unalterable as the stars in their courses and are found alike in the socialists who condemn, and those who uphold the established order of society; that human society cannot adopt any form we please, but must, if it is to subsist, follow certain rules, accept certain principles, and find room and place for all sorts and conditions of men. In following a theory the socialist may forget human nature. Experience tells me that the socialist often does forget human nature.[63]

Here Askwith is, of course, invoking classic liberal pessimism, or realism, about human nature, but we have to recognise that this is more than a reactionary formula when it comes from a liberal industrial lawyer. For one thing, it follows from this that the realisation of equity in practice depends on a sensitivity to these same human and material constraints. The defence of reason against the multifarious forces of disorder cannot be reduced to a question of the authoritative application of law. There is also the dimension of consent and agreement, in which reason can be elicited and the elements of a tacit social contract confirmed. Macassey was consistently aware of this in his published work on industrial law, and it is one element in the caution and tact he displayed as a dilution commissioner. The other element, to be sure, was a hard-headed appraisal of the consequences of exacerbating an exceedingly tense labour situation. But he believed in the fundamental reasonableness of the ordinary man, if he could be given a chance to understand the limitations built into the situation in which something was being demanded of him. Macassey could claim with Askwith that experience had taught him a thing or two about human nature.

Askwith's behavioural assumptions also have implications for the origins of legislation that is rational both in the positive sense and as an instrument of a reasonable social philosophy. Good legislation can only be conceived in a state of expert detachment: in one important sense good law is made in spite of and not by virtue of political conflict. One group of politicians might provide a better opportunity than another for getting into the statute books, but unreason, exorbitant demand, of its nature enters through politics. Quite typically, Slesser, writing in the 1940s, remarks on the 1906 parliamentary Conservatives:

> Their behaviour was quite without principle; if there was ever a measure which might reasonably have been rejected, it was the Trade Disputes Act, which gave a complete immunity to Trade Unions for all wrongs committed by them, not even limited to those done during a Trade Dispute; it was not even a Government Bill, yet the Conservatives, despite the protests of their lawyers, let it pass.[64]

Edwardian social reformers of all sorts served under the obligation imposed on them by the 'realistic' assumption that rational law and social policy derive from the effective independence of a 'responsible' élite.

The 'Asquithian' group in the ICF is less clearly defined. Sir Donald Maclean, Chairman of the non-coalition Liberals from February 1919 to 1922, could not himself be described in any other terms. A solicitor, he won Bath in the 1906 election, and was Member for Peebles from 1910. He was virtually unknown until the accidents of 1918 imposed the burden of Asquithian parliamentary politics upon him, a burden which remained after Asquith's return to the House. Even unsympathetic opinion had to acknowledge that he did the job well, as the colourless, financially competent manager the Party, or a disintegrated fraction of it, needed at the time.[65] He had more urgent matters to deal with in this period than ICF Council meetings, but he remained on the Council, one has to suspect, for reasons that fused churchmanship and politics. There can be no doubt about the former. He had Presbyterian connections and took up the cudgels over education, bishops in the House of Lords, and Sunday closing. His letters to his wife pay regular attention to Sunday sermons and churchgoing. But he was always concerned as a good party man with the sliding electoral base of the Liberal Party, the uncertainties registered in internal party divisions, and in the ambiguous liaison with the Labour Movement. He is reported defending Asquith's 1907 budget.

> . . . as regards the question of old age pensioners, he noticed with some surprise and amazement that some spokesmen of the National Labour Party—although he denied the right of any small body of men to call themselves the Labour Party, since he regarded himself as much a Labour member as anybody else— raised complaints as to why they did not start immediately some scheme of old age pensions . . .[66]

And speaking to the Annual General Meeting of the Central Council of the Scottish Liberal Federation in April 1923;

> The Labour Party was not the common enemy of the Liberal Party . . . The common enemy was the conditions which produced these extreme forms of political belief . . .[67]

The Labour group on the ICF almost without exception emerged from the Edwardian Liberal Party, or were implicated in the Lib–Lab association at some stage, or else were middle-class recruits to Labour in the drift that has been partly analysed by C. A. Cline.[68] The Liberal Party was in disarray, possibly temporary, but at least these people were all arguably continuing on the 'straight road—where it (is) difficult to get lost'.[69] In terms of a public association with electoral implications, Maclean's membership of the ICF is not surprising.

However, Asquithian sentiment involved a good deal more than middle-range electoral worries or concern for the personal fortunes of a defunctive philanderer, whom even Maclean identified as a liability by 1922.[70] There was within the Party at large a revulsion against the compromises with fundamental principle which the War had forced on it, and more specifically a revulsion against Lloyd George coalition politics, expedience, absence of principle. Hichens' old Chairman, Charles Hobhouse, who suffered the indignity of being the first ex-minister ever to lose a deposit, departed after the coupon election of 1918 with a distaste for the Coalition shared by many Liberals. Bentley draws attention to the extraordinary bitterness of the feeling that principle and party had been betrayed, expressing itself in private harassment and verbal hostility towards Liberals in the Coalition.[71] The hostility was to continue as party divisions failed to heal. At the time of the 1922 election, Masterman was writing privately that 'the . . . thing was to get rid of L. G. and his crapulous crew *at any cost*', even at the cost of a Tory victory.[72] For many honourable men of system, Lloyd Georgism had served its turn, planting fruitful possibilities for the future, but the post-war Lloyd George was something else again.

The symbol of this internecine conflict was the issue the 'coupon' was in the end all about, the affair of the 'Maurice letter', which appeared in *The Times* and other leading newspapers of 7 May 1918. The details of this incident are intricate and were, at the time, obscure, very largely because it was by compounding obscurities that Lloyd George won a debating victory in the House. Positions taken up over this dispute ultimately determined membership of the Asquith and coalition camps.[73] Nancy Maurice, one of General Maurice's daughters, has presented her father's case in great detail.[74] Peter Rowland has summarised the incident in his massive biography of Lloyd George.[75] Very briefly, Maurice, who was Haig's Director of Military Operations, took the sensational step of denouncing as inaccurate three statements made in the House of Commons, one by Bonar Law and the other two by Lloyd George. Lloyd George's statements had to do with the strength of the British army on 1 January 1918, and with the number of white divisions in Mesopotamia, Egypt and Palestine. Maurice asserted that these statements were 'known to a large number of soldiers to be incorrect, and this knowledge is breeding such distrust of the Government as can only end in impairing the splendid morale of our troops at a time when everything possible should be done to raise it'. Maurice expected a Select Committee, but was dramatically outmanoeuvred by Lloyd George, and found himself within a few days dismissed from the army. Rowland's judgement is that Lloyd George won a triumph in the debating chamber, but only by pulling every trick in the book, to the embarrassment even of strong supporters like Milner, Hankey and Kerr. He could not admit the truth in Maurice's charges and interpreted them as a cunning move in his own feud with General Sir William Robertson.

The incident blew the lid off 'fermenting hostilities between the civilians and the High Command which need not be touched on here,[76] beyond noting Maurice's almost totally uncritical devotion to Haig, and Haig's close connections with Asquith. Lloyd George's furious suspicion of cunning on Maurice's part seems very wide of the truth. 'A highly cultured and scientific soldier', as Hankey described him,[77] Maurice was also astonishingly naïve in the way he failed to develop his initial gesture, which he appears to have thought of as an ultimate moral stand which would speak for itself without further support. The day before the letter appeared, Nancy, then eighteen, was handed a letter from him in the course of which he wrote

. . . I am persuaded that I am doing what is right, and once that is so, nothing else matters to a man. That is, I believe, what Christ meant when he told us to forsake father and mother and children and wife for His sake. It has been a difficult decision for, as you know, I love the Army and I have you all and Mother to think of, but it is made now, and you must help me to make the best of it.[78]

Maurice became, briefly, a journalist, and later biographer of Haldane and author on military matters, Principal of the Working Men's College in 1922, Professor of Military Studies at London in 1927, and in 1933 Principal of Queen Mary's College. He was appearing on church platforms from 1919 and it is interesting to note that reports of these occasions refer to the warmth of his reception, while summarising contributions which were on the bluff and banal side even for the exhortatory sessions arranged by William Temple's Life and Liberty Movement at the time.[79] It was the honest Christian soldier his hearers identified with, the man who had stood up for principle in a public world becoming increasingly loathsome. The emotions which crystallised round the Maurice affair within the non-coalition group were vividly shared. A note from Asquith to Maclean:

My dear Maclean,
. . . This is the Maurice trap over again. By refusing facilities unless the motion is to be regarded as a vote of censure, the government practically prevents fair debate and a free vote.
We know what unscrupulous use was made of the Maurice affair.[80]

A great many people with no understanding of these procedural iniquities saw the Maurice affair as a symptom of something rotten.

Maurice, with his wife, was a very active member of the ICF throughout the period. His membership was loaded with implications of which he was fully aware. He was the authority on the Just War against the evils of Prussianism. He was an expert, not only on technical matters, but also on the *esprit de corps* which sustained the armies. He had a theological interpretation of the war which a great many people welcomed, a degenerated version of the argument to be found in Gore and other liberal theologians about the presence of God in History and the working out of His purpose. Finally, and most aptly, he was the grandson of the great F. D. Maurice, and never tired of placing himself in that line, advocating fellowship and co-operation, in the spirit of Kingsley, Ludlow and Maurice.

Values brought to the surface by the Maurice affair were very important to the ICF movement in this decade. Studdert Kennedy himself wrote and spoke of the 'shameful episode' of the 1918 election.[81] But these values appear in a network of interconnecting preoccupations, some of which have already emerged in the course of introducing the component groups. Thus, the ideal of system, efficiency, rational combination, crops up in several closely related contexts. The original F. D. Maurice's concern with the organic society, patriotism and its basis in physical and spiritual health, is picked up in the social imperialist line that reaches into the new managerial philosophy articulated by Hichens, and the social policies of the reformers, Fabian and others, who remain to be identified, and also in a theory of industrial law, which incorporated union activity into a systematised process of collectively oriented comparison and adjustment.

The reformers, it has already been suggested, had a natural place in the ICF, as the most energetic and effective element in the old CSU. Gertrude Tuckwell had been on the Commission on lead poisoning in china and earthenware, the subject of a CSU campaign. Closely associated with her was Constance Smith, co-author of *The Worker's Handbook*.[82] Others in the ICF group included Miss M. E. E. James of the Bethnal Green Board of Guardians, Barbara Drake, Beatrice Webb's niece and Fabian author of *Women in Engineering* and *Women in Trade*, and E. C. P. Lascelles, an authority on dock labour and employment.[83] Tuckwell and Smith directly continued the Dilke tradition, which saw a rational wage structure as the key that would integrate workers in unorganised sectors into the economy. Dilke had introduced his Wages Board Bill year after year from 1898, and the Trade Boards Act was finally introduced by Churchill in 1909, proving, according to Tuckwell, its orthodox character and high economic worth.[84] She describes the problem for industrial legislation in terms of the 'chaos of unregulated labour', and the solution in terms of a logical response to the specific complexities of the modern industrial state.

> The gaps in our legislation are many, but, on the whole they are now apparent, and the trades or classes of trades which have been regulated are in comparative order, and, where administration is effective, form an object lesson of the successful safeguarding of industrial interests.[85]

The destruction of Dilke's political ambitions as a result of the Crawford divorce scandal[86] had created the archetypal reformer, a man with neutered political ambitions, but immense energy, specialist knowledge, a clear reading of the logic of state intervention and a capacity for translating that into a workable system of constraints. Tuckwell and Smith may have seen themselves as working for the completion of his programme, but their work anticipated the more massive welfare legislation of a later period. At

the 1921 Congress, Tuckwell's twenty-five years of work for the
Women's Trade Union League was acknowledged by a special
presentation.[87]

The last major group of laymen on the ICF Executive and Council
consists of Labour parliamentarians and trade unionists. The non-
union parliamentarians were thoroughly middle class, and fugitives
from more conventional political loyalties. One or two, like Edith
Picton-Turbervill, lecturer and prolific author (*The Musings of a
Laywoman, Christ and International Order*, and the remarkably titled *Christ
and Woman's Power*, etc.) leave a slightly eccentric impression. In 1929
she became Member for The Wrekin, a constituency in which
Bottomley had successfully run two candidates since 1920 for
Rothermere's Anti-Waste Party.[88] One or two of the others were
unquestionably distinguished. E. N. Bennett had been a Fellow of
Hertford College, a war correspondent in the middle east in the late
nineties, and a volunteer in South Africa, before becoming the
Liberal MP for Woodstock in 1906. His *Problems of Village Life* appeared
in the Home University Library in 1914, under the editorship of
Gilbert Murray, and he joined the ILP three years later. Fenner
Brockway asked him to contribute to a 1918 election pamphlet for his
fight at Lancaster, 'What Soldiers and Sailors think of Fenner
Brockway'. It cites Bennett's decorations, including the Serbian
Order, bestowed for 'splendid and gallant service', and his message:

> Our country stands badly in need today of sincere and unselfish
> politicians like Fenner Brockway. I strongly urge ex-soldiers, who
> have been shamefully deceived and exploited by the government,
> to give Fenner Brockway their votes, and not to be led away from
> supporting Labour ideals by prejudiced and unfair attacks upon
> him. Thoughtful and fair minded people, whether soldiers or
> civilians *are bound to admire men who were prepared to suffer for their
> principles*, even if such principles may for the moment be
> unpopular.

He himself ran for Westbury that year, and was to take Cardiff
Central for Labour in 1929, and to continue in support of
MacDonald after 1931. Bennett's main interest, the farm worker, got
little attention from the ICF, despite the great impact on Gore of
Joseph Arch, the organiser of farm workers in the 1870s. Bennett's
concern as a believer with the supernatural emerges in a highly
cultivated interest in psychical research.[89]

It will be more convenient to discriminate the Labour trade
unionists individually and in greater detail at a later stage, since
several of them devoted considerable time and attention to the ICF
while occupying union offices, and in one case, that of Frank

Hodges, played a significant role in the industrial disputes of the period. The list of names reads like a fragment of an inventory of the trade union right wing. C. W. Bowerman, 'courteous Charlie' as he was called according to an acidulous Walter Citrine,[90] was Secretary of the TUC from 1911–23 and Secretary also of the Compositors Union and official Labour candidate for Dartford in 1906, where he 'made it clear that he "had always been an active voter in the Liberal and Radical interest" '.[91] He was the clear winner on that occasion. E. L. Poulton, General Secretary of the National Union of Boot and Shoe Operatives, was President of the TUC in 1921. H. H. Elvin and F. Hughes of the National Union of Clerks were both lay preachers. Hughes had put in several years for the ILP in Birmingham, had been Glasier's election agent in 1906, an election in which Labour candidates 'stressed their nonconformity more than their socialist qualifications',[92] and himself ran for Bordesley in 1910 with an appeal for the Liberal vote over the budget, tariff reform and drink. The elderly George Edwards, founder in 1906 of the National Union of Landworkers, moved from the Liberals to Labour, and was MP for Norfolk South from 1920.[93] C. G. Ammon of the Postal Workers was a methodist and a close friend of Henderson's.[94] Frank Hodges, perhaps the most interesting of the group, who became the ICF Treasurer in 1923, the year he entered Parliament as Member for Lichfield, had been a miner, went to Ruskin College, taking part in the rebellion that led to the founding of the Labour College, and in 1918 defeated Noah Ablett to become Secretary of the Miners' Federation of Great Britain. He may have been recruited for the ICF by Kempthorne, Bishop of Lichfield, though he was on friendly terms with Hichens, who recognised him as an essentially sound, though occasionally wayward labour leader.

This overview leaves a number of lay members of the ICF unaccounted for. They were all prominent churchpeople. Major Birchall, an Estates Commissioner for the Church, was a Unionist MP, who did voice criticisms of the ICF at Council meetings. The Tory radical Lord Henry Bentinck was one of the three Trustees throughout the period. Lord Parmoor, Beatrice Webb's brother-in-law, was Vicar General of Canterbury from 1902, a distinguished lawyer, a Unionist MP, Liberal Peer and Lord President of the Council in the first Labour Government. Beatrice Webb was fond of him and admired his taste in women—'He chose the most charming of the Potter sisters'. She wrote a brief progress report on his somewhat cranky career in 1919.

During the war Parmoor has developed into a political idealist. Whatever may have been his reasons for being against the war at the beginning, the horrors of it, and the revengeful spirit of the peace, have turned him into something very like an International Socialist. So does evil company corrupt good manners. All the men who held fast by the capitalist creed he used to believe in have been eager to crush Germany and impose their countries' material power on the world ... The Church has bitterly disappointed him in its casuistical support for the powers that be. 'I really do not know where I stand on all economic questions', he said to me the other day; 'all I know is that I disagree fundamentally with all those with whom I used to act in the House of Commons'.[95]

He was the most eminent representative of an internationalist concern that was of great importance in the ICF. Mrs Hudson Lyall, a life Vice-President of the Mother's Union and Vice-President of the Primrose League, was to become an important figure on the London County Council. There were others, but the main elements have been sufficiently identified.

The parsons, more a category than a group, can for the present be disposed of more briefly. They included many figures from the CSU, Gore, Temple and A. J. Carlyle among the better known, and also Frere, Fry, Moore Ede and Donaldson from those mentioned in Adderley's letter to the *Church Times*. But Kirk spread his net wide and several of the *Church Socialist League* figures, P. E. T. Widdrington, Adderley, and even C. Stuart-Smith, until his death in 1924, came in to try and influence the direction of the organisation's activities. Politically on the other flank, and somewhat isolated, was Canon W. H. Carnegie, Sub-Dean of Westminster, who had married Mary Endicott, the American widow of Joseph Chamberlain, whom he had known from his ministry in Birmingham. The Rev. F. R. Barry, MC, was to describe him as belonging 'more to the Edwardian past than to the century of the common man' and noted that his rare Chapter votes 'would not be cast for an innovation'.[96] Barry himself, later Bishop of Southwell, was one of a significantly high proportion of ICF parsons with distinguished war records. The non-partisan stance of the ICF applied no less to theological divisions, and there was an important group of socially concerned evangelicals which included Guy Rogers, MC. J. A. Kempthorne, Bishop of Lichfield since 1913, was a particularly keen Vice-President throughout the period. The Archbishops of Canterbury, York and Wales were Presidents.

For all its apparent comprehensiveness, however, this was not by any means a representative group of parsons of the Church of England. Its general characteristics will be considered in greater detail in Chapter 6.

This, in rough outline, was the coalition of prominent figures that began negotiations with Studdert Kennedy in January 1920. With the

2 J. A. Kempthorne, Bishop of Lichfield (*Staffordshire Sentinel*)

critical exception of the trade unionists, it was socially homogeneous, as the passing references to family and other connections will have suggested. The delays over the appointment were not the result of uncertainties on the part of the ICF. 'Woodbine Willie' began appearing on ICF platforms immediately after the war, and the Executive was convinced that he would more than pay his way if his full-time services could be secured. The Executive Minutes for May 1921 record that:

> The Committee considered the urgent need of the present industrial crisis and agreed to invite the Rev. G. A. Studdert Kennedy to join the staff as Fellowship Messenger at a stipend of £600 a year and travelling expenses.

3 The War and 'Woodbine Willie'

THE CRISIS, THE CHURCH AND THE PADRES

This chapter sets out to do three things. It describes in broad terms how the post-war crisis with which the ICF was to engage was seen at different levels within the organisation. It identifies certain consequences of the war for the conditions in which an active and organised response, on the part of the Church of England, would have to develop, and, finally, it places 'Woodbine Willie' in this context as an attractive candidate for the task envisaged by the officers of the ICF.

We need only allude to some of the obvious symptoms of disorder which fuelled the anxiety behind the Executive's resolution of May 1921. The slump which followed the replacement boom of the post-war months had made a shambles of the promises of Reconstruction. The pressure on wages provoked threats of direct action. Massive unemployment threatened to swamp a frail system of insurance designed for quite different conditions, while public works and emigration seemed to many to be at best weak palliatives. There were acute and pervasive anxieties about subversion, revolution and bolshevism, which were by no means confined to the propertied classes, for there was ample evidence of sharpening polarisation and disintegration. In mid-April 1921 the Triple Alliance had collapsed and with it for the time the threat of a general strike, but the coal strike was continuing. At the beginning of April the out-of-work donation for 300,000 soldiers came to an end, leaving many of them ineligible for unemployment insurance, whilst another 900,000 civilians came off the uncovenanted eight weeks benefit at the same time.[1] It was observed that the former soldiers were quite unlike any other mass of unemployed, since they were not only bitterly disappointed by the false promises of Reconstruction, but were accustomed to discipline, professionally aggressive and conditioned to stop at nothing. In October 1920, there had been a violent confrontation between police and unemployed in Whitehall, and similar events could be predicted with confidence. They duly took place over the following year in several Lancashire towns, and in Sheffield, Dundee, Bristol, Leicester, Cardiff, Glasgow and Trafalgar Square.[2] In *Forward* of 14 May, in the course of a depressed attack on ' "direct action" as a remedy for every social and political ill', Ramsay MacDonald noted the relative incidence of the economic pressures, whilst drawing on standard imagery of radical agitation which was much in use at the time.

> Meanwhile, Capital suffers comparatively little. It suffers no famine and no canteens have to be opened for it. It cancels the rooms it took for a week-end's golfing at Porthcawl, and it dines and golfs at home instead.[3]

There were orthodox assumptions available which seemed to make sense of the economic crisis and carried authority. For the thoughtful and socially concerned who could get beyond the gut reactions to disturbing manifestations, there was an area of detachment and apparent objectivity in which the basic structural problems could be confronted and logical consequences drawn for various forms of action. At the level of a general understanding of the dynamics of the crisis, economic historians have passed severe judgements on these orthodoxies. The most expert and experienced economic opinion within the ICF was unapologetically orthodox.

In 1919–20, instead of restricting inflation, the Government added to it by a budget deficit, but then, from April 1920, applied 'immense deflationary pressure' in an attempt to recover control of the market and prepare for a return to gold at the old parity, a policy which 'greatly aggravated the effects and extent of the slump', though it did have the technical effect of reducing the floating debt.[4] Pre-war experience with the labour market was forgotten.[5] The consequences for unemployment of a 'bank rate of near panic level'[6] in the year leading up to April 1921 were taken to be less important in the framework of orthodox economic analysis, than the consequences either of unbalanced budgets for exchange rates and prices, or of continued indulgence in the various forms of 'waste' which were to be lopped off public expenditure by the 'Geddes axe'. Budget priorities in the early twenties were City priorities, and it was believed to be sound and realistic to place the costs of recovery elsewhere and then to face the consequences of having done so with whatever material and moral resources were available after the commitment to a deflationary economics had been made.

Informed opinion was not homogeneous, but it is impressive evidence of the strength of what passed for realism at the time that even industrialists who were as sympathetic as Hichens, in principle and other things being equal, to high wages on economic grounds, could defend the 7 per cent Bank Rate under the circumstances. On 1 February 1921, the *Financier* started mobilising opinion against the 7 per cent rate, printing telegrams, generally cautiously worded, from people like the industrialist Roscoe Brunner and the President of the Manchester Chamber of Commerce. Hichens' contribution on 2 February hardly added to the ground swell of support the editors claimed to have uncovered.

> Dear money is undoubtedly injurious to trade, but plentiful money is even more essential than cheap money. If, as is probable, the results of lowering the Bank Rate would be to cause foreigners to withdraw their deposits on a large scale we should lose more than we should gain.[7]

His overall analysis of the crisis was elaborated and repeated in the course of the year in a series of interviews and newspaper articles, and in the annual report to the shareholders of Cammell Laird.[8] It could be summed up in a favourite phrase, cutting our coat according to our cloth, and started from the central problem of foreign trade, the loss of markets in Central Europe and Russia as a result of chaotic conditions, and our hopeless competitive position in the markets available. In the basic iron and steel industries, British prices were higher than German or Belgian, quite simply because their wages were lower and their hours longer. Furthermore, the systematic interdependence of market and production did not end there, since there was no practical way of insulating particular sectors. Cheap coal was essential to the steel industry and there was no way in which the price of coal could be materially reduced unless the wages of the miners came down. In the coal industry as much as 80 per cent of the costs of production were absorbed in wages. Even in transport the wage bill accounted for the bulk of costs. Economies would have to be made in every possible direction, but the key to recovery could only be a reduction in wages.

He insisted, however, and this exposed his new liberal reflexes, on an even-handed attack on wages; salaries and dividends must be included. In good times profits increased first and a rise in wages followed after. By the same industrial law, in bad times profits fell first and then wages. Unless this principle was recognised and seen to obtain, we could expect neither recovery nor industrial peace, because there was no way round the problem of scarcity and the disadvantaged would not suffer what must be required of them if burdens were not fairly shared. We must, in short, compete or go to the wall, and the recovery of our competitive position called for a collective recognition of the costs, which would initially include

punitive wages, and even unemployment under grinding conditions
for substantial numbers, since it was literally impossible to provide
funds to pay for unemployment benefits once large numbers moved
out of employment and the tax base was strained to breaking point.
We could not base wages on the cost of living, but on what we could
get.

Economic analysis proved the inexorability of these constraints,
but the solution had to be found in another, moral arena where we
decided how we should respond to the laws of cause and effect, in the
light of a rigorous analysis of material contingencies. Management
and labour must get round the table, in the knowledge that it was
useless for opposite camps to throw bombs at each other. All either
side need bring, in the end, was commonsense and good will.

Hichens from time to time felt compelled to put down people who
were effectively in agreement with his analysis of the limits of
economic policy, but suffered from attacks of hope or indignation or
intellectual weakness which stifled 'commonsense'. For example, the
scheme submitted to the Government by Frank Hodges (an
increasingly 'sound' Labour leader), as Secretary of the Miners'
Federation, in October 1921, provided one occasion for confident
sparring, in which the proposed subsidy for the coal industry was
revealed as a mere shift in the incidence of taxation, which would
reduce incentives into the bargain.[9] Hichens was also irritated by
progressive voices from among the clergy and the social workers
which demanded legislation for a living wage but did not offer to
effect the necessary multiplication of loaves and fishes.[10] They tended
to draw on nebulous expert sources. L. T. Hobhouse's discussion in a
pre-war symposium, which was intended for CSU reading lists,
blandly evades the problem of redistribution and political conflict in
relation to the living wage.

> ... I do not think we should be guided too much by our
> experience of the labour market. The labour market is a place
> where people with property bargain with people without
> property, and I do not take the result of that bargain as a measure
> of what working people are worth, or can be made capable of
> under fairer conditions.[11]

But these were in the end differences of vantage point and rhetoric
and did not derive from a fundamentally different or analytically
developed interpretation of the constraints imposed by the crisis. It is
striking how seldom ICF supporters made any allusion at all to
Hobson's underconsumptionist theory. He had been important to
pre-war Christian Socialists like Scott Holland on the issue of
Imperialism,[12] but his interpretation of the problem of redistribution

was too challenging and academically heterodox to be safely handled as an integral part of the 'broad assault upon *laissez faire* and the protean individualist fallacy'.[13] Everyone called for retrenchment, sacrifice, reform, but not for the abandonment of positions that had been laboriously prepared over several decades. The crisis visibly threatened institutions and structures which, like the Trade Boards, were barely established, or else were in the process of emerging from the old Poor Law administration, and it was such evolving structures, with their rules, their legitimacy and their representative personnel that constituted the reality of 'both sides getting together round the table'. Active in this cause, in the 1920 Poor Law Conference in the Metropolitan District, the Bethnal Green delegation, headed by Miss M. E. E. James, an ICF Executive member, presented a paper supporting the formation of a Conciliation Council to represent the Metropolitan Boards and their employees, expressing general support for Whitley Councils, consultation through trade union representation and the systematic reduction of friction. Rude voices were raised on the same occasion. Walter Day, a Labour Guardian from Paddington, excoriated the

> Boards of Guardians and Charity Organisations and other pernicious institutions which are merely symbols of the capitalist system of paying back to the victims of their robbery and exploitation a few crumbs that can keep them quiet and in ignorance of the real position.[14]

But social reformers from Toynbee Hall and elsewhere, who themselves criticised the Poor Law Administration and the Charity Organisation Society both on practical and philosophical grounds, might well have taken this kind of thing merely as an invitation to administrative chaos, rather than as the prelude to an era of workers' soviets. Recovery for them meant re-establishing material and psychological conditions in which, for example, the Trade Boards would not find their functions eroded, as they were to be in 1922 on the advice of the Cave Committee,[15] and which would permit a rational restructuring of Poor Law functions and the implementation of existing recommendations such as those of the Maclean Committee, chaired by Donald Maclean, also of the ICF, as has been pointed out. These were published in 1918, but not in the event acted on until 1929.[16]

ICF supporters and activists with less practical experience or pragmatic sense, like very many others, simply recognised in the unrest, the March declaration of a State of Emergency, and the Government's counter-preparations, such as the Special Defence Force, 'the makings of a civil war'.[17] There is the recurring imagery of a straightforward moral drama, the wicked flaunting of wealth, the undeserved indignity of unemployment and deprivation, and the understandable but fatal temptation to seize and to destroy.

It was the idea of war that concentrated the attention of ICF activists of all sorts. For some it was the possibility of civil war, but for all at least a state of conflict and disorder, domestic and international, in some profound sense analogous to the 1914–18 Armageddon, a pointless, evil, endless waste. They denied its inevitability and promoted what they saw as the collective moral choice that would redeem the situation, by attempting to anchor the language of economic and social analysis in religious categories, or at least in values and assumptions that could not at the time be extricated from the categories of religious belief.

There appeared to be two interrelated aspects to the crisis, a revolutionary threat to structure and to institutions, and an imperative need to renew motivations serving to sustain the moral community.

Churchmen, of course, were by no means the only contributors to the flood of exhortation on behalf of a 'new spirit'. However, in attempting to invoke the crowning sanction of institutional authority and of doctrine, they encountered serious difficulties.

For many contemporaries, including committed Christians, the Church itself, as a corporate body, seemed a sadly disoriented guide to the social message of the gospel, in part because of the nature of its involvement in the war effort, but also because the war had shown it up as an institution of no relevance at all to the vast majority of those who went to the front. The subject of the impact of the war has been obscured by the vigour of popular cliché, sharply articulated by Robert Graves in *Goodbye to All That*,[18] but also hotly debated in the press between the wars. More than seventy pages of a folio Army Book 124 are filled by reviews and controversial letters, collected between January and March 1930, following the publication of C. R. Benstead's novel *Retreat*, in which the central character is an inadequate temporary chaplain.[19] However, a number of recent studies have assembled material on the medley of responses to the war from within the Church, and on some of its consequences for the Church as a formal organisation, for its system of beliefs in a limited theological sense, and for more diffuse beliefs with which it was associated in a period of accelerated secularisation.[20]

The dismal picture that emerges from these accounts is to some extent biased by the nature of the records. Whatever the writer's point of view, shell-making vicars and recruiting bishops are ripe for journalistic exploitation. Published acknowledgements of the role of the Church from military men and politicians have acquired increasingly discordant reverberations with the passage of time, as

have many of the pronouncements and confidences of patriotic
bishops and keen Assistant Chaplains General at the Front. One
quote illustrates the point for two of these groups.

> Sir Douglas Haig came to our Headquarters, and when, with the
> rest of the staff I was led up to him, he spoke to me so kindly and
> said 'Tell your chaplains that a good chaplain is as valuable as a
> good General'.[21]

Haig's goodwill towards the narrator, Assistant Chaplain General to
the First Army, is easy to understand in the light of Blackburne's
account, which brims with topping and splendid generals, charming
staff officers and wonderful subordinates, relentless ebullience
drowning every vestige of dismay or uncertainty about the role of the
Church as a prop to military morale. Winnington-Ingram, Bishop of
London, who visited the London Rifle Brigade in France at
Blackburne's suggestion and Field-Marshal Sir John French's
insistence, was a skilful publicist, if a naïve one, and what one of his
biographers describes as his 'intense patriotism'[22] found expression
in a popular bellicosity that seems to have been an effective aid to
recruitment. But is is also true that many other less prominent
churchmen interpreted the Church's national role with a degree of
insensitivity to the implications of some of the activities into which
they threw themselves. Marrin points out that Roger Lloyd's
historical survey grossly underestimates the extent of the
involvement of the clergy in recruitment and related activities.[23] The
general sense of Masterman's reaction must have been common. 'I
remember his complaining that a service at Westminster Abbey
seemed like an activity at Wellington House' (the headquarters of
Masterman's propaganda department).[24] No doubt there were
zealous figures in addition to Bishop Hensley Henson who retained a
critical perspective on their recruiting activities, but the Church had
suffered from wartime improvisation and compromise.

The sense of irrelevance and failure in relation to the spiritual
needs of men at the front was most painfully experienced by the
temporary chaplains, though it was frequently registered by others as
well. George Coppard, for example, who ended the war as a
corporal, remembered hearing Studdart Kennedy (*sic*), and even a
story he told. It was told on scores of similar occasions and appears in
Rough Talks by a Padre at the end of a section headed 'This ain't exactly
what ye'd call a b—— mother's meeting, is it, sir?' But Coppard's
main point is the irrelevance of religion to the ordinary soldier with
whom he served.[25] On the other side of the class divide between
commissioned and non-commissioned ranks, Major R. S. Cockburn,
MC, wrote extended comments on opportunities missed by the

Church (and by the High Command) at the front. The men are predisposed to respect the padre. 'He represents God.' But 'the Church has done little beyond mystifying these men, irritating them, giving them cigarettes and magazines and burying the dead. And this is the tragedy'.[26] Spontaneous references to the Church, lay and clerical, convey a sense of shocked disappointment and positive disillusion. The more sensitive accounts of the work written by padres themselves share a sombre sense of discovery and raise questions about the peacetime Church and a post-war England.[27] The central discovery, what came to be called the 'inarticulate religion' of the trenches, became something of a commonplace as a result of the popularity of Donald Hankey's *A Student in Arms*.[28] Younger brother of the Secretary to the War Cabinet, he was killed on the Somme in 1916. At its simplest the phrase referred to a manifest presence of Christ in the loyalties, comradeship and self-sacrifice of the ordinary soldiers, and an implicit judgement on the failure of the Church to reveal this for what it was or to guide its development.[29] So Dennis Jones, Precentor of Manchester Cathedral, wrote that 'their love for God and all things good, when once revealed is true, childlike and sincere'.[30] Neville Talbot, a keen supporter of the ICF even after his departure as Bishop of Pretoria, saw no evidence of a heralded revival of Christianity, but an inarticulate development of natural religion, a hidden Christianity, in the non-calculating, self-regardless co-operation at the front. Christ's sacrifice epitomises the sacrifice of those who 'have trustfully given themselves to death for others'. 'There is everywhere about, over here, a diffused Christianity in men who are better than they know.' This perception could promote wishful thinking. Jones supposed that 'those who return will have seen a new world . . . Men will be less bigoted, more broadminded, courteous, and humble, more zealous for the truth, and keen for freedom to spread over the broad world'. Others were less inclined to take comfort and reflected with greater realism on conflicts in the society from which war had detached them.

> I find many people talking as if the camaraderie of the trenches between officers and men would of necessity solve Labour troubles after the War. But there is an element of pathetic delusion in that expectation. What trench life has proved is that when officers and men are divorced from the artificial relationships of our industrial and commercial system they discover each other as men, and arrive at a new appreciation of each other.[31]

The Rev. Tom Pym, MC, subsequently on the ICF Council, looked ahead to the intensification of class hostilities in a society that would not reproduce the sense of common purpose and common danger informing the army.[32]

Temporary chaplains for whom the experience of the trenches constituted both a challenge and an accusation returned with a sense of corporate identity and a number of broadly agreed objectives. There was the question of the Church itself as an institution, a spiritual failure, compromised in its material endowments, which reflected the inequalities of the society at large and the differential spiritual opportunities these entailed. Pym, for example, argued for a movement among individual clergy to pool financial resources and live off them till the Church was either disestablished or free to put its own house in order.[33] There were also immediate issues to be taken up, such as the overt use of the Church as an agent of social control among the demobilised.[34] There was nothing new about impatience with the Church's concern with temporalities, the disfunctional structure of its hierarchy, or the obsolescence of some traditional forms. Many of these issues had been discussed, for example, in papers edited by Douglas Eyre, a lay member of the ICF after the War.[35] But the army padres injected a novel element of radical brashness, which Archbishops Lang of York and Davidson of Canterbury, confronting a deputation to Lambeth in October 1918, found vulgar and tasteless, though maladroit and childishly easy to dispose of.[36] Davidson himself, of course, took an instrumental line on reform, which operated through technicalities and procedures, the law and finance.[37] On the other hand, the large social observations which fuelled the reformism of the padres, though they may have indulged in a 'good deal of ephemeral romanticism' about the liberties of the wage-earner in the industrial system,[38] were a more durable legacy and shaped a number of post-war careers. F. R. Barry, MC, later Bishop of Southwell, was to claim for the wartime Chaplain's Department that it did something to re-establish the clergy and what they represented in the respect and affection of the workers.[39] Of the contributors to F. B. Macnutt's *The Church in the Furnace*, which became a kind of tract for front-line reformists, Barry, Pym, Macnutt himself and Studdert Kennedy joined the ICF.[40] The book was referred to by the contributors, according to Dora Pym, as the 'Fat in the Fire', or 'Parsons on the Stove'.

Like the late Victorian slum and settlement clergy, a small but articulate proportion of the temporary chaplains returned from the war guilty at the 'failure' of the Church as a national institution, traumatically initiated into the dilemmas of a socially effective faith, and with some collective sense of issues requiring attention. They shared what seemed to many of them, at the time at least, a fresh perception of the implications of the gospel, and one that emerged

half-formed from an experience shared by many thousands of
ordinary men, rather than deriving from the specially equipped
religious individual, and which therefore required to be translated
into the language of faith if it was to take root.

The war made less of an impact on British theology, however, than
its enormity and the content of pre-war liberal theology might lead
one to expect. There is no sort of equivalent to Barth's 1918
Commentary on the Epistle to the Romans (translated into English in 1933),
with its doctrine of total corruption.[41] The paper by Eric Milner-
White, DSO, another of Macnutt's contributors, on the Spirit and the
Church in History, in *Essays Catholic and Critical*, a volume written 'in
conscious succession to *Lux Mundi*',[42] suggests an adjustment made
without serious intellectual difficulty.[43] J. K. Mozley, who made two
contributions to that volume, discusses in another book the
implications of the war in the light of the work of Schweitzer and the
eschatologists, with particular reference to the notion of a finite God.
The dedication is a joint one, to P. T. Forsyth, the theologian, and G.
A. Studdert Kennedy, a close friend from boyhood. His argument is
that the war had thrown into high relief the supreme but familiar
ethical question, 'whether morality is the nature of things, and
existence moves forwards towards a moral end', by challenging us to
place 'the righteousness of the cause within the great framework of a
righteous world'. The war, in short, made the paradoxes of faith
more visible, but changed nothing.[44] Archbishop Ramsey's survey
actually refers to the 'theological gap' felt by some during the period
of intellectual and religious unrest ushered in by the war, suggests
that William Temple's teaching on the suffering of God in *Christus
Veritas* (1924) was 'evoked no doubt by sensitivity to the distresses of
the time', but claims that the most direct impact of the war was on
popular teaching, in Studdert Kennedy's *The Hardest Part* specifically,
which was 'written for readers sensitive to the agony of the world,
[and] spoke of God as the greatest sufferer of all'.[45]

So it was in the literature emerging directly from the war itself that
there were developments that might be used in a post-war context, at
the level of a popular and unsystematic theology, a concentration on
the idea of a suffering and human Christ, on the incarnation and a
sacramental interpretation of reality. This was an intensification of
an extended process in which *Lux Mundi* had been important before
the turn of the century, a shift away from emphasis on sin and
atonement to a more compelling sense of immanent presence.

This wartime development in the religious interpretation of reality
needs to be distinguished from an undoctrinal tendency for
articulate people to manipulate and explore images in the literary
tradition they had inherited, in their attempts to understand what
was happening to them in the war. Letters, verses and narratives

inevitably turned to imagery from Old and New Testaments which made destruction intelligible, and to the powerful associative content of the image of the passive suffering of Christ, and also of course to Bunyan. Examples have been collected by Wilkinson and Fussell.[46] But a difficulty with Wilkinson's collation of literary and religious or, if one can use the word neutrally, parsonical uses of this imagery, is that we are referred to obvious and inevitable similarities between, for instance, some of the verse of Owen and Studdert Kennedy,[47] but less is made of fundamental differences. This point will have to be elaborated, but the plain man's sacramentalism, most powerfully developed by Studdert Kennedy among the padres and familiar to many from his verse and his preaching, had to do in the first instance with beliefs rather than the literary modalities of allusion, irony and paradox, whatever, precisely, his listeners derived from it. Studdert Kennedy's contribution to the Macnutt symposium, a piece on the religious difficulties of the private soldier, reappeared in a modified form in his *Rough Talks*, under the title 'Why aren't all the best chaps Christians?', and was twice reprinted as a pamphlet in early 1939.[48] It was an attempt to transcend divisions and repair the bridge between the Church and the lost and inarticulate 'Christians' of the trenches. This theology could at some level be assimilated by a wider audience than was attending to the more established voices of the Church.

However, the feeling that the war had provided the occasion for a fresh and authentic voice of prophecy—the word was quite frequently invoked—was confined to more committed believers. Wider attention to this reassertion of faith depended in part on an important paradoxical consequence of the war. There is no doubt that the derogatory image of the Church at war corresponded with the experiences of a great many servicemen, and confirmed latent hostilities and suspicions. At the same time, the individual priest who 'succeeded' was seen against this unpromising background in an impressive contrast, which was no doubt unfair to many painful and unglamorous ministries in the trenches, but was nonetheless an important element in general attitudes to the Church. The fact that such figures were few in number made the contrast all the more striking. There were about 6000 chaplains in the Department on Armistice Day.[49] Kempthorne's Diocese of Lichfield provided no less than 500 out of 600 priests for various national service projects.[50] According to the Journal of the Chaplains' Department, ninety-seven padres, fifty-seven of them Church of England, were killed in action or died of wounds. Another sixty-nine, forty-one of them Church of England, died as a result of war service. Many were decorated. The distribution of honours in a military conflict serves various purposes. In January 1918 J. M. Shakespeare, Secretary of the Baptist Union, complained that in the New Year's Honours List a disproportionate sixteen out of nineteen DSO's granted to members of the Department serving in France went to Church of England Chaplains. A month later the Chairman of the Interdenominational Advisory Committee was able to announce that there would be a supplementary list to rectify inequalities.[51] Some kind of quota must also have operated for the Department as a whole, and possibly a version of Gresham's Law with regard to the distribution of medals applied towards the end of the war. But padres from all denominations earned an honourable place in the history of the conflict by taking on the distinctive role for which Siegfried Sassoon's friend Joe Cottrill admired the Rev. M. Peel:

> I am sorry to say that the Padre—The Hon. Rev. M. Peel, M.C., got killed—he was up with the lads again at the very front of the fight and got sniped by a Bosche—the stomach and died immediately. He is a great loss. I have not much room for his crowd as a rule but Peel was the finest person I have ever known . . . He was bound to get killed sooner or later, as he was absolutely indifferent to danger and in fact courted it. Surely a splendid man and one of whom the Church should be proud.[52]

The Rev. T. B. Hardy, who gratefully acknowledged that his interpretation of the task had been shaped by a discussion with Studdert Kennedy, received the DSO, the MC, and the VC, all inside ten months before being killed.[53] Of those who survived, several of the most distinguished either joined the ICF or actively supported it. They included C. M. Chavasse, MC and Croix de Guerre, son of the evangelical Bishop of Liverpool, and twin brother of the only soldier to win the VC and Bar during the war;[54] Guy Rogers, MC, one of the new evangelicals; C. S. Woodward, MC, at a later date successively Bishop of Bristol and of Gloucester; T. Pym, MC, Head of Oxford House Camberwell; F. R. Barry, MC, Head of the Knutsford clergy training school for ex-service ordinands; and David Railton, MC, who initiated the scheme for interring an unknown warrior in Westminster Abbey.[55]

Bishop Henson of Durham directed a firm warning at those chaplains who felt that they were returning from the extremities of war with special revelations for the Church of England.[56] Congregations would not have been unduly impressed by the mere fact of military service, but Henson may well have been concerned at the potential influence of some of the outstanding figures, who had undeniably lived up to the sternest expectations. A small but articulate proportion of these returned with the visions of a practical reconstruction of church and society which disturbed him. The anomalous man of God, wearing military honours more commonly bestowed on those who have maimed and killed to good effect, had a place in the mythology of the Great War which ensured at the very least respectful attention.

G. A. STUDDERT KENNEDY

By the end of the war audiences were turning out to listen to Studdert Kennedy with high expectations. Before it he had been known inside the Church as a slum parish priest with the common touch and the imagination to offer pastoral care to every kind of individual in unself-conscious and sometimes eccentric ways. He tended to give what he had to the poor with a literal and sometimes catastrophic obedience to scriptural injunction. He sang and talked in pubs, ran a refuge for the down and out, and attended to the individual miseries of the many people who approached him.[57] A. V. Baillie, one of whose curates he was in Rugby from 1908–12, describes his activities with approval in a passage from which Purcell quotes at length, though he does not include Baillie's devastating but unelaborated judgement on the preacher's later career.

> After he left me, people were so dazzled by the amazing force of his eloquence that they took him seriously, which did him a great deal of harm.[58]

Baillie's mother had been a much loved lady-in-waiting to Queen Victoria, and the Queen was his godmother. He was Dean of Windsor from 1917–44. The retrospective judgement seems to fall as much on his former curate's admirers as on the man himself, a high Tory's distaste for the lay company Studdert Kennedy was identified with.

The dangerous talent with large audiences was given every opportunity to develop, so that by 1919 he was a major platform attraction, who seldom disappointed his audiences' expectations. He had also built up a large readership. Chronic asthma made it impossible for him to survive front-line conditions for extended periods. In June 1916, he was with the 157th Brigade of the 46th Division, in the following year with the 17th Brigade of the 24th Division, when he witnessed the mining of the Messines Ridge and was in the attack, an experience which earned him the MC, but initiated an alteration in his attitude to the war. In 1918 he was in the final advance with the 42nd Division.[59] However, the Foreword to *Rough Talks* was written at the HQ Physical and Bayonet Training, BEF, and the Introduction to *The Hardest Part* at one of the three Infantry Schools to which Bishop Gwynne, Deputy Chaplain General (and brother of the Editor of the *Morning Post*) sent him at different times. Large numbers of men passed through all of these. He was, in addition, drafted into the National Mission of Repentance, which began in the autumn of 1916, as an itinerant messenger to the armies in France. In some ten days at least 15,000 men listened to him, probably several thousand more. The Mission was regarded as a failure by leading churchmen, but it greatly extended his reputation in the army. The Archbishops followed it up by appointing five distinguished committees, and the report of the fifth of these, on Christianity and Industrial Problems, became the charter document of the *Industrial Christian Fellowship* in 1919. Gore and Tawney were both on the committee.[60]

Rough Talks is the record, with two additional chapters, of six appearances in Rouen during the Lent of 1916 before a large number of soldiers. The climax on the sixth evening, entitled for the occasion 'Christ or the Kaiser', was impressive, and there is no need to accept his own interpretation of his impact in order to recognise from his letter home that he had worked powerfully on his audience.

> Some may forget it, but surely not all; some will remember that Good Friday night for years. I won't ever forget it. It sounded strange to hear men cheer Christ—strange to us, and not perhaps what we would do, but you would have loved it, and so I am sure did He. There was the awe, the hush, the silence, and then the roar and it meant real homage from men who were, hundreds of them, going to the death.[61]

The situation was highly charged and exceptional, but this was the kind of response he could generate. Essential ingredients of such performances were, as they are for all good theatre, totally ephemeral, though one student of pulpit oratory has attempted to convey its general effect.[62] But there can be no doubt that by the end of the war, he was a spellbinder in the same class as the best political speakers of the day, and that he already had an attentive public which included large numbers of ordinary ex-servicemen and others.

His verse and prose were read by many who had never seen him. Encouraged by Macnutt, he had begun producing verses while in France. Gwynne had a number printed and distributed in the trenches, and they started appearing in small pocket editions, his familiar *nom de guerre* 'Woodbine Willie' appearing in brackets under his name on a yellow cover. *Rough Rhymes of a Padre* sold 30,000 copies in the course of a few weeks. Sales reached 70,000 by 1924. *More Rough Rhymes* followed, *Peace Rhymes of a Padre*, *Songs of Faith and Doubt*, and a collection, *The Sorrows of God*. The verse made an important contribution to his popularity at this time. He used it as a vehicle for his basic themes and reached many who would not have read his other books. Increasingly, he was to work it into his discursive writing and his speeches, along with frequent quotations from Browning, but also from others ranging from Milton to Conan Doyle, and it became an integral part of his rhetoric in the post-war decade. In addition to the two prose works already referred to, he produced *Lies* in 1919, which ran into eighteen editions by 1937 and was in its sixth by January 1921, and *Democracy and the Dog Collar* came out in that year, though sections from it had already been heavily used on the platform.[63]

For the officers of the ICF he had further valuable qualifications. He was not a reformist troublemaker of the kind that had irritated the Archbishops. He believed that a number of reforms were overdue, found certain prescribed forms of words meaningless, even blasphemous in their context in church ritual, but felt no levelling rancour towards the hierarchy, and his refreshing eccentricities—he is said to have delivered one entire sermon in blank verse, and he had no inhibitions about provoking laughter and mild outrage from the pulpit—thinly disguised an obedient churchman. Furthermore, his attitude to doctrinal and interdenominational diversity, like his impatience with the institutional preoccupations of the reformist platforms, identified him with a lay rather than a clerical perspective. 'The real duty of a good Catholic is not to wear vestments and hate Nonconformists, but to love everybody and wear Christ.'[64] During the war, a similar view of schism and dissension was encouraged by Haig, because it was in accord with his own simple faith and also because it had implications for the effective integration of the Chaplains' Department in the military structure.

> We had quite a large party of clerics at lunch . . . I had only two wishes to express. 1. Chaplains should preach about the object of Great Britain. No selfish motives. 2. Chaplains must cease quarrelling among themselves.[65]

For other reasons a pragmatic interdenominational commitment was no less essential to the ICF.

What was the substance of the appeal which commanded this degree of attention? The answer is not as straightforward as the recollections of contemporaries can suggest. Malcolm Muggeridge, for example, recalled that

> At Selwyn a good number (of ex-service undergraduates) were ordinands, mostly in the Woodbine Willie, or padre style; a version of Christianity which emerged from the 1914–18 War,

enormously sincere, ardent, and at the time seemingly vital, but which subsequently, for the most part ran into the sand. This invariably happens when it is attempted to relate a transcendental faith to an earthly hope—in this case, pacifism.[66]

But the man the ICF was recruiting was no simple pacifist. In an introduction to the reprint of 'Why aren't all the best chaps Christians?', written on St Andrew's Day, 1938, its editor Ronald Selby Wright observed that he had 'altered words and phrases here and there to remove some of the bitterness that was felt at the time of its being written against some of our former enemies who are now happily our friends. Such bitterness was afterwards strongly repudiated by Studdert Kennedy himself'. The implication is that the acerbities were an unfortunate but entirely understandable concession by a naturally enthusiastic temperament to the psychological pressures of the war. It is indeed the case that, with his friend the Rev. Dick Sheppard, also a preacher with a very large following,[67] and also on the ICF Council, he was to make a contribution to the climate of opinion reflected in the political innocence of Wright's introduction. His anti-war speeches seem to have been unforgettable. But their emotional violence must be seen in relation not only to his experience of the horrors of war, but also in relation to an ambiguous revulsion against his own involvement in the military process. During the war he had been a highly effective patriotic preacher, who had gone further than some in translating Haig's expressed wishes into combative incitement. *Rough Talks* provided everything the authorities could ask for.

> You could not make machine parts out of Britons; they would give the fitters the devil of a time because they would not fit. Britons can be led, they can't be driven; Germans can be driven, but can't be led. There you have the difference between the two people in a nutshell. The British officer goes before his men and cheers; the German officer comes behind his men and snarls. (*RT*, 40)

> The great German crime is the denial of this sporting spirit and its universal application. (*RT*, 28)

> When the nation was up against it, with its back against the wall, men struck and claimed holidays. They refused to recognise the peril; they would neither be driven nor led. It has been a humiliating spectacle this strike in time of war, and it is a sign of decay in the national spirit. It means that some of our workmen are not fit for freedom and its high call . . . The master who would make a fortune out of his country's loss, and the man who would

imperil his comrades' lives to make a higher wage, are both traitors and murderers, and ought to be shot. (*RT*, 86–7)

Finally, we stand for Peace. That is a word which must be uttered now with bated breath. It is a sacred name which is glibly taken in vain by so many sloppy, cowardly and thoughtless people, who think it can be bought and bargained for, before it is earned. They cry out against War, not because it is wrong, but because it is so damned uncomfortable. (*RT*, 61)

There is a good deal in the same vein. The pugnacious Britisher loves freedom and fair play. The Prussian commits atrocities and is a cog in an inhuman machine. The Prussian is honest, but it is the devil's honesty, based on a denial of all ideals except the rightness of might. In August 1914 God called in a voice of thunder across the sea to come out and share His sorrow and save the world, and England answered 'I come'.

These crudities tend to be quoted in a local context which makes them seem idiosyncratically violent.[68] They were in fact commonplaces deriving from sources that were addressed with greater urbanity to another class of reader. Social Darwinist premises had been heavily employed by German intellectuals and politicians before the war to provide a 'philosophical' justification for the bid for World Power status, and German historians were preoccupied with the State and its purposes, in its foreign relations particularly, to a degree that was plainly menacing.[69] Lay perceptions of this were influenced by writers like Norman Angell and J. A. Cramb, Professor of Modern History at Queen's College, whose 1913 lectures ran into ten editions between June and September of the following year.[70] Studdert Kennedy read Angell (*HP*, 32), and echoes him (*RT*, 58–9), while a number of confident allusions to Treitschke, who was not translated until 1914, and also perhaps his occasional reflections on Napoleon, could easily be drawn from Cramb, though a number of commentaries were published in that year. Cramb points to the clearness and self-consistency, of contemporary Napoleonism in Germany, its repudiation of Christ's law of self-effacement, and its transfiguration of 'the tedious, half-hypocritical morality of an earlier generation ... Corsica, in a word, has conquered Galilee'.[71] Against this threat we must pit a society still free, though physically and morally vulnerable, and an empire redeemed by the disinterested and progressive intentions of its rulers. The conflict is an ethically radical one.

Behind the eve of war alarmism there were more long-standing preoccupations which had involved the Church generally and drawn on the Maurician tradition in particular. Dilke's social reformism

went hand in hand with a commitment to the beneficent
imperialism of an organic society. The misuse of national human
resources through malnutrition and the neglect of training was seen
as a major contribution to the gap between national power and
pretension.[72] A decade later, Major General Maurice, the intensely
partisan author of his father's life and letters,[73] picked up the theme
in *National Defences*, an authoritative popular text.[74] Throughout the
Edwardian period the Prussian example of the advantages of a tightly
organised society excited both fear and admiration among
educationalists, military men, Milnerites, Fabians and Liberal
Imperialists who participated in the pre-war quest for national
efficiency. Haldane's army reforms, his interest in the modern,
'scientific' soldier and in the development of the Territorials
reflected these concerns. Followers of the cult of efficiency recognised
the congruence between their own loosely agreed formula for
national survival and elements in the broad church tradition, with its
hierarchical paradigm for social order, sustained by natural
relationships and common values. The Church could provide the
moralised organic doctrine to justify expedient collectivist
developments, whilst fending off the threat to certain liberal values
which was implicit in the secular social Darwinism of such a popular
writer as Benjamin Kidd, whose *Social Evolution* established him as a
leading sociologist on its publication in 1894. Motives were no doubt
mixed, but it was natural and inevitable that Major General Maurice,
for instance, should appeal directly to the morality of his clerical
friends in an argument which at the same time emphasises national
interest and commercial rationality. A. V. Baillie, Studdert
Kennedy's superior at Rugby, kept in his library a copy of *National
Defences*, inscribed by the author for Baillie's birthday in 1897, when
he was vicar of St Margaret's Plumstead. With more calculated
intent, the Webbs hob-nobbed with Bishops Creighton, Talbot and
Lang on the Church's modern function as the guardian of national
communal aspirations and on the potential role of its leaders in
national reconstruction.[75] Indeed, as late as 1921, Haig spoke up for
something very like J. R. Seeley's National Church and was
applauded for it by Inge. Maurice got into difficulties for echoing
him at a Life and Liberty meeting.[76] Studdert Kennedy had long been
sensitive to the appeals for a consecrated nationalism. He had even
been in uniform before the war as an unco-ordinated but
enthusiastic volunteer, and to the end of his life would invoke
Haldane on the subject of leadership with something approaching
reverence.[77] The harsh statements about Prussians and shirkers were
the popular expression of a respectably consolidated attitude.

So the parade ground talks had a context. However, for him the
importance of the battle at the Messines ridge was not that the entire

system of beliefs and assumptions implicated in this context was suddenly invalidated, necessitating a radical inversion of commitments. On the contrary, the essential features of his system of beliefs remained remarkably constant. He had, however, come up against a realisation that what had for him been a passionate commitment was itself infected with the madness of war in ways he had not been able to recognise. His commitment had been theatrically and by all accounts effectively displayed. Colonel Ronald Campbell, CBE, DSO, of the 4th Army School ('Pokey' Campbell) recorded that he

> used to take him to the troops in the field as one of a troupe (called by Studdert Kennedy 'the travelling circus'), which included Jimmy Driscoll, the champion boxer, two champion wrestlers, and an N.C.O. who had killed eighteen Germans with a bayonet. After these thugs had given a demonstration of the methods of killing and self defence, Woodbine Willie would finish up with twenty minutes' talk which never failed to get a wonderful response from his audience, leaving them with their 'tails up' and ready for battle.[78]

According to Purcell he would himself spar with Driscoll and demonstrate unarmed combat.[79]

The clerical memoirs either make no comment or are sentimentally apologetic about this piece of *guignol*. But it is not difficult to see its implications for a sensitive man subsequently attempting a drastic reassessment of his wartime ministry. The relevance for the content of his public speaking is that, however widespread a kind of tow-path enthusiasm may have been among young parsons with the padre style, the post-war message of the preacher himself incorporated unresolved tensions and a deep strain of pessimism, personal guilt about the war, frequently expressed in speeches later in the decade, and an ambivalent treatment of the wider social implications of his sacramental theology. Speaking in the Central Hall, Westminster, on Armistice Day 1921, he said:

> . . . If they killed your husband—in Christ's name, forgive. They were mad. I was mad—crazy. We got decorated for doing things that we did when we were mad . . .[80]

But the same tensions reveal themselves in other areas. In Mozley's view, encapsulated in the abstract language of a professional theologian, the inescapable paradoxes of faith had emerged in the war with unforeseen intensity. But given a continuous thematic reference in Studdert Kennedy's output to the question of action in a specific and contemporary social order, the tensions have further implications.

The system of beliefs, an assertively simple theology and a social theory that was far from being original, is not in itself difficult to outline. The theology was doubtless unbalanced, a 'pure patripassianism . . . that of Mr H. G. Wells, not of the Creeds' was how one reviewer, presumably Charles Raven, put it in the month of Studdert Kennedy's death,[81] but it was, nonetheless, essentially orthodox. Canon Raven, who was on the ICF Executive, was also, like Adderley, both a Christian Socialist and an authority on Christian socialism,[82] and he seems, too, to have responded as equivocally to Studdert Kennedy as Adderley had done.

The main themes in the preacher's social theory are set out here descriptively rather than analytically, in a more condensed form than he had occasion to use himself, by drawing on material that was already available by the end of the war, *Rough Talks* and *The Hardest Part*. This will identify his general position as a popular version of a perspective that was being propounded with greater refinement by others. We can make use of an immediately contemporary text, L. T. Hobhouse's *The Metaphysical Theory of the State*,[83] which shares none of the strictly theological preoccupations, but draws on broadly congruent guiding assumptions. They locate the preacher's message in a philosophical tradition. But Hobhouse also provides a suggestive parallel at a literary level, in one brief but striking and well-known passage, where he presents himself and his intellectual activity very vividly as an integral part of the harsh military conflict across the Channel. In *The Hardest Part* Studdert Kennedy does something similar, employing the ideas which have reached him more or less indirectly from some of the same sources. It is worth setting passages from both side by side in order to provide a representative example at an early stage of a characteristic projection of a philosophical theme into a concrete situation. It was in large measure this sort of facility, better illustrated than anatomised, which the ICF recognised as an invaluable asset. The chapter concludes by identifying some of the central ambiguities referred to above as they reveal themselves in this distinctive idiom.

The organising concept behind the preacher's anti-Prussianism is a conflict between two ideas of history, a concept which integrates his treatment of many other themes, his hostility to striking workers, for instance, and even his direct and cathartic discussions for soldiers out of the line of the standard problems of sex and drink (*RT*, 112–17).

I dare say you think I am exaggerating the part which ideas have played in causing the struggle, and are thinking to yourselves that the real causes are money and race conflict . . . I want you to understand that I am not blind to the enormous part which money and economic conditions have played in wars of the past, nor am I out to deny that they played a part in this war and its causes, but I am sure that apart from militarist theories, fostered by false teaching, and the wholesale rejection of the moral basis of Christian civilisation, purely economic causes would never have led Germany to risk all her prosperity on a throw of the dice in war. (*RT*, 58–9)

The false teaching, to which Frederick the Great, Napoleon, Bismarck, Darwin, Haeckel, and the materialistic evolutionists all contributed was distilled by Treitschke and his kind into a theory of state power and state will, a collective purpose which must be pursued by violence, and into which the individual was absorbed, an idea of collective survival and dominance to which he abandoned his will and his power of choice. This was scientific barbarism, the substitution of a mechanical, willed causation for the more unpredictable but ethically fertile causation of individual choice.

We thought we would have to worship an engine—an engine!—not even an engine-driver. Personally, I might have managed an engine-driver. Engine-drivers are alive, and do strange things. I knew one who used to get drunk and spit in unexpected places. I did not worship him, but I did like him. He was at any rate a person. But worshipping an engine, a mechanical system, makes me feel like a cog—a little cog in a big wheel. That is what it does make a man feel. It is soul-destroying, because it denies liberty. It is German, that's what it is; in fact, it's the devil. It is as intellectually impressive and as vitally futile as Pan-Germanism, because it has no psychology, and does not believe in souls. (*HP*, 22–3)

For us the possibility was not merely one of defeat by a diabolical military machine, but of a damnation which could overtake us on the road to victory, because war forced its unwilling victims themselves to devise an engine of collective will and in the process to modify the nature of what they were defending. There was more to protect than territory and independence. There was a totally different conception of the social collectivity, of the public good and of the meaning and end of history. On the broadest view, the process of history was an evolution towards union, interdependence, combination at levels of increasing scope and generality. It was a thoroughly confused process because of human error and the dynamics of interminable conflicts, liable to ruinous reverses, but progressively uncovering possibilities, patterns of co-operative social interaction and new forms of material organisation. More specifically, the collective realisation of the larger process was embodied in hierarchies of social institutions, starting with the family, which more or less successfully balanced the good of the individual against the good of the whole, and since the whole was an organisation of individuals rather than an abstract system of functions serving superordinate ends, it was in and through individuals that the larger process was understood and acted out. This was the truth that scientific barbarism would destroy, thereby foreclosing human development, or, in his own language, the redemptive process.

Patriotism in this context is not at all the Mafeking emotion that had nauseated liberal churchmen like Scott Holland and Gore at the time of the South African war.[84] The audience at Rouen was assured that:

> We have gained a new patriotism because it has suddenly become fashionable to give all and get nothing. Public opinion has become so nearly Christian as to condemn selfishness as sin. To give up all for England has ceased to be quixotic and become just commonplace. Duty as a matter of course comes first . . . We stand now, as we should always stand, at attention, waiting for the word of God's command. We are once more a patriotic people. (*RT*, 150)

Patriotism was a collective discovery of the organic nature of society, and that included a willing acknowledgement of the differentiation of functions essential to the society's survival, a unity of clean hearts behind a leadership of clear heads (*RT*, 162). Freedom, in some fundamental sense, had been achieved and demonstrated in the wholesale 'christian' condemnation of selfishness, the liberating decision to submerge the lesser good in the good of the larger unity, a discovery of the true meaning of duty, a provisional advance in the process of redemption. In passages like this he is looking well beyond the next big push. Somehow the front-line images of redeeming significance, loyalties, obedience, sacrifice, leadership, discipline must serve to sustain us in the fractured and ambiguous conditions of peace.

Hobhouse is, of course, much more rigorous, but he could be taken as a model for this general position. The error he seeks to dispose of is Hegel's metaphysical theory of the state and Bosanquet's English version of it.

> Briefly, we are morally free when our actions conform to our real will, our real will is the general will, and the general will is most fully embodied in the state. These are the governing positions of the metaphysical theory which we have to examine.[85]

Against this he sets up a balanced appraisal of T. H. Green's *Principles of Obligation* (1895), with its insistence on the obligation of each man to 'realise his own perfection as an integral part of the common good',[86] which necessarily entails reciprocal relations between state and society in which the scope of the individual is protected by rights.

> The truth is that the State is only one element in the society of human kind. It is an organisation which men have built up, partly with conscious purpose, but largely through a clash of purposes which has settled down into an order exhibiting some permanence, but constantly threatened with more or less revolutionary changes. In this order there is nothing sacrosanct. On the contrary, government, law and the institutions lying behind and supporting them are far from being the most successful of the experiments of mankind. They call for radical criticism, and to deify them is to establish false gods, gods who at the present time figure as veritable Molochs before whom our sons are made to pass in millions through the fire.[87]

In the metaphysical theory, collective will was reified in the momentum given society by current institutions and the preferences of current holders of power, and prohibited the expression of a plurality of purposes. But in a free society, this complex of psychological forces, many of them selfish and sometimes violent, did over time produce 'the institutions and traditions of society (which) imply a certain social mentality',[88] a process which modified individual expectations, drawing people with varying degrees of disinterested awareness into the shaped reciprocities of a social organism, as against locking them into the functional requirements of a social mechanism.

The uncompromising tone of Hobhouse's polemic against German idealism, however, is misleading. His reputation in this regard, Rodney Barker suggests, 'has been sustained, or encapsulated in the memory of Hobhouse's outburst (in the Introduction to the book) against the Zeppelins which disturbed him in his garden as excrescences of Hegelianism', a passage which will be quoted below.[89] But Green's ambiguities left it open to his followers to make what Richter describes as 'the most discrepant deductions',[90] and Hobhouse himself was in fact firmly attached to Green's idealist notion of 'positive freedom' which entailed a sanitised version of the theory of the general will which he was attacking.[91] Studdert Kennedy in his turn inherited the ambiguities of the Green tradition and liberated the individual in the name, effectively, of positive freedom, though he did not use the term. The individual was truly an individual only as a member of the purposeful social whole. The dialectical paradox of Plato's Republic was brought home to roost by the followers of Green, even when they claimed, like Hobhouse and William Temple, to have worked themselves loose from the habits of Oxford idealism.

Hobhouse's rationalism, 'a derivation of idealist conclusions from empiricist premises', needed to call on no specifically Christian beliefs.[92] For Studdert Kennedy an interpretation of Christian dogma was fundamental, and his guiding preoccupation with the incarnation of Christ, God's participation in the process of the development of man through his suffering in the person of Christ, was a point of departure constantly revisited as a source of energy for a rehearsal of one familiar theme or another. He would refer to his beliefs as the hypothesis on which he gambled, and his determination to assert, express and induce others to share a sacramental sense of reality colours his entire output. There were standard critical and theological arguments available which he used. Thus, an organic theory of social evolution could be presented as a general paraphrase of the paradigm which existed in the divinely inspired history of the Jewish people. The Bible recorded a groping evolution towards a truer conception of the nature of man's unity in God, in the course of which much confusion was occasionally transformed by cumulative moments of insight, by the words of the prophet Hosea, for instance, and the twelve verses of Isaiah 53, and ultimately by the Incarnation and what that entailed for an understanding of the nature of God (*HP*, Ch 4). The paradigm revealed that the premise on which Christian history was based was the existence of individual choice, the freedom to err and the capacity, through the Grace of God, for discovery and regeneration. This interpretation, at least at one level, accounted for the existence of suffering. History was God's decision to endure the consequences of creating the necessity of free choice and to suffer with man the apparently arbitrary evils of our fallen condition.

This argument, extensively developed in modern biblical criticism, provided a framework for the interpretation of scriptural authority, and a larger coherence for the cosmic drama of the Incarnation. But what for Studdert Kennedy compelled assent was the human example, above all the suffering of Christ. A correspondence between the sufferings of Christ and the passive endurance of trench warfare by ordinary soldiers was obvious to the point of banality,[93] though superbly exploited by a few writers, notably by Wilfred Owen in a rich set piece contained in a personal letter.

> For 14 hours yesterday I was at work—teaching Christ to lift his cross by numbers, and how to adjust his crown; and not to

imagine he thirst until after the last halt. I attended his supper to see that there were not complaints; and inspected his feet that they should be worthy of the nails. I see to it that he is dumb, and stands at attention before his accusers. With a piece of silver I buy him every day, and with maps I make him familiar with the topography of Golgotha.[94]

But in the framework of a sacramental interpretation of history, the correspondence had quite different implications and the reasons for dwelling on it and evoking it were different also. Owen used it to explore a situation and his own role in it. Studdert Kennedy interpreted, explained, and in one sense justified the common situation in terms of a higher reality which was allegedly manifested in the historical Christ and simultaneously in the dumb victim of the war. The cost of regeneration and progress in the light of the Divine purpose was suffering. Its victims were unaware of its significance and intensity, because it was more than merely *like* the suffering of Christ, it *was* that suffering. The fear that had to be suppressed before going over the top had been experienced by a human Christ in the Garden of Gethsemane, who re-enacted that victorious encounter in every battle. At its simplest and least articulate, in comradeship and self-sacrifice, the suffering revealed the Christlike impulse to deny self in the interests of a higher unity. At least during the war, the preacher saw in the new patriotism the same impulse appearing at a higher level of collective awareness, a sense of unity, in harmony with the Divine intention, and increasingly alive to its roots in individual conduct.

All men are learning to worship patient, suffering love, and the muddy bloody hero of the trenches is showing us Who is the real King. The darkness is being cleared away, and men at last are growing proud of the Cross. Beside the wounded tattered soldier who totters down to this dressing station with one arm hanging loose, an earthly king in all his glory looks paltry and absurd. I know nothing in my real religion of the Almighty God of power. I only see God in Christ, and these men have shown me—*Him.* (*HP*, 71)

The sacramental assertions in passages such as this suggest the more fortuitous parallel referred to earlier with Hobhouse's vision of the material expression of Ideas. Driven by an urge to provide a straightforward illustration of the formative activity of ideas within the material contingencies of history, Hobhouse wrote a sensitive introductory letter to his son, Lieutenant Oliver Hobhouse, a pilot in the RAF in France. Elaboration and nuance retreat as the existential

situation of the middle-aged philosopher emerges. The young
airman is reminded of their sitting together reading Kant in the 'cool
Highgate garden in those summer days of peace',

> ... because three years later I was reading his great successor in
> the same garden in the same summer weather but not with you.
> One morning as I sat there annotating Hegel's theory of freedom,
> jarring sounds broke in upon the summer stillness ... Gunfire, at
> first distant, grew rapidly nearer, and soon broke out from the
> northern heights hard by. The familiar drone of the British
> aeroplanes was pierced by the whining of the Gothas. High above,
> machine guns barked in sharp stoccato and distant thuds
> announced the fall of bombs. Presently three white specks could
> be seen dimly through the light haze overhead, and we watched
> their course from the field. The raid was soon over. The three
> specks faded away, and below the hill the great city picked up its
> dead. The familiar sounds resumed their sway, the small birds
> chirruped from the shrubs, and the distant murmur of the traffic
> told of a world going steadily on its accustomed course.
>
> As I went back to my Hegel my first mood was one of self-satire.
> Was this a time for theorizing or destroying theories, when the
> world was tumbling about our ears? My second thoughts ran
> otherwise. To each man the tools and weapons that he can best
> use. In the bombing of London I had just witnessed the visible and
> tangible outcome of a false and wicked doctrine the foundation of
> which lay, as I believe, in the book before me.[95]

This memorable expression of idealist convictions has much in
common with Studdert Kennedy's sacramental idiom. An equivalent
passage in *The Hardest Part* is in fact more complex and dramatic. It
includes the equivocal and corrupting aspect of commitment, a pre-
echo of Biblical history, and both ironical and reverential allusions to
the Divine Will and Authority, as well as the standard imagery of
innocent Edwardian pastoral and the identification of the
philosopher or metaphysician in the ranks of the combatants. The
first chapter of *The Hardest Part* is a preliminary series of reflections set
in the assembly trenches on the morning of 7 June 1917, just before
the attack on the Whyschaete–Messines Ridge.

> ... What a glorious morning! So still. Now the birds are just
> awaking in English Wood. How soft the silver dawn light is, and
> this grey mist that hangs so low makes all the open meadow land
> just like a dim-lit sea, with clumps of trees for islands. In the east
> there is a flush of red—blood red. Blood ... Beauty ... God's
> Fruits. I wonder what—

* * *

God Almighty! What's that? It's the Hill gone up. Lord, what a noise! and all the earth is shaking. It must be like that Korah, Dathan and Abiram business in the Book of Numbers up there . . . We're all laughing. We're enjoying it. That's the stuff to give 'em. It is a glorious sight, one silver sheet of leaping flame against the blackness of the trees. But it's damnable, its a disgrace to civilisation. It's murder—wholesale murder . . . What's that, lad? Shout a bit louder. It is, you're *right*, it is the stuff to give 'em. They can't stand much of that; they'll have to quit.

* * *

How wonderful that sky is, golden red, and all the grass is diamond-spangled like the gorgeous robe that clothes a king. Solomon in all his glory. Look at that lark. Up he goes. He doesn't care a tuppeny dump for the guns. His song is drowned, but not his joy.

> God's in His heaven;
> All's right with the—

What awful nonsense! All's right with the world, and this ghastly hideous—But, by George it's a glorious barrage, and English girls made 'em. We're all in it—sweethearts, mothers, and wives. The hand that rocks the cradle wrecks the world. There are no non-combatants. We're all in it, and God, God Almighty, the loving Father who takes count of every sparrow's fall, what is He doing? It is hard to fathom . . .

There are, however, the central and recurring themes which he cannot take up with the same command over the implications of his rhetoric, most notably the theme of the individual in a democratic society, which is touched on intermittently in *Rough Talks*. The question of the effect of such writing on his admirers at the time will be taken up later, but the material can be illustrated here from characteristic examples, which range from a contrived chapter in *The Hardest Part*, which candidly expresses anxieties while indulging in evasions that are a consistent feature, to the emotional disorder of some of his popular verse.

Each chapter of *The Hardest Part* opens with a detached exordium in the form of a compact description, often of a random death, which sets up a paradox for the ensuing reflections on a doctrinal theme, such as the Sacrament, Life Eternal, or Prayer, and directs the response to it. Opening the chapter on God and Democracy, he recalls a service in a tent between battles.

. . . The thanks of the Commander-in-Chief had been conveyed to the troops for

their gallantry in the recent action, and parade finished with 'God Save the King'.

The chapter proper starts with a slightly daring admission.

> I never was thrilled by 'God Save the King' before. As a rule it leaves me cold; to-day it sent a tingling down my spine and gave me a lump in my throat. I wonder why. I suppose I am a bit upset really; hell is bad for the nerves. The parade was pretty awful too, so many splendid chaps absentees; it gets on one's nerves . . .

God Save the King, he says, is certainly not the British army's confession of faith. Whatever the army really has in that line would

> . . . all centre round the ideas of Democracy and Freedom . . . They do believe in Democracy. They are not quite sure what it means, but whatever it means, they believe in it . . . This is their faith, vague and shadowy, but enormously powerful and big with mighty issues, good and evil, for the days that are to come.
>
> I was driven to this truth about the British soldier by my wanderings as a preacher through the bases and the armies in the field, and I was driven against my will, for, in many ways, the prospect frightens me.
>
> Any form of democracy is bound to throw such an enormous weight of responsibility upon the ordinary average man, and he, splendid fellow as he is, seems to be much more alive to his rights than to his responsibilities in the free democracy that is to be.

This, very early in the chapter, is the only reference to the idea of 'rights' or political demands of any kind in a democratic polity, apart from a passing and characteristic reference to the 'pioneers of social betterment' and the slights they had suffered from narrow-minded, ignorant and conventional Christians. The rest celebrates at a vague elevation and with some repetition our national repudiation of tyranny.

The pageantry of kings had had its day. Democracy had arrived as part of the development of man. Whole populations had begun to acquire education. Societies had, so to speak, grown up, and it was merely pathetic for states and churches to try to retrieve their absolute authority. The reason of man had revolted from the repulsive fatalism which had been justified by the doctrine of an Almighty God. Now

> in their hearts all true men worship one God—the naked, wounded, bloody, but unconquered and unconquerable Christ.

This is the God for whom the heart of Democracy is longing, and after Whom it is blindly, blunderingly, but earnestly groping . . . Christ pronounced the doom of Kaiserdom.

This leads to a warning.

The British Demos is astoundingly Christian, but it is exposed to awful dangers as it advances in freedom and takes up the inevitable burden of responsibility.

Finally, a peroration resolves the opening rhetorical dilemma with disarming formality, in an image of transmuted stability, the fullness of a familiar inheritance, which is also a 'type' of abnegation for every man to contemplate as he confronts the dangers ahead.

Perhaps, after all, I ought to be thrilled by 'God Save the King'. Our English kings are public servants now. The King of the British is a monarch of free men. A patient, painstaking, public servant upon whom great burdens of responsibility rest. If any king survives it will be ours, for he is very nearly a 'Christian king'. The crown of our British Kings is a crown of golden thorns. Perhaps our English 'God Save the King' is a fit song for the Army of the Free. I think I will always love it more since I heard it sung by men who stood at attention with death behind them and death before.

The 'astoundingly Christian Demos' is of course the central figure in the sacramental interpretation of the 'inarticulate Christianity' of the trenches, and the correspondence here between soldier and Christ was not, as has been pointed out, merely religiose. However, the actual expression of 'Woodbine Willie's' sacramentalism in this crucial area is decidedly unstable, and reflects more obviously than anything else a deeply ambivalent attitude to the ordinary man, the ranker. In the abstract, of course, and given a universal application, this is the essence of theological orthodoxy; every individual is capable of both good and evil. This is how he appears in a chapter on God and The Church.

> . . . *He was still kneeling up on one knee in a shell-hole, grasping his rifle, with his face turned towards the Green Line which two days before had cost our battalion many lives to win. His forehead was pierced with a bullet which had evidently killed him instantly. His identity disc bore the name of Pte. Peter—*
> . . . Evidently rose to advance and got it clean through the head. It's a fine fighting face; no saint, but a fine man. A gentleman in his own way, as every British Tommy is. If faces go for much he was no saint. Heavy fighting jaw; thick sensual lips; deep lines

round the eyes and mouth. They all tell the same tale. This was man Peter—fine man, Peter, but no Saint Peter. I should not think he was a pillar of the Church. Not the sort of stuff we build them of. Yet, I don't know . . .

But later, inevitably, this ambiguous potential is associated with the threat of a massive social deviation, to which the failures of the Church have contributed, but whose agents will be collective and undisciplined social forces, an expression in the mass of our fallen condition.

> . . . So Peter has left the Church, and found what his soul needed in his union, his club, his cause—the cause of the down-trodden and oppressed . . . Everywhere the followers of Christ are outside the Church . . .
> . . . She knows her weakness, and that means much; she knows she has betrayed her Lord, but at any rate in this war she has gone out to weep bitterly.
> And let me whisper this, lad: she loves you, she really loves you, and she is not the Church of a class any longer at heart. She means to reform. (*HP*, Ch viii)

Elsewhere, however, the ordinary soldier is celebrated in an unqualified transfiguration, a variant in verse of a passage of prose quoted earlier (p. 67). It is hardly necessary to point out that the image is of disciplined and collective patience and suffering.

> Still I see them coming, coming
> In their ragged broken line,
> Walking wounded in the sunlight,
> Clothed in majesty divine.
>
> For the fairest of the lilies,
> That God's summer ever sees,
> Ne'er was clothed in royal beauty
> Such as decks the least of these.
>
> Tattered, torn, and bloody khaki,
> Gleams of white flesh in the sun,
> Raiment worthy of their beauty
> And the great things they have done.
>
> Purple robes and snowy linen
> Have for earthly kings sufficed,
> But these bloody sweaty tatters
> Were the robes of Jesus Christ.
>
> ('Solomon in all his glory')

Finally, in a poem like 'The Gift' it is simply impossible to arrive at a coherent reading at all. One can follow no sequence of thought or association in order to link the Calvary of the opening lines with the crucifix of the last, with Rob McNeil and with the Hun he wanted killed, which does not define an emotional and intellectual morass. There is no question of explaining the difficulties as one might the contradictions in a Browning monologue. His frequent imitations of Browning do not reach that level of psychological complexity. But the confusions were acceptable and, one must argue, were part of the attraction for his readers. In this particular case, in the context of the Just War, which was undertaken with Divine sanction, they are compounded, but there can be no missing the guilt associated with the death of the central figure, and the hopeless attempt to submit it to the redeeming power of the sacramental idea.

> Dead black against a blood-red sky
>> It stands,
> With outstretched hands,
>> The Calvary.
> What can it mean
> Beyond the vain recalling of a scene,
> A shameful scene of centuries ago?
> And yet, if that be so,
>> How can it be,
>> For you and me
> A thing of any worth at all?
> We've seen men die,
> Not once, nor twice, but many times
>> In agony
> As ghastly to behold as that.
> We've seen men fall,
> And rise, and staggering onward fall again,
> Bedrenched in their own blood . . .
> . . . Do you remember Rob McNeil
>> And how he died,
>> And cried,
> And pleaded with his men
>> To take that gun,
>> And kill the Hun that worked it dead?
>> He bled
> Horribly. Do you remember?
> I can't forget,
> I would not if I could,
> It were not right I should

He died for me.
He was a God, that Boy,
The only God I could adore.
And that reminds me I have something here
He wore:
He gave it me that night,
But because my heart was sore
With grief, I have not dared to look at it.
But here it is, a little leather case,
A picture, maybe, of the face
That smiled upon him as a babe,
    All wondering bright,
    With mother light,
Of tenderest pride and Love.
The face that oft would dimple into laughter
At his first baby tricks.
It is her gift: but look at it—
A little silver Crucifix.

        ('Her Gift')

4 Anglican Social Gospels and the Testimony of Science

TAWNEY AND CUNNINGHAM

Gore, Temple and Tawney were dominant figures on the more radical flank of the Church of England in the interwar period. There were strong personal ties between them, dating in the case of the two younger men from boyhood at Rugby and their subsequent careers at Balliol.[1] All three were associated, in different ways, with the ICF. Tawney, 'a discriminating satellite in the outer orbit of the Church of England',[2] joined the Council but only for a year, in 1923–4, and attended neither of the meetings. Gore attended committee meetings and three Council meetings in 1920–1, while Temple, who became Bishop of Manchester in January 1921, attended a Council meeting in 1920. Like Gore, he continued his formal membership and encouraged the organisation, which was active in his diocese, but apart from certain public activities at the time of the General Strike, neither man was identified particularly closely with it. Indeed, the ICF was just one element, though an important one, in the consortium which Temple drew into the organisation associated with his 1924 Conference on Politics, Economics and Citizenship in Birmingham (COPEC). The support of such widely known Christian Socialists was, nevertheless, of prime importance to the ICF and both Gore and Temple were major influences on its Messenger. An influence in some respects more fundamental, though unacknowledged and submerged, was, it will be suggested, that of the Rev. William Cunningham (d. 1919). Like Tawney, he was a distinguished economic historian.

A number of quite evident intellectual debts will emerge in this chapter, to three members of this distinguished anglican quartet and to the social scientists discussed in the final section. But the intention is less to trace specific influences in detail, an unprofitable undertaking at this level of eclectic absorption, than to locate the ideological centre of gravity of the ICF, particularly in the output of its Messenger, by developing a number of contrasts and comparisons.

His general orientation had little in common with Tawney's, but was close to Cunningham's. With Gore and, more intimately, with Temple, he entered into personal relationships that affected his most central preoccupations as a believer, and he reflects these two powerful personalities in selective and rather complex ways. All four of them, however, despite significant contrasts, saw themselves as heirs to a common and peculiarly English tradition of social thought, which included many intellectuals, such as Hobhouse, who were outside any direct anglican tradition. It is with a brief consideration of T. H. Green, its most influential exponent, that we must begin.

Freeden's point on the multitudinous intellectual activity of Edwardian liberalism is well taken, that 'at the very most Idealism must be regarded as one element amidst a general progressive movement in ideology, philosophy, economics, science, and practical politics',[3] but Green's importance to our particular sector of this movement was substantial, and it is from his ambiguities that the relevant variations in emphasis largely derive. These variations are strands in a mediating 'religious' bond, itself an ambivalent one, between liberalism and socialism, which is of substantial importance to the general movement.[4]

Green's main influence was diffuse, operating, Freeden suggests, more through an emotional atmosphere, which formed motivations for engaging in social reform, than through an intellectual rationale.[5] As a social connection, the tradition is powerfully represented in the ICF. There were a number of leading figures from the public schools with places on the Council, including Canon A. A. David, Headmaster of Clifton and of Rugby, Bishop of St Edmundsbury (1921–3) and F. J. Chavasse's successor as Bishop of Liverpool, also T. C. Fry, Canon of Lincoln and formerly Headmaster of Oundle and of Berkhamstead, who is unflatteringly recalled by Graeme Greene, a relative by marriage and son of his successor at Berkhamstead.[6] Among these was W. W. Vaughan, Headmaster of Wellington and of Rugby. He married the daughter of J. A. Symonds, the Renaissance historian, whose sister had married Green, a close friend from the 'Old Mortality' essay society at Balliol. Vaughan was additionally related to Green, whose mother was the niece of Vaughan's grandfather. The Balliol connection with Green was represented by the two Masters, A. L. Smith and A. D. Lindsay. In addition to the social reformers referred to earlier, many of the ICF people had worked at Toynbee Hall and the settlements under the atmospheric influence represented by these connections.

The intellectual legacy, which was heavily worked, consisted of a system of categories which Green had explored with considerable density but, Richter suggests, a degree even of deliberate ambiguity.[7] Green's heirs were constantly reviewing the concepts of Personality, Freedom and Community and, the notion at the heart of his metaphysics, the teleological definition of Obligation. Human life was a struggle for perfection in a material context of unfolding rationality, which was perceived with increasing clarity by the evolving consciousness of mind and realised increasingly, but always imperfectly, in customs, laws and institutions. Seen in terms of this purposive unfolding, evil and injustice must be necessary means. Purpose, since only individuals have Personality, was individual, a man's relationship with God, or rather it was sustained by the individual, but realised in terms of one's contribution to a social process and a corporate struggle and evolution. Whether God in a Christian sense was necessary to Green's scheme is not clear, and his ambiguity on this point may have been a characteristic attempt to blur the grounds for conflict.[8] But the fundamental political ambiguity in his rationale derived from an unexamined relationship between freedom and obligation. 'In abandoning the older view (of freedom) so long held by liberals, Green gave up a concept which, whatever its difficulties, was still an effective weapon against dictators and all others who would destroy liberty in the name of some allegedly higher principle called "positive freedom".'[9] But, since he assumed that Will, the energy of the higher self, and not force, was the basis of the State, enacting the grand and rational design, he had no logical place for any paradoxical conflict between individual and society. The notion of positive freedom made an inexplicit appeal, in an irenic assimilation of conservative doctrine, to a benign organicism. This was qualified in a number of ways: since rights were collectively defined they had to be practically maintained against a natural tendency to relapse, so there was no objection to ordered trade union activity, for instance, and the evolutionary argument entailed a consistent development of education, though of course on terms defined by the instruments and agents of evolving mind.

It was above all Green's unstable resolution of the tension between individual and society that invited the 'discrepant deductions' of his followers. Some, like Hobhouse, who acknowledged the necessity for compulsion by the State and the problem of reorganising constraints in a complex society,[10] moved towards a more radical and progressive interpretation of the role of state interference in furthering the good of the community. The variant developed by D. G. Ritchie, one of Green's outstanding pupils, which particularly appealed to the combative mentality of Scott Holland, accepted social struggle and competition as the expression of a consciously directed selection, which was subject to error, of ideas that established bearings for the course of collective evolution.[11] The successful rational action of the reformer, in this view, was the society's freely chosen involvement in the development of the divine purpose. Others fell back more on Green's uncritical acceptance of capitalism as a sufficient economic mechanism for the times, though saddled with a legacy of specific problems of distribution and discrimination which were not, however, intrinsic to it. In each case a position was being defined which would dispose of the 'individualistic' premises of an unacceptable social theory and reconstrue modern scientific developments, which had appeared to make man part of a deterministic process of natural evolution, in ways consistent with a moralised view of individual and collective choice.

Richard Tawney, drawn into the Green tradition through the idealism of Edward Caird, the tutoring of A. L. Smith at Balliol and the socially oriented liberalism of Gore, provides a critical preliminary bearing. But the brevity of his association with the ICF underlines the fact that it is as a decisive contrast that Tawney is illuminating. It is only on a superficial reading that his social theorising has much in common with the thinking of the clerics most closely associated with the ICF, a fact that may help to explain the curiously furtive and manipulative relationship he maintained with the Church.[12]

Much that was important to Gore and Temple in the Christian derivations from Green meant little to Tawney; the teleological apparatus, evolutionary theory, the sacramental theology and Gore's sense, shared by Temple and Studdert Kennedy, 'that the clauses of the creed stand or fall together'.[13] But at his most general he could be quoting any of them: '. . . society should be organised primarily for the performance of *duties*, not for the maintenance of *rights*, and the rights which it protects should be those which are necessary for the discharge of social obligations'.[14] Industrial war was inevitable in a society whose industry 'has '(no) end or purpose other than the satisfaction of those engaged in it'.[15] If industry was to serve society it had to be organised, under whatever appropriate formula, in terms of functional professional service and not on the fortuitous and divisive criterion of ownership.[16] Justice was a function of unity and purpose.[17] The individual could only realise himself through fellowship with others, and so on.

The Acquisitive Society became required reading for socially concerned clerics, who also called on his *Religion and the Rise of Capitalism*, based on the Holland Memorial Lectures of 1922, as a conclusive historical indictment of the anti-social principles on which contemporary society was based. A few followed what Tawney saw as the logical consequence of accepting his argument by joining the Labour Party (from which Temple resigned for the sake of appearances when he became Bishop of Manchester). Many more saw in his polemical work a valid application of the gospel to the failures of society. But the small print of Tawney's analysis was persistently neglected and the standard assimilation of Tawney to the reformist stream of Anglican social theory is misleading. Terrill's analysis of Tawney's thought as a system of ideas, consisting of mutually qualifying and supporting elements, places Tawney at a significant distance from many of the clerics who drew on him. There were of course more radical perspectives in British politics. Tawney's treatment of his central category of equality is somewhat elliptical. But he was unquestionably a man of the left, in outright conflict with a right-wing theorist like W. H. Mallock over the nature of what Temple referred to as the 'Mind of the Age'.[18]

Tawney's social interpretation of the gospel is based on a fundamental political premise, which is ignored in the perspectives of Temple and Studdert Kennedy, that any social action involves structured relations of interest and power, that this structure is the central term in any problem involving social change. It follows that the large goals of purpose and unity must be functions of a 'politically rooted fellowship',[19] which cannot be a product either of William Morris's vitalistic hope or of vacuous programmes for transforming wills and sacralising social relationships. Behind the churchmen's attempts at the latter there was indeed a theory of power, but an unsatisfactory one, a harmonic, rationalistic conception, within which liberal theorists, Hobhouse for instance, were writing before the war, and which Tawney found 'too rationalistic, optimistic, and atomistic to cope with the social conflicts engendered by agglomerations of economic and political power'.[20]

Like the clerics, Tawney related the terms Equality, Personal Fulfilment and Fellowship to a seamless fabric of social relationships, but his texture is very different from theirs. He nowhere relies on the quantitative Shavian argument for equality (the straw man with which Mallock, and Studdert Kennedy in his wake, take issue), and he does relate rewards to services, but what he envisages is a politically transformed society in which a totally undeferential psychology of fellowship was guaranteed by a reorganisation of the social structure. Vastly reduced differentials, the inevitable corollary of a drastic, glacial flattening of the peaks of hierarchy and authority, would rationalise and humanise social energies by directing them from acquisitive competition to other socially constructive rivalries.

The conviction with which this case is made reflects on aspects of Tawney's personal character and experience. Unromantic about the working classes, realistic about empirical variations in ability, he had no faith in the special qualities of any actual or potential ruling class in relation to the exercise of social power. Direct personal experience had developed his unpatronising sense of the human qualities of ordinary people, and he felt no anxieties about socially destructive bacilli cultured in the medium of the new democratic mass. After the war, in which he fought as a sergeant,[21] he was in no doubt that his own role was not primarily to improve the masses, but 'to help equip them to bid for power',[22] so he moved beyond the sticking point of progressive liberals like Hobhouse.

Studdert Kennedy never refers to Tawney and does not engage with his discussion of equality at either a theoretical or an empirical level. He does, as we shall see, make good use of Mallock, who selected data on inequality on an entirely different basis in his appeal to the 'oligarchic principle'.

Tawney's reading of the historical process which made his position a reasonable one to take up was profoundly different from that of his fellow economic historian William Cunningham, Fellow of Trinity College Cambridge and Archdeacon of Ely.

Cunningham, who described Green as 'my master in all that I care about in philosophy',[23] had in 1884 entertained hopes of being elected to the Cambridge Chair of Economics to which his teacher Marshall was appointed. The subsequent tension between them, which prompted Cunningham's resignation from his university lectureship, is a significant episode in the history of economics as a social science.[24] He would have regarded contemporary economic anthropology, with its sensitivity to the social values, structures and priorities of particular societies, more kindly than the abstract and generalist conceptualisations of the pure economist, and he shared many assumptions with the conservative tradition in anthropology, its holism and organicism, its sense of the social system as a network of constraints evolved in response to specific material conditions and constituting a rational order which is bound to suffer in complex and unanticipated ways if it becomes the victim of abstract and inevitably partial theories.

Studdert Kennedy never refers to Cunningham, but it does seem to be the case that his comments on economic subjects consist in the main of loans either from Mallock or from the economic historian, and he is entirely sympathetic to Cunningham's distillation from the idealist tradition. He sets out the same general position, without nuance or, obviously, scholarly development, but with a similar balance of emphasis, and the correspondence is close enough at times to suggest direct paraphrase. It is hard to believe he was drawing on Cunningham indirectly.

Cunningham writes of the same Nature, imperfect in the process of redemption but dominated nonetheless by wisdom and goodness.

Nature 'red in tooth and claw', the terrible waste of animal life, the degradation of human life through sordid struggle from which there is no relief—these are things which alienate some men from any religious belief, and tempt them to withdraw more and more from contact with grim realities . . . [But] all are only working for a good that lies beyond the range of our vision, and it will be our wisdom to try to co-operate in this working.[25]

There is much truth in the charge that Nature is red in tooth and claw. It is hard to see God in a cobra or a shark.

Nevertheless, the heart of the ordinary man will always turn away from these things and come back to the glory of a summer dawn and worship the Maker of it . . . Progress has everywhere and at all times been accompanied by strife and warfare. It is the eternal law of nature. (*HP*, 18)

Both encountered a similar ambivalence in social evolution, in the implications of the war (in which Cunningham lost a son), and the often unconscious realisation of the Divine Purpose in economic progress. Both were sustained by the 'continuous story of the growth of religious consciousness', the operation of the Spirit concentrating the attention of individuals, in ways often misperceived in the intellectualism of theological controversy.[26] For both the question was whether this process was to penetrate the natural evolution of a struggling society, as it might if, for instance, both unions and management engaged with great public issues with a view to the best outcome for society as a whole; integral to the fight for standards of pay was the fight for standards of work. Certainly, no mere change in external conditions could set the labour war at rest.[27] The historian's quarrel with the mechanistic science that serves a deterministic theory of evolution had, of course, a special application:

The economic *must*, whether standing baldly by itself or wrapped up in verbiage about inexorable economic laws, was responsible for much misunderstanding and bitterness in connection with economic legislation throughout the nineteenth century. Those who are contented to view society as a mechanism are not competent to deal wisely with national life, even in its economic aspects.[28]

Marshall, he pointed out, had attempted to improve on the classical economists in this respect.

Professor Marshall has made a gallant attempt to recast Political Economy, so that it shall be better accommodated to meet the popular need of positive guidance. He has endeavoured to enlarge the scope of Political Economy by abandoning the view that it confines attention to material wealth, and to the motive which it calls into play.[29]

Studdert Kennedy, who observes that 'Economics, which is thought out and written in terms of money, is largely a tissue of lies' (*WG*, 157), makes one allusion to Marshall. It is tempting to relate it to this specific source and see in the patronising touch a subtle transposition of tone.

> Have you ever tried to plough through Professor Marshall's *Principles of Economics*? If you did I bet you got tired of thinking then—I know I did—but mind you, it's a good book still. Now listen to what that dry but extremely sound old gentleman says on page 22:
> 'Though it is true that "money" or general purchasing power or "command of material wealth" is the centre around which economic science clusters, this is so not because money or material wealth is regarded as the main aim of human effort, nor even as affording the main subject matter for the study of the economist, but because in this world of ours it is *the one convenient means of measuring human motive on a large scale*.' (*DDC*, 70)

Cunningham was a careful student of F. D. Maurice. He adopted a Maurician position on the national community, and his concept of equality was a long way from Tawney's, far less preoccupied by the disparities of actual social existence. Fellowship, Maurice had taught, transcends such differences; secular social movements live off them and the envy they generate. Democracy as the will of the majority had been an 'object of dread' to him,[30] as it was to Cunningham and Studdert Kennedy.

> Individuals perform different functions in society ... The insistence on equality between individuals may even become positively injurious if it leads to efforts to keep all individuals alike; measures imposed with a view to the maintenance of equality may prove to be inconsistent with the liberty of each citizen to take advantage of the opportunities within his reach for the development of his powers. The attempt to enforce equality of treatment among individuals must tend towards the maintenance of a dead level, and of stereotyped mediocrity.[31]

As a differentiated organism, society depended on the existence of some directing power and the existence of a principle of subordination but, 'insofar as free labour can be introduced, and the principle of reward, which appeals to free men is substituted for the principle of compulsion there is an attraction and a stimulus for the individual to do his best and to improve his position.'[32] It was the case, furthermore, that the modern community provided greater opportunities for wholesome personal ambition than had ever been the case before, so 'class relations are not arbitrary',[33] but a constructive response of ambitious ability to stimulus. At the same time, 'there is no task, however humble or however high, that may not be thought of religiously, as a vocation assigned to us by God, and each man is called to cooperate with God by diligence in his vocation'.[34]

The directing power of the state acted, within its limitations, on behalf of the whole, and should 'pursue a policy, and coordinate the energies of the nation in such a way as to secure the best results'.[35] This might well involve state intervention to protect the economically weak, because 'from the strictly religious point of view, it must be recognised that gross and brutalising surroundings are actively hostile to spiritual influences of any kind, and present most serious obstacles, which we must desire to remove'.[36] 'The Statute of Labourers was one example of such intervention, and the whole history of nineteenth-century legislation in regard to the work of women and children in factories is an example of intervention on behalf of the employed.'[37]

But the first concern must be to protect the general economic viability and growth of the society.

> ... the important thing economically for the maintenance of society and for its progress is that there should be favourable conditions for production; the more distribution is improved so as to be as little unequal as maybe—or so that whatever inequalities exist can be justified as reasonable and right—the better; but if production is injuriously affected, there will be less material wealth available, and a diminution of average material well-being.[38]

This entailed stimulating the inventiveness of the exceptional few and protecting the capitalist in his task 'of organising and directing and supervising the labour of the country'.[39] If private capital was regarded as the enemy, and the individual's power of accumulation was checked, we risked a general decay in material prosperity, for 'even if the growth of capital can be secured authoritatively instead of voluntarily, there would be a danger that the prevailing type of individual character would be lowered'.[40] The authorities must look also to the delicate reciprocities of trust on which credit depended, which a stable society could evolve over years, but lose in an instant because of some 'trivial disregard of its obligations on the part of the state'.[41]

A representative anthology of observations from Studdert Kennedy traces the same course.

> I say that I am unequal, and am going to remain unequal, and I don't want to abolish the inequality which I believe will always exist. (*DDC*, 107)

> There is no lie more utterly devoid of truth than the lie of the equality of man ... There are, and there always will be, enormous natural inequalities among men in respect of strength of body and brain power. When you raise men above the bread-and-butter level, and teach them to love God and man; then you can get them to see what human inequality means—get them to see that superior ability is God's call to service, that strength is a summons to protect the weak. (*DDC*, 198)

> If ever the day comes when no man removes his hat to another, and is the better for doing it, it will be a bad day for mankind. We shall never all be equal except by levelling down. Mankind can never be levelled up without ceasing to grow, for growth depends, and always has depended, largely upon the exceptional individual, the personality to whom the rank and file of men look up, and whom they delight to honour. (*WW*, 5)

> The conflict between the organic and the mechanical conception of human society is one of the most real issues in the world, and to my mind there is only one side to take, and that is the side of the organism. (*DDC*, 161)

> Discipline is an absolute necessity in any co-operative effort. That is, there must be in every co-operative effort those who command and those who obey, those who direct and those who carry out their directions. (*L*, 58)

> It is not true that what are called the 'upper classes' are only upper through luck, inheritance or fraud. They are upper partly through essential superiority of brain power and ability. While classes are at present indeed largely artificial, there are natural classes springing out of natural inequalities. (*DDC*, 198)

> I want the miner to feel when he is down there in his pit that he is not merely working for his wage—working for Friday night—a wage slave—but that he is a Priest of God, a Priest of Love called by God to produce warmth and power for his brothers in the world. I want him to feel that he is as much a priest down there in the dark,

filthy black and streaming with sweat, as I am a priest when I stand at the altar and plead for the wants of men. (*DDC*, 99)

The outcry against organisation and rational regulation of our corporate life is largely the refuge of moral cowards from the insistent call of God. (*WW*, 31)

Seventy five percent of our people are out of touch with organised religion, and with the worship of God, and one of the chief reasons for this is that our industrial civilisation blasphemes against the beauty of God. (*WW*, 9)

The history of the Labour Movement as a whole makes it clear that the best work that was done for it in the nineteenth century was done for it by men who were not of the working class, but had been convinced that their cause was a righteous one, and that still remains true. (*DDC*, 55)

The problem is not solely a problem of distribution, it is also a problem of production. It is important to improve the method of distribution, but the main thing is to get wealth to distribute. Karl Marx ... was either wilfully or ignorantly blind to the part that exceptional brain and exceptional ability played in the Industrial Revolution, and the inevitable part that they must play in modern production ... Our great need at the present minute is an enormous output. We must increase our production. What stands in the way? The old enemy—War ... as an analysis of modern production by highly complicated machinery combined with scientific organisation, the Marxian analysis is absurd. It leaves out *the* great factor—the brain work of the exceptional few. (*L*, 49–50)

But, pardon me, he does perform a very distinct service. That's where half the trouble lies. You [Organised Labour] tend to mix up 'Capital' and 'Capitalists', and to make no distinction between profits and profiteering ... Either the community must learn to save or the saving must be done by private individuals, and it is intensely hard at present to get a community to save ... Saving is harder than working. For ten men that can work there is only one that can really save. It demands a higher order of intelligence and greater self-control, and is one of the great means of educating people and bringing out those virtues. A man who saves does deserve a reward, does deserve to have his savings secured to him. (*DDC*, 112)

The power of money is always and everywhere the power of credit ... the power of trust between man and man, and between bodies of men . . . *the further this development proceeded, the more vital became the mental and spiritual factor in economics.*

. . . You cannot consistently foster and encourage the anti-social passions of mankind—fear, hatred, suspicion, reckless falsehood, and an utter disregard for the value of human life—for five years, and expect at the end to find trust, confidence, mutual understanding and forbearance which are the spiritual realities underlying credit, unimpaired. (*WG*, 159–60)

Dr Norman laments the virtual extinction within the Church of the tradition of social theory for which Cunningham spoke, and refers respectfully to the critique in which he drew attention to the weakness of the charter document of the ICF, with its woolliness and its readiness to frame specific 'Christian' maxims about economic relations.[42] Such relatively trivial symptoms of politicisation indeed continued to appear. But Cunningham's general position, a position that is profoundly political, as of course is Dr Norman's, in its deeper structural implications, had in fact a vigorous popular life. It is in the context of ideas more fully developed by this distinguished conservative cleric that we can best understand the 'Truth of Co-operation' proclaimed in the ministry of the preacher (p. 14 above) who, though undeniably provoking hostility in some sections of church opinion, can hardly be said, in this context at least, to have been crying in the wilderness.

GORE AND TEMPLE

Gore was a radical activist on the spectrum of 'discrepant deductions' from Green. Episcopal interventions in industrial disputes have been made to serve more questionable tactical purposes than students of christian socialism always recognise, Bishop Westcott's intervention in the Durham miners' lock-out of 1892 being a case in point.[43] But Gore was persistent and well-informed. In 1906, when he was complaining of the failure of attempts to give the CSU a new lease of life, he was associated with practical reformers like Tuckwell and Masterman on issues included on Labour and Liberal programmes. He 'plotted and goaded' Birmingham City Council into action over bad housing, chaired a conference between Birmingham master-bakers and their workmen, 'laboured indefatigably in the interests of the chain-makers', who were the subject of an inquiry by Tawney, and fought management when the unions were attacked in Reading in 1911.[44] Here, characteristically, he set up an expert fact-finding commission. A year later the Committee on the Moral Witness of the Church on

Economic Subjects published a report under his chairmanship, but drafted by William Cunningham, which offered a general analysis of the causes of privation and discontent, and proposed remedies for both.[45] It quoted a statement from C. G. Ammon of the Postal Workers' Fawcett Association, containing evidence, on the one hand, of intolerable condonation of systematic injustice by the State, significantly enough, in the form of the Postmaster General, and, on the other, of sustained social responsibility by a union whose members had been pressed beyond fair limits. Ammon was to become an active member of the ICF.

But the structure of Gore's radicalism was opaque to many who applauded, and many who condemned, its public expression on such occasions. It was not, as has often been supposed, merely a clerical variant of Oxford idealism, any more than it was an ingratiating attempt to bring 'labour' inside the Church. Gore himself is partly to blame for this misreading, because he wrote vaguely, particularly about the central category of personality. This was a dangerous thing to do, since in more general usage, to which Temple made larger concessions, the concept did not retain its theological root in the personal nature of God's redemptive concern for man, which was of central importance to Gore. At the same time, though this applies less to Gore than to other members of the *Lux Mundi* school, he was bound to make concessions to the language of philosophical idealism. The distinctive character of his social interpretation of the gospel has often been misperceived from positions outside his own rational Catholicism.[46]

He sets out the same central position as the idealists. 'We are to interpret the beginning in the light of the end; not the end in the light of the beginning.' And he cites Haldane's *Reign of Relativity*; 'The higher is the explanation of the lower, and not the lower of the higher'.[47] But he distinguishes evolution from progress and entirely misses the optimism that derives from Green. 'Evolution is as compatible with retrogression as with progress, as we were warned by Huxley long ago. It must accommodate itself to the facts. The facts of human history suggest nothing at all like necessary or uniform progress.'[48] The evolutionary principle was at work and must be recognised in specific historical developments, in democracy and the labour movement, for example. Where it was recognisably at work we must act with it; it was craven to flinch from conflict and foolish not to acknowledge its creative potential. Industrial unrest and militancy in themselves did not alarm him.

If the position of this vast majority has been gradually improving during the last hundred years, that has been because they have, in a measure successfully, combined to rebel against their slavery in

its extremer forms, aided no doubt by the assistance of some
merciful and rational men of the privileged classes, but relying in
the main on their own efforts, and fighting continually against the
organised resistance of the mass of the well-to-do.[49]

At the same time there was no immanent validation of
'progressive' movements and forms, though there was 'nothing in
the socialistic idea of the constitution of society antagonistic to
Christianity'. To the extent that this movement for state ownership,
which was how on a strict definition he saw it, expressed ethical
motives, indicted selfish luxury, embodied social obligation and
fellowship, it was at one with 'the prophets of Israel (who) are on the
side of the poor',[50] and who bore witness to 'the idea of the equal
spiritual value of every human soul in the sight of the common
Father'.[51] In so far as the movement was sectional and materialistic it
was at risk. A commitment to ameliorative reform was instinctive
with Gore, but his primary point of reference was not its intrinsic
rationality. His historiography was biblical and complex. The
incarnation of Christ was an essential and unique occurrence, a
sacramental drama against which everything else had to be
measured, since it was at one and the same time a judgement on our
permanent condition of sin, and a demonstration of divine
expectations. An apparently congenital pessimism is fully worked
into his theology. Gore's writings convey an oppressed sense of the
universality of sin, an awareness which Christ came to broaden and
deepen.[52] The fulfilment of obligation through social and political
activity was for him more important in its sacramental significance
than as a perceptible addition to a demonstrably sluggish
evolutionary progress. Social improvement uninformed by belief
was ultimately inconsequential.

As a political agitator Temple stands no comparison with Gore. He
was heavily indebted to Gore's theological coherence and to the
devotional conviction which churchmen recognised in Gore's
biblical scholarship and his rationalistic exposition of the credal
claims of high Anglicanism, but Temple's social concern in this
period is expressed in a faithful replication of idealist arguments at
the level of a general readership. One can only accept Craig's claim
that there was more to his religious philosophy than that,[53] for the
theological affinity with Gore was substantial. But he was far more
inclined to assimilate and review the philosophical machinery and
elaborate on its implications in general discussion. He was not, by
the end of the war, greatly impressing the professional philosophers.
A. E. Taylor, by no means an unsympathetic critic, found in the logic
of *Mens Creabrix* the unexamined prejudices and commonplaces of 'a
social group of Oxford tutors', and made damaging criticisms.[54] Less

exacting readers of Temple's work over the period will have found a comprehensive general guide, saturated in the Oxford Greats Platonism with which the idealist scheme has a natural affinity.

> Keeping a steady hold on the Love of God as our one all-sufficing principle, and making a wise use of the conceptions of Personality and Evolution, which play so large a part in our modern thought, we shall be able to catch more of the meaning of the revelation of God in Christ than was possible, perhaps, in earlier times. The seat of the problem is our wills; they need transforming.[55]

Evolution was a function of Purpose, and the problem of understanding Purpose 'is not so hopeless as it looks at first. Scientific principle requires us at least to take seriously the hypothesis of a Purpose in the world, and, therefore, a real Will behind the world'.[56] He repeats the standard reappraisal of evolutionary theory in terms of survival through effective co-operation, rather than competition,[57] indeed engaging in an athletic attempt to assimilate fashionable scientific theory on the evolution of mind to his own *a prioristic* teleology for the development of the divine purpose. He draws on C. Lloyd Morgan and S. Alexander, who was a friend and colleague of L. T. Hobhouse, with a specific interest in relating biology and the theory of evolution to the insights, political and other, of Green and the idealists.[58] He and Morgan provided Temple with a fresh cultural injection, a booster to the earlier philosophical dose of Oxford idealism, in the form of a thoroughly academic account of the basic structural principle of reality, the 'nisus', or 'sense of straining towards deity' in natural phenomena. (Studdert Kennedy also draws on Morgan, but his corresponding argument emphasises group psychology.)

The social 'nisus' towards Deity was expressed in the emergence of mind, through a process that was located in the individual but operated in the fellowship of the collectivity.

> ... the more fully Purposive we are—that is, the more complete our Personality—so much the more will the future preponderate over the past in our interest. The later in time has upon the earlier a far greater influence than the earlier upon the later ... as Lord Haldane has said, explanation is to be sought in a system of Ends rather than of Causes.[59]

The argument about Personality, which he had first set out in 1911,[60] was the classic organicist argument of the idealists, more thoroughly so than was the case with Gore. Personality was a self-conscious and self-determining system of experience, in fact or in potential, but purposive only in and through social interaction. A man's 'whole being is a condensation of society. He is his fellow-men's experience focused in a new centre',[61] for the essential basis of society is community of purpose.

> . . . in the fact which we call society, the citizens, the members, are the organs of consciousness . . .
>
> Duty, Obligation, Ought—all express a relation of the individual to his fellow-members in Society; . . . Society itself is a union of individuals whose several wills are at one in a common purpose; and . . . the aim of Society, as of the individual, is freedom and self-government.[62]

However, to use Alexander's words, 'a complete determination by the personality on all its sides is more attainable in the good man than the bad one'.[63]

Contemporary social and political applications of these generalities are developed along lines that would surely have gratified Haldane and the other Liberal Imperialists. Social class was a corporate group, generating fellowship and developing the individuals within it, but to 'substitute class for nation as the primary object of loyalty is ethically retrograde; those who advocate it, and still more those who, by maintaining an unjust social order, cause many to tend in that direction, are the worst enemies of true progress'.[64] In *Mens Creatrix* he had anchored this functional moralism in contemporary political realities by quoting at some length on two occasions from *The Commonwealth of Nations*, a study compiled for the *Round Table* from the contributions of its members by Lionel Curtis, the most intimate of Hichens' friends in the Milner kindergarten. He was at the Ministry of Reconstruction by the end of 1916, with Kerr, Beveridge, Webb and Haldane.[65] Curtis, Hichens and Max Balfour were known in South Africa as 'the three musketeers'.

> The quickening principle of a state is a sense of devotion, an adequate recognition in the minds of its subjects that their own interests are subordinate to those of the State. The bond which unites them and constitutes them collectively as a state is, to use the words of Lincoln, in the nature of a *dedication*. Its validity, like that of the marriage state, is at root not contractual but sacramental. Its foundation is not self-interest, but rather some sense of obligation, however conceived, which is strong enough to over-master self-interest.[66]

Haldane, we might note here, is a continuous ghostly presence in this study. He was an important mentor in the eyes of dominant figures in the ICF, 'a combination of leading politician and thinker on the fringe of original thought', a prophet of the organised state, but also the practical exponent of an evolutionary politics and the most coherent of the Liberal Imperialists.[67] As a group, Matthew shows, their domestic policies had been far from progressive, and they used imperialism in a domestic context as an antidote to the development of class antagonisms. Haldane became MacDonald's Lord Chancellor in 1924.

Gore's engagement with political realities, required by an inner prophetic righteousness, is tough and circumstantial. Temple, revolving his general theoretical formula, is sentimental.

> . . . the inner history of the movements shows plainly that the real energy came from spiritual discontent rather than from material greed. This has been most emphatically true of the Socialist movements . . . a sympathetic observer very quickly detects that what really galls is not so much the small proportion of the results of industry allotted as the reward of labour, but rather the sense that the employees are treated as 'hands' and not as 'persons', so far as the industry is concerned. Their personality apparently is for their leisure time.[68]

The same tentative, evasive and schematic treatment of conflicts of material interest is reflected in the imagery he employs to domesticate the actuality of competition.

> Consider the English Cotton Industry . . . The whole process goes on simply and solely because the public wants cotton goods; it exists for public service. And it is co-operative in its very nature. All the groups of people who take charge of the processes set out above are co-operating, whether they know it or not . . . Competition and Co-operation are logical opposites, but they are not incompatibles. Consider a game of football . . .[69]

Temple made regular use of this sporting metaphor, when appearing with Hichens, for instance, at a large COPEC meeting. It was also used, though rather more inventively, by Studdert Kennedy.[70]

It is this vein that lies below Temple's surface radicalism, a collectivism which he sees emerging out of the co-operative freedoms of Will, which requires that 'the parts must be controlled by the whole which they constitute, and to that end must truly constitute the whole by which they are controlled', an argument which promptly cues the standard idealist thesis on education and the legitimacy of the Authority vested in those best prepared by

education to act as the Guardians of the collective will.[71] An
intelligent and wholehearted sensitivity to obligation is the binding
medium of society:

> ... the temper of a movement that rests on rights will be
> aggressive, violent, contentious; and the temper of a movement
> that rests on duties will be persuasive, public spirited,
> harmonious.[72]

The same view is less compactly expressed in *Personal Religion and the
Life of Fellowship.*[73]

The validation of the general argument on the collective
development towards co-operation lay in history, on which he drew
with historicist assurance. Contemporary politics provided us with
the encouraging spectacle of the two teams constructively locked into
the game.

> The party conflict is very superficial; Mr Baldwin and Mr
> MacDonald have far more political ideas in common than either
> shares with the Duke of Wellington. The Mind of the Age really
> guides both parties; but each party only possesses part of it. It is
> well that each should have its turn, and that all should do their
> best both to strengthen and to guide the party with which on the
> whole they sympathise.[74]

Between Temple and Studdert Kennedy there is a strong
presumption of reciprocal influence, though the evidence available
only hints at its nature and extent, and it is not discussed in studies of
the future Archbishop.[75] There are obvious echoes and paraphrases,
particularly from Temple's more quotidian philosophising, in
Studdert Kennedy's work, but Temple was himself fascinated by the
preacher, admiring without reserve the integral and exceptionally
unself-conscious nature of his intellectual and emotional
commitment, even attributing to him a degree of mastery of
economics and psychology in particular, which is hardly born out by
the published record.[76] In Temple's *Personal Religion* there is a solitary
extended footnote in which he refers to the previous volume in the
same series, Studdert Kennedy's *The Word and the Work*, with a
reminder of the powerful emphasis on the significance of
Redemption with which that essay concludes, and points out that he
himself is deliberately aiming, at this point, 'to effect a continuity of
expression, as there is a close kinship of thought between that
volume and this'.[77] The seminal passage is undoubtedly one of the
most confident elaborations of the Messenger's central themes, a
rejection of the idea of God as a 'super super Napoleon', an intense

concentration on the suffering, 'the Love, the pure and peaceable wisdom, and the selfless humility of Christ'. It is written with an unself-conscious fervour that is not to be found in Temple.

Craig identifies a retrograde tendency in Temple's theology in this period, particularly in *Christus Veritas*. The criticism is technical in relation to the present discussion, but it bears on the general content and emphasis of Temple's religious philosophy at the time, which Temple himself criticised severely in the 1930s. He came to look back on his concentration on uplift—love, service, fellowship, a rhetorical apparatus which Studdert Kennedy never moved away from—as unrealistic and, in its social and poltical implications, evasive.[78] One can reasonably suspect that his response to a powerful personality organised, unlike his own, round a devotional rather than a theological core, contributed to and perhaps prolonged this phase of his development. In any event, the Messenger's relationship was with the unreconstructed Temple, and it was by no means a passive one on Studdert Kennedy's part.

But whatever the balance in the relationship, one can sum up these contrasts by saying that the eupeptic optimism of Temple's writing in this period is absent in Studdert Kennedy, whose harrowed sense of man's fallen condition corresponds more to that of Gore; but that, at the same time, his assumptions about the structure of reality, the importance to him of a 'Christian theory of evolution' encompassing nature and society, is essentially that of Temple, shares some of the same sources and even borrows passages on central concepts such as Personality. However, this combination of strains results in a far bleaker assessment of the potentialities of secular progressive thinking. He makes significantly heavy use of the organic analogy with society, and the specific applications of his perspective to current political conflicts reveal its decidedly conservative loading.

Where, too, the thinking of Gore and Temple develops along a steady trajectory from the pre-war period, the Messenger's writing is the product of a specifically post-war malaise, a response to the lost sense of purpose, the disillusion of Reconstruction, to the increasing numbers of nominal Christians who, like Wilfred Owen, who had 'murdered [his] false creed' before the war, having abandoned a scheme to get ordained,[79] had come to believe that they had been saddled with an untenable set of religious sanctions. Studdert Kennedy's gradually shifting adjustment to the war provides the most powerful imagery of moral disorder and collective wickedness.

I was always interested in military history . . . I carried the interesting facts into my first battle, and there they came to life, they roared and thundered, they dripped with blood, they cursed, mocked, blasphemed, and cried like a child for mercy. They stood up before me like obscene spectres, beckoning with bloody hands, laughing like fiends at my little parochial religion, and my silly parochial God. I can remember running over an open space under shell-fire trying madly to fit in the dates, and every shrieking shell kept yelling at me with foul oaths: Now do you understand, you miserable little parson with your petty shibboleths, this is W–A–R—War, and History is War,—and this is what History means. How about gentle Jesus, God the Father, and the Peace of God—how about it? (*L*, 5)

In *Lies* he writes of the War as a necessity wickedly forced on us, exacting distortions of the truth and inhuman behaviour. By 1923 he sees himself refusing to accept that necessity: 'I see a day when I and my son will face one another with that choice between us—and maybe he will choose the other way from mine—and I shall have to watch him go, because I cannot make him see the Valley of the Somme' (*WG*, 88). There is a continuous ambivalence, however. Great deeds were done with a new sense of national purpose; but the unity was essentially false. Wars brought unity and co-operation; 'So it is all through history. God makes even the wrath of man to serve Him. Competition destroys itself and gives birth to wider cooperation' (*L*, 21). But war 'creates nothing' (*L*, 38). And yet; 'From the bottom of my heart I believe that this work of destruction, however painful it may be, must be accomplished to the bitter end, to lead the children of our generation to the worship of the true God' (*L*, 143). Increasingly, however, he inveighed against the War as a wicked retrogression, the culmination of a shameful inventory across the past century. In theological terms, war fever was the prototype of all sin, 'the misuse of faculties good in themselves',[80] a symptom of the ascendency of passion over will in the imperfectly developed Personality, submission to a drug in which the struggle of reality was forgotten.

> . . . the moaning of the boy in the corner like the moaning of a damned soul. 'The pain—the pain—my Gawd—the pain. For Gawd's sake gimme somefing to stop the pain.'
> There was no morphia. That was the horror. Someone must go for it. I went. I went because the hell outside was less awful than the hell in . . . I ran, and as I ran, and cowered down in shell-holes waiting for a chance to run again, I thought—thought like lightening,—whole trains of thought came tearing through my mind like non-stop expresses to God knows where . . . If I bring it back, I will be to him a saviour from hell. I'd like that. It's worth while. I'm glad I thought of that. I can't pretend that it was that I

came for. It wasn't. Still I'm glad. He wants to forget, to forget and sleep . . . Fancy putting heaven in a pill box and putting it by your bedside. Beastly dangerous. How can men resist when things get bad beyond bearing. Don't we all want to forget . . . All men want to more or less. Drugs—the world is full of Drugs. (*L*, 226–7)

The struggle towards the Freedom of the individual Will was in every case almost impossibly hard.

At the same time he reiterates an idealist historiography which cannot be distinguished from Temple's. There is an emergence towards freedom and relatedness, drawn forward by Divinity, but retrogressions occur at any stage or level. He seems to be using Morgan's 1923 volume to consolidate the general idea of retrogression scientifically a year before Temple's *Christus Veritas*, arguing that 'the possibility of this false freedom appears to exist in some measure wherever what we call "life" exists', and in one of his rare footnotes, which invariably appear to be insistent afterthoughts inserted at a late stage in the manuscript's preparation (late 1923 in this case), that 'wherever there is energy there is life and inanimate nature does appear to have the power to resist God in some way or other, as it certainly has the power to resist us. Creation seems to involve the gift of self-existence and therefore the temporary limitation of the Creator' (*WG*, 140). His various developments of this theme suffer from comparison. 'All parasites are an abomination unto the Lord. That is settled' (*WG*, 58). Presumably the fleas, equally with the dishonest financiers of this passage, are self-existences in defiance of the End which explains the Beginning. The general philosophical weakness of teleological argument, its tendency to serve as a vehicle for preferences independently arrived at, is impossible to disguise in popular exposition. But, where Gore was able to live with the inscrutabilities of the Divine Purpose, here Purpose has to be established as a universal immediate and salient category, and the full urgency of the argument is most obvious when he is writing about the Duty of the individual in relation to contemporary society (*FFU*, 37 ff, 98, 210 ff; *L*, 23, 170 ff; *WG*, 45 ff, 106–20).

The teleological argument is applied to religious history, as has been pointed out already, but not in the form of the diffuse immanentism which can avoid a culmination, in one sense outside time, in the Incarnation of Christ. The Messiahs of earlier religions were expressions of a universal 'Messianic passion', Temple's 'nisus' at a critical stage of development, but this was ultimately satisfied only by the Incarnation (*FFU*, 106).

The teleology is applied in a schematic and vulnerable way to material progress. The industrial revolution was 'the result in the

main neither of capitalistic enterprise nor of manual labour, but of
inventive genius', which was a pure and absolute gift of God
(*FFU*, xii). It drew on the coal providentially stored to provide energy
for it, a providence celebrated in his poem 'The Collier's Hymn'. The
message of the telegraph and the railroad was that we were within
reach of the social unity and co-operation in which knowledge,
mind, would be applied to the elimination of natural limitations on
the creator, and to the material consequences of an imperfect social
and economic system (*L*, 175; *FFU*, 51). But to achieve this we must
realise true Democracy, a public opinion structured by awareness of
duty, forming a society of volunteers, not conscripts, where freedom
signifies a willing identification of responsibilities (*L*, 65–6; *DDC*,
passim).

> A man may work impossible hours at impossible tasks, but if his
> heart is in his work, if he sees the reason of it and loves the master
> whom he serves, that man is free. This freedom which is willing
> service is the freedom toward which the world is growing—
> painfully, blindly, blunderingly growing. (*L*, 68)

But contemporary realities threatened a further ruinous
retrogression. The Industrial Armies had grown up (*L*, 32) and the
philosophy of the hen-run obtained.

> Mutual distrust and suspicion, class-war fostered and fomented
> from abroad, selfish greed and personal ambition for power, are
> putting all industry more and more on a war basis. (*L*, 237) If that
> fat-headed feathered fowl had had the sense to spend the time
> scratching poor old Mother Earth that she spent scratching sister
> hen, she might have had six fat worms instead of a quarter of one,
> dusty and full of grit. (*L*, 17)

In the ICF Council meeting of 12 January 1921, Studdert Kennedy,
seconded by Elvin, proposed a motion advocating conciliation and
arbitration, as the only Christian way, referring to industrial war and
barbarism and admitting strikes only as a 'last resort'. Gore
proposed an amendment, recognising the power of the strike in the
uplift of the workers, and was supported by A. J. Carlyle. Miss Picton-
Turbervill suggested redrafting.

TRUE AND FALSE PROPHETS: MALLOCK AND MARX; MCDOUGALL AND FREUD

The allusions of a popular writer may be straightforward appeals to

1 Charles Gore in 1925

2 Cosmo Gordon Lang, Archbishop of York (centre) and William Temple, Bishop of Manchester (left) *(The Dean and Chapter, Manchester Cathedral)*

3 Lionel and Hermione Hichens at
the launch of HMS _Rodney_, built
by Cammell Laird, December 1925
(_Mrs Hichens_)

4 Lionel Hichens attending King George V and Queen Mary during a
royal visit to the Cammell Laird works in Sheffield (_Mrs Hichens_)

5 Major General Sir Frederick Maurice (centre), with General Vazoff of Bulgaria (left) and General Prince Schonburg-Hartenstein of Austria (right), leaving Buckingham Palace after an audience with the King in June 1936 (*The Royal British Legion*)

6 Gertrude Tuckwell, JP (*TUC Library*)

7 Sir Lynden Macassey in 1917
   (National Portrait Gallery, London)

8 Lord Henry Cavendish Bentinck,
   around 1900 *(Local Studies,
   Nottingham)*

PARLIAMENTARY ELECTION, 1910.

BREADWINNERS
NOT
LANDOWNERS.

THE PEOPLE
NOT
THE PEERS.

TO THE ELECTORS OF THE
BORDESLEY DIVISION OF BIRMINGHAM.

9 Fred Hughes, on his 1910 Election Address *(Birmingham City Library)*

10 C. G. Ammon, campaigning in Camberwell North, 1922 *(BBC Hulton Picture Library)*

11 E. L. Poulton (left) and C. W. Bowerman, at the 1921 Congress at Cardiff *(TUC Library)*

12 Frank Hodges and his wife, travelling to Canada in 1924 *(BBC Hulton Picture Library)*

13 H. H. Elvin (left) with Ernest Bevin, on taking over as Chairman of the TUC in 1937 *(BBC Hulton Picture Library)*

14 The Rev. P. T. R. Kirk,
Director of the ICF *(ICF)*

15 David ('Navvy') Smith, in
uniform as 'Lay Chaplain'
to the recruits in June 1915
*(Birmingham Parish Church
Magazine)*

16 The Rev. G. A. Studdert Kennedy with his wife, leaving
for Berkeley Divinity School, New Haven, October 1923
(BBC Hulton Picture Library)

17 A Crusade work site meeting *(ICF)*

18 Part of the crowd at the Castle Street pitch, Tredegar, during the
Monmouth Crusade, 1928 *(ICF)*

authority, but they may also be contributions to rhetoric, like Studdert Kennedy's standard allusion to Herbert Spencer, an instance of the conventional short-hand frequently employed since the 1880s to trigger vague anxieties about virulent individualism. Such rhetorical allusions can raise quite difficult questions about their purpose and their cargo of meaning, as in a passing reference to Lamarck (who was, of course, of positive importance to Spencer himself); 'I am sure that Lamarck was nearer than Darwin, and that what is behind the Universe is a will or a wish ...' (*HP*, 24). An informed reader might identify a reference to the argument developed by D. G. Ritchie in such works as *Darwinism and Politics*. Studdert Kennedy paraphrases this elsewhere: '—not that we inherit spiritual ideas, not that there is any inheritance of acquired characteristics, but that we are, whether we like it or not, born into a world which has a spiritual history' (*L*, 109). But Lamarck was also a standard reference in general discussion, though a more obscure one than Spencer, and is alluded to in passing in the heavy synoptic manuals read by Studdert Kennedy, such as Theodor Merz's Hegelian history of thought and McDougall's *Body and Mind*.[81] If a scholar like Hobhouse could be 'guilty of trying to legitimate his own political values by appropriating the prestige of the evolutionary argument',[82] perhaps it is not surprising that the preacher should do something very similar in more allusive and elliptical ways. However, even Studdert Kennedy's most obviously opportunist thickenings of the text are skilfully assimilated, along with other material that has been more unobtrusively adapted. A number of allusions, probably including one to the Italian syndicalist Labriola, and certainly including a reference to Marx, comes from a major source of argument who is himself acknowledged only once by Studdert Kennedy, W. H. Mallock.[83]

Mallock died in 1923 and for a couple of decades his prolific output dropped out of sight.[84] His unique assimilation of elements of liberal ideology to a conservative perspective was comprehensively attractive to Studdert Kennedy, who not only digested the general argument but skilfully adapted detail for a wider audience than Mallock could reach through his books or such periodicals as the *Nineteenth Century* and *Fortnightly Review*.

Before turning to the general argument, we can look at this transposition of material in a couple of instances. They illustrate a close identification with Mallock's outlook, and a thoroughly professional approach to popularisation, in verbal economy, energy and sense of audience.

Twice Studdert Kennedy quotes from Sidney Webb on the projected outcome of Democracy in 'the recovery of what John Stuart Mill calls "the enormous share which the possessors of

industry are able to take of the total produce" '. Webb uses this
quotation frequently, sometimes making it clear that Mill was
himself quoting, from Feugueray.[85] One of the preacher's allusions is
in *Democracy and the Dog Collar* (*DDC*, 38–9), a book which emerged from
some of his most applauded platform presentations in the form of a
dialogue between Organised Church and Organised Labour, and
there is another in the fourth chapter of *Lies*. In *Lies* he recalls his first
reaction to a persuasive demagogic appeal:

> I wanted to start at once. I looked around for a brick or a bomb to
> shy at the first man I saw in a motor or top hat. The dirty dogs I
> thought, bricks are too good for them ... The solution seemed
> simple and easy. Destroy the inequalities and level incomes down.
> Fairer distribution; that was all that was required. Mr Sidney
> Webb put the thing into words for me exactly when he said,
> 'There is a growing consensus of opinion that the inevitable
> outcome of Democracy is the control of the main instruments of
> production by the people themselves, and the consequent
> recovery of what John Stuart Mill calls "the enormous share"
> which the possessors of industry are able to take of the total
> produce'. There was the problem and its solution in a nutshell. I
> used to roll that off at meetings, and John Stuart Mill made it so
> intellectually respectable. But alas! facts are cruel things, and care
> nought for respectability, intellectual or otherwise. I investigated
> and I am doubtful about that 'enormous share' ...

This suggests a first-hand monitoring and evaluation of Fabian
pronouncements. But the allusion apparently derives from Mallock's
Limits of Pure Democracy, which had been published in the previous
year. ' "Every day" says Mr Sidney Webb, "there is a growing
consensus of opinion" ' etc.[86] Mallock continues after the quotation:
'Now, this short statement, which seems simple enough, is in reality
a combination of three', and he proceeds in his briskly pedantic
manner to itemise, first, the distinction asserted between workers
and mere 'possessors', second, the assumption that 'democracy'
would rationalise distribution and third, the assumption that the
share of the possessors is 'enormous'. He then proceeds to argue that
'even if all these statements were correct, there would be no integral
connection between the first two and the third', that the accuracy of
the third can be empirically tested, and that there is an even more
fundamental difference between the first two.

The passage in *Lies*, avoiding this analytical cleverness entirely,
moves directly to the empirical question.

We forget so easily a simple thing that makes all the difference—

there are so many poor and so few very rich. I find that there are
only 1500 people in Great Britain with an income of over £20,000.
If the people were to recover their 'enormous share', it would give
them about fourpence a week extra. Now I don't mind revolting
to secure the millenium, but I refuse to revolt for four packets of
woodbines. (*L*, 47)

This is shortly followed by a reference to the large quantities of
factual information reproduced from official sources in books like
Grey and Turner's *Eclipse and Empire* and Mallock's *Limits of Pure
Democracy*. The passage just quoted is an admirably polemical
condensation from page 155 of Mallock, who writes;

Let us, however, suppose that the robbery of the poorer classes by
the richer is imputed, not to a little cluster of super-millionaires
only, but to the semi-millionaires as well—that is to say, everybody
whose income was as much as £20,000. The number of this class in
America was approximately 3000. It was in the United Kingdom
approximately 1500. If we suppose that every one of such persons
stole the whole of his income, and the people 'recovered' what
would vulgarly be called 'the lot', the results would be doubtless
superior to those we have just considered. The weekly 'tip' would
in America be raised to tenpence halfpenny, and in the United
Kingdom to fourpence.

Mallock's statistics, with their 'air of verisimilitude', were not taken
too seriously at the time by statisticians,[87] but it is fair to point out,
with Mason, that objectivist rhetoric of this sort was standard among
socialists as well. If one passed over the equation assumed here of
capital with past ability, these figures were an effective resource in
popular debate.

The other text recommended must be Gray and Turner's *Eclipse or
Empire?*[88] Gray was in orders, had taught at Winchester and became
Headmaster of Bradfield. Sir Samuel Turner, twice mayor of
Rochdale, ran cotton mills and asbestos works. Their book blames
the scandalous housing of the poor on the ill-organised condition of
the body politic, accuses the unions of taking over the powers of a
supine State, speaks of the romance of Business, of Man the creator
taming Nature to his will, with Science at his elbow, invokes
efficiency, the elimination of waste, good will and self-discipline.

The State ought to express *ourselves* ... She must in fact be the
foster mother of every activity in all industrial and scientific
spheres. And we, in turn, ought to realise that we are the servants
of the State—that she is our Over-Soul, the great constructive

power which, so far from stifling, develops individual energies.[89]

The glossary contains alarming figures which show the rate at which British inventions, neglected here, had been taken up and developed abroad. The general analysis endorses the Messenger's position on the hard facts of social organisation at every point.

A second, more concealed adaptation of Mallock opens the following chapter of *Lies*, where about a thousand words of Mallock's first three pages are condensed by about two-thirds. Mallock's second paragraph opens:

> 'Man is born free, and is everywhere in chains.' Such are the opening words of the most celebrated work of Rousseau; and though the philosophy of Rousseau himself is by this time largely obsolete, these words to-day are significant in a sense far deeper, though quite other, than that which their author and his disciples imputed to them.

He proceeds to dissect his quotation, concluding that;

> ... in this insane proposition that 'man is born free', and in the wide effects produced by it on the thoughts and temper of multitudes, we have a signal example of the condition of moral and mental chaos to which language used ambiguously is able to reduce mankind, causing their demands and arguments to resemble the cries of animals vaguely conscious of anger, disease, or wounds, rather than a rational diagnosis of what is really the matter with them.

His next step is to analyse the idea of Democracy with the same sense of logic and practical realities. Studdert Kennedy's loan, however, begins by combining the opening quotation and the conclusion.

> ... It is a perfectly topping sentence, but I am not sure what it means. It rouses indignation and pity, and paints a wonderful picture. Everywhere you see the masses of men groaning in slavery ... (*L*, 55)

In place of Mallock's withering sarcasm;

> ... the only kind of baby that is free is the baby that is left to die, and the only kind of free adult is the solitary on a desert island,

we get whimsical deprecation:

> A free baby would only succeed in giving its mother forty fits, and
> then solemnly starving itself to death. (*L*, 56)

But where Mallock's discussion proceeds to raise structural and
political issues, the preacher hangs on to Rousseau and the idea of
Liberty, 'one of the biggest words in the English language', and
moves into a passage, quoted earlier, on the higher freedom.

> Does it, then, only stand for a dream? Or does it stand for reality?
> It stands for the greatest of all realities, and therefore the reality
> which is the hardest to define. First let us recognise this great fact,
> that if men are to unite in order to work there must be discipline.
> Discipline is an absolute necessity in any co-operative effort. That
> is, there must be in every co-operative effort those who command
> and those who obey, those who direct and those who carry out
> their directions.

The theme is more frequently recalled by Mallock, and by Studdert
Kennedy, than it had been by Cunningham.

Marx was not a serious problem for Cunningham and he says little
about him, but in the post-war climate 'Marx' served a purpose
which 'Spencer' had served for an earlier generation. The name
represented the same mechanical and deterministic 'science', a
repudiation of personality, freedom of choice and distinction, and
was, in addition, credited with one menacing contemporary success
in the Bolshevik revolution. Particularly in the early years, the ICF
was preoccupied with what he was taken to signify, and the
organisation's encounter with marxism will have to be discussed in
greater detail. But the substantive content of Studdert Kennedy's
published allusions can be dealt with briefly, with some further aid
from Mallock.

All Studdert Kennedy's allusions to Marx in *Democracy and the Dog
Collar* (dedicated to the working men of Britain, 'who were her
soldiers once') and *The Wicket Gate* (dedicated to Kirk and the staff of
the ICF) are conventionally and crudely abusive, where they are not
trivial.

> . . . *Das Kapital* is really the Bible of the working classes; they swear
> by it and don't read it, and could not understand it if they did. I
> am fed up with the whole performance. I believe that old
> gentleman ought to be buried. He was not really a prophet, he was
> only a disease. (*DDC*, 59)

> . . . as woolly-headed as Karl Marx. (*DDC*, 89)

> Of course Marx was logical. He was a German, and all Germans
> are logical, and that is why they are often such silly fools ... We
> can break clear of economic determinism and claim our moral
> freedom. (*DDC*, 91)

The ICF could field more deliberate arguments at Mallock's middle-
brow level. In 1922 Macassey published his *Labour Policy—False and
True*. But the Messenger's only reasonably composed allusion is in
Lies (*L*, 49–50), again in the fourth chapter, and it is derived from
Mallock (who is enthusiastically acknowledged by Macassey).[90]
Quoted above (p. 85), it refers to Marx's supposed blindness to the
role of exceptional brains and exceptional abilities, and it is
elaborated in a footnote. This is one of Mallock's most regular
arguments and Studdert Kennedy seems to have been referring to
pp. 101–4 of *The Limits of Pure Democracy* when he wrote this passage.

The Messenger took Mallock very seriously as a hard-headed guide
to the intractable realities confronting warm-hearted but
intellectually subornable social reformers. Indeed, it is hard to see
where he would have been without this support, for Mallock was
uniquely serviceable. He makes no attempt to integrate religion with
his social philosophy, so his analysis of social and economic
constraints could be calibrated with other elements in Studdert
Kennedy's own thinking as an independent and seemingly objective
system of relations of fact. Mallock, also, was unique among leading
anti-socialist writers in that he did not attack socialism from a
position of extreme individualism. He was totally unlike Spencer in
this respect, was quite unconcerned with the freedom of the
individual as a general good, and pragmatic about state intervention,
which was in any case regularly argued on grounds that were
independent of the debate over Individualism and Socialism,
particularly where 'social' rather than 'economic' issues were
concerned. As with Cunningham, reform, of necessity conceived and
directed by the state, was a desirable activity, but its grounds were not
distributive. The issue was the increase of national wealth, which
involved maintaining a rational structure of motivations and
incentives and an effective gradation of labour, while at the same
time avoiding risks that are endemic to hierarchically stratified social
relations, by social responsiblity and stewardship, on the one hand,
and realistic adjustment, on the other. This includes the recognition
of organised trade unions as an estate of the realm. The energy
behind this rational order is taken to be the genetically rare quality of
ability, inventiveness and directive skill. Round this central assertion
Mallock built a strictly economic justification of inequality: the
middle-class industrialist operating within a steadily expanding
political economy is the hero of this society. It was an argument with

particular appeal to the new recruits to the conservative party from suburban villadom, an expanding pool of aspiration, with its own brand of radicalism in its sense of the rewards due to industry and talent in an orderly world and its resentment at the conspicuous consumption of unearned wealth. Mallock's argument combined elements that were attractive also to many liberals. A programme for avoiding either class war or the ruinous alternative of a raw form of individualism, it exalted the idea of individual development within an organically structured community, whose harmony and functional balance would be maintained by judicious state intervention. The breadth of his appeal makes Mallock an important contributor to the larger capitalist ideology, within which, for instance, Joseph Chamberlain's defensive reformism was conceived, socialist in the loose sense of being a reaction against the crudities of a doctrine of *laissez-faire*, which had never dominated actual practice, but uncompromisingly hostile to a thoroughgoing collectivism, to the continental socialism of confiscation and violence, and to the labourism and egalitarian radicalism that seemed to herald such developments in British politics. Within this broad perspective, substantial structural change is seen as a recipe for collective suicide, whilst the impediments to a rational survival are psychological and moral. What distinguishes the more conservative emphases from the more progressive are the terms in which this collective moral dilemma is presented. Mallock is hardly at all concerned with equality of opportunity, but consistently anxious about the problem of inducing people to know and willingly keep to their place. He 'could never persuade himself that a movement which aimed at equality was motivated by anything other than envy'.[91] For him social problems were the outcome 'of a desire of those in inferior positions to change existing social arrangements'.[92]

Studdert Kennedy entirely accepts the objective necessity for the political economy Mallock describes.

> Oligarchy—or the rule of the few over the many—is a practical necessity in all democracies. Oligarchy is the soul of trades unionism, which is supposed to be the quintessence of Democracy. When the oligarchy of trades unions fails, unionism fails and you get chaos. (*L*, 73)

Certain ills of capitalism he freely abuses—sinfulness compounds the inherent limitations of material relations, and, like Mallock, he is harsh on irresponsible privilege. He too expresses deep anxieties about the psychological forces released by unrealistic material demands.

There is all the bitterness of thwarted desire in the contempt
which the 'have nots' display for the 'haves'. Give them the
chance, and they would change places to-morrow and be as
blatantly vulgar and as stupidly tyrannical as those who are in
possession to-day. The champions of the 'Bottom Dog' are only
out to make him 'Top Dog', not to make him a New Man.
(*FFU*, 59)

Mallock's assumptions about human irrationality, however, were
nominalist and sectarian. Studdert Kennedy's religious philosophy
called for a comprehensive scientific account of human behaviour
which would validate the theological interpretation of individual and
collective weakness. This he found in the work of William
McDougall, particularly in *The Group Mind*.[93] While the attention
Studdert Kennedy gives to political and economic issues betrays
impatience and irritation, psychology is a field of absorbing interest,
and his work is littered with allusions, some of them thoroughly
recondite, to psychologists of the day. But his reactions to the new
science have a distinctive structure, polarised by the attractions of
McDougall's social psychology, on one side, and the threats
emanating from the supposed discoveries of Freudian or Jungian
psycho-therapy, on the other. McDougall is a guide to be trusted;
Freud, or perhaps 'Freud', like 'Marx' is a disease visited upon us.
   A number of clerics were attempting to assimilate, or domesticate,
the new speculations on the covert dynamics of behaviour.
Grenstead's 1930 Bampton Lectures could draw on a substantial
literature bearing on the psychology of religion,[94] and at a more
popular level, two leading ICF figures, T. Pym and F. R. Barry, wrote
on psychology and the Christian life.[95] Canon Raven's reflections on
the subject, however, were severely mauled by H. Crighton-Miller of
the Tavistock Institute.[96] But Studdert Kennedy had little systematic
interest in this sort of approach, though he uses the standard
arguments on such issues as the transcendence of impulse through
sublimation (*FFU*, 167; *WWC*, 32). More often, he voices anxieties
about the danger of irrationalist derivations from Freud or a
misreading of Freud. The consequences of the abuse of sexuality for
the individual, the family and society are a central element in his
message for the ICF, a common theme in his verse, and the theme of
at least one mission conducted in the midlands with the assistance of
'Navvy' Smith.[97] His pastoral concern in this area, however, carried
him further than the official 'pure-living' campaigns which seem to
have been a major preoccupation of the Interdenominational
Advisory Committee of the Army Chaplaincy Service. His novel, *I
Pronounce Them*,[98] is about the difficulty of Christian marriage, and
shocked many readers because of its 'excessive sympathy' with loyal

but irregular relationships.[99] His final book is concerned with the principle of 'creative conflict', which operates at every level, sexual, economic and international.[100] An understanding of anomalous sexual behaviour, gained in part from the monumental studies of Havelock Ellis and others, was doubtless important in his pastoral work with individuals. Whilst this aspect of his concern with the irrational bases of behaviour accommodates to his general view— disordered sexuality, like war, is a sympton of misdirected will, with consequences that can be identified at a number of different levels— the psychological theory primarily concerned with it seemed to him narrow, unbalanced and open to misinterpretation. Early in the decade he is dismissive and hostile:

> The teachers of [this natural animality] are largely followers of Freud, the psychologist, who have never read his books, and dabblers in psycho-analysis with the most elementary sort of knowledge of what it all means. It is a ghastly thing for one who has studied and come to understand the powers of suggestion to contemplate the unnatural alliance which has been formed between the specialist in his study and the fool in every street to debauch the minds of the people with a flood of new sex teaching. (*FFU*, 148; and see his poem, 'The Psychologist'.)

Towards the end of the decade he is taking Freud to task for mistaking abnormal for normal psychology, but acknowledging his 'deep and true' observation that civilisation has been built up on the sacrifice in gratification of the primitive impulses (*WWC*, 32). Given his frame of reference, there can be no recognition of the socially radical implications of Freud's 'abnormal' psychology, and he is not prepared to accept developments in this quarter as validly scientific. McDougall's social psychology satisfied him on this score, and perfectly complemented the other elements in his system of beliefs.

Above all, McDougall's 'scientific' filtration of Hobhouse's social theory—*The Group Mind* is deferentially dedicated to Hobhouse—[101] exactly matched a fundamental tension in the Messenger's own thought, between an evolutionary belief in a rational social order and a concurrent conviction of the irrational, unpredictable, passionate and suggestible nature of man as an individual. In each case the offered solution is the same, a paradoxical commitment to rationality as a corporate quality which is, however, somehow to be realised through effective management by an élite that is expert and socially conscientious, and therefore redeemed from the common condition. The guardian-expert, for McDougall, is the agent of an immanent, yet vulnerable process:

To thwart democratic or crowd behaviour [the terms were
synonymous for McDougall], he invested absolute control in an
evolutionary movement toward corporate national ends.[102]

This orientation pervades the Messenger's work, but direct and
explicit derivations can be found in *The Word and the Work* (44 ff and
74 ff) and *Democracy and the Dog Collar* (209 ff).

Alluding to the works of Le Bon and Trotter, with which Studdert
Kennedy was familiar,[103] McDougall identifies the central
evolutionary paradox of progress and retrogression.

> We seem to stand before a paradox. Participation in group life
> degrades the individual, assimilating his mental processes to those
> of the crowd, whose brutality, inconstancy, and unreasoning
> impulsiveness have been the theme of many writers; yet only by
> participating in group life does man become fully man, only so
> does he rise above the level of the savage.[104]

The complexity of mind is the instrument of impulse. The individual
achieves personal harmony by learning to balance self-regarding
and social pressures in an ascending hierarchy of situations,

> . . . in which each larger group includes the lesser; each group
> being made the object of the extended self-regarding sentiment in
> a way which includes the sentiment for the lesser group in the
> sentiment for the larger group in which it is comprised. Thus the
> family, the village, the county, the country as a whole, form for
> the normal man the objects of a harmonious hierarchy of
> sentiments of this sort, each of which strengthens rather than
> weakens the others and yields motives for action which on the
> whole co-operate and harmonise rather than conflict.[105]

The psychological development of the individual in this schematised
social structure is seen as analogous to the collective development
over time. One can speak of the 'national mind' of a highly evolved
state, a construct which is maintained by an intellectual aristocracy
capable of engineering present sacrifice in the interests of the
collective future. Leadership at every level, as much a moral as an
intellectual quality, the point at which group consciousness is most
highly evolved, is critical to this purposive collective development. In
default of such leadership, the group moves towards its lowest
common denominator and becomes a herd or mob. McDougall is
generous with his illustrations, and Haig, Foch and Joffre are
introduced as the outstanding figures who ensured the moral unity
of the allied armies,[106] whilst Haldane is applauded for his sensitivity

to group psychology in forming the territorials. One of Studdert Kennedy's revelatory footnotes in *The Word and the Work* underlines the importance he attached to this aspect of the argument and directly relates McDougall's argument to his own preoccupation with the war as the supremely paradoxical manifestation of collective purpose. McDougall has a good deal to say about the British army.

> . . . the more fully the consciousness of the whole group is present in the mind of each member, the more effectively will the whole impress its moral precepts upon each.
> . . . Thus Lord Kitchener, by issuing his exhortation to the British Army on its departure to France, did undoubtedly exert a considerable influence towards raising the moral level of the whole force . . . the organisation of the whole group, with its hierarchy of offices which confer prestige, gives those who hold these higher offices the opportunity to raise the moral level of all its members.[107]

Studdert Kennedy's footnote comes in a section drawing directly on McDougall:

> That was the secret of the popular adoration of Lord Kitchener at the beginning of the War. He was pictured as the man of Power who swept obstacles out of his way with a wave of his hand. That strong face with the slight cast in the eyes summed up in itself all that we wanted to be. Therefore his name was a name to conjure with. He was the apotheosis of ourselves. God rest his soul. We laid a heavy burden on his back. (*WW*, 78)

There is little except the scientific idiom to distinguish McDougall's social psychology of group sentiments and leadership from Temple's fusion of Plato and Oxford idealism. Temple, indeed, invoked McDougall's authoritative endorsement. Both proceed inevitably to the same conclusion. Beyond the nation lies the higher collectivity, whose realisation will subsume a redeemed patriotism and a pure and noble imperialism. Studdert Kennedy echoes them both:

> . . . you [Organised Labour] do not really decide upon the vastly important question as to what your next unit of co-operation is. Is it to be the class or the nation? In striving to make united classes you tend to make divided nations, and that is one of my great criticisms of your present policy. (*DDC*, 230 ff)

The failure of the statesmen to recognise the emergent opportunity

for integration at an international level is treated with sustained
bitterness in a lengthy poem by 'Woodbine Willie', 'Dead and
Buried'.

> . . . Yet my heart was still unbroken,
>   And my hope was still unquenched,
> Till I bore my cross to Paris through the crowd.
>   Soldiers pierced me on the Aisne,
>   But 'twas by the river Seine
> That the statesmen brake my legs and made my
> shroud.

>   There they wrapped my mangled body
>   In fine linen of fair words,
> With the perfume of a sweetly scented lie,
>   And they laid it in the tomb
>   Of the golden-mirrored room,
> 'Mid the many-fountained Garden of Versailles . . .

McDougall provided 'scientific' support for a kind of psychological
reductionism which was to take more sophisticated forms towards
the end of the interwar period. His social psychology, though this was
masked by his reputation as an experimental scientist, was rather
blatantly a conservative and élitist 'political polemic aspiring to be
social science'.[108] Francis Mulhern's comment on the political
contribution of the literary critic Denys Harding to F. R. Leavis's
journal *Scrutiny* is apt in the present context, though *Scrutiny*, needless
to say, as the voice of a freshly recruited presence in the intellectual
élite, was not looking to the clerisy of the Church for an insight into
the energies that might sustain a new moral order, or to the
enlightened man of affairs as their most articulate agent.

> The social, repressed in the scheme of his analysis, returned in the
> form of an abstract ideal, to be pursued (or not, as the case might
> be) by the abstract individual. Social progress was now to be
> achieved not by the working out of contradictions in the social
> structure but by the striving of individuals towards an ideal of
> 'social integration' which, represented by none, excluded none.
> Thus, despite his claim to the contrary, Harding denied the
> rationality of political conflict: its very existence testified to the
> 'custom of domination' and precluded 'social integration'. His
> solution was to abolish it; for in society so conceived, political
> struggle could only be individual moral effort.[109]

5 Verse and Rhetoric

The content of Studdert Kennedy's message cannot be isolated from its persuasive form, and one would expect an analysis of this to throw some light both on the more elusive aspects of the content and on the nature of the response to his published work and his public appearances. It might be suggested, however, that an excursion into literary criticism is likely to reflect individual reactions based on aesthetic criteria irrelevant to the author's intentions in a case like this. Nevertheless, whilst these intentions need to be recognised and appropriately acknowledged, the hazard of being suspected of making claims to an inappropriately superior refinement of sensibility and taste must be accepted. The Messenger dealt with ideas whilst playing on emotions. A 'literary' response is therefore a necessary and integral element in an analysis of the public life of these ideas, and part of a broader judgement about their significance.

Studdert Kennedy's verse has not found its way into anthologies of writing from the war. But unlike other highly popular versifiers of the period who have long since sunk without trace, such as John Oxenham, who was much quoted in church circles and warmly reviewed in the *Atheneum*[1] his verse is still read, recited in sermons and, with some regularity, on religious broadcasts. It has revolted the two distinguished poets and literary critics, I. A. Richards and Roy Fuller, who have given it some attention in passing.[2] Both of them were seriously concerned with the implications of a ready response to such writing. It is now incredible that the vapidities of Oxenham's *Bees in Amber* should have run to 203,000 copies by 1923, though we are assured by Stead that such volumes were appearing by the score,[3] but the preacher's verse does not invite the same kind of inattentive reading. As I. A. Richards discovered from the reactions of his own students towards the end of the twenties, it tends to provoke a strong response in one direction or another. His discussion of the grounds advanced by some of his students for approving of the one poem, 'Easter', which they were asked to consider in detail, draws attention to the untrained sensibility's vulnerability to a fluent use of 'stock' poetical imagery, and to sentimentality, by which he intends the inflation of emotion, its disorder and forced emphasis in relation to the situation in the poem. Roy Fuller's lecture harks back directly to Richards' discussion of 'Poem IV' in *Practical Criticism*. But, like Raymond Williams who identified a disquieting passivity in Richards' concern with the reader's psychological organisation,[4] Fuller is dissatisfied with the earlier discussion and his own discussion of sentimentality more explicitly develops the concept in relation to a kind of writing that can diminish awareness of social circumstance and social relation.

> . . . we can expect the characteristics of sentimentality in poetry to express themselves in one or other or all of the following modes. First, reactionary emotion. Secondly, anti-scientific feeling. Thirdly, deficiency of realism.[5]

The general issues raised in this critical development are obviously of fundamental importance and have a bearing on this body of verse, but Fuller is unfortunately brief, for our purposes, on 'Woodbine Willie', who is used as a whipping boy only because of his appearance in Richards' classic study. It is also unfortunate that the poem considered by Richards himself, by his students and by Fuller is not quite the one Studdert Kennedy actually wrote. Richards doctored the poem for teaching purposes by removing a reference to the war in the second stanza and by removing the last stanza altogether, so that it ended with four lines of Swinburnian pastiche (still in 1929, a modern idiom for his young students), and missed the doctrinal climax.

> One solace there is for me, sweet but faint,
>   As it floats on the wind of the years,
> A whisper that spring is the last true thing,
>   And that triumph is born of tears.
>
> It comes from a garden of other days,
>   And an echoing voice that cries,
> 'Behold I am alive for evermore,
>   And in Me shall the dead arise.'

The complete poem would surely have cropped up for discussion in Richards' chapter on doctrine in poetry, which explores the problem of a reader's response to substantive beliefs expressed in poetry and also raises the particularly difficult question of sincerity in this connection. There is no simple or symmetrical relationship among these critical categories. It is hard to see on what basis the sincerity of the preacher's beliefs could be questioned, but what is to be said about the shape they took and the response to them in a literary form of such manifest deficiency and apparently enduring popularity?

Both Richards and Fuller go out of the way to acknowledge 'Woodbine Willie's' modesty. In the Appendix to *Practical Criticism* which reveals the authorship of the thirteen poems his students were asked to evaluate, Richards writes of Poem IV:

> I am greatly in debt to the author, who wrote; 'You can use any of my poems for any purpose you like. The criticisms of them could not be more adverse and slaughterous than my own would be.'

And Richards recalled, some months before his death in 1979, that he included this note in order 'to indicate my admiration and regard for his generosity of spirit—so different from the angry reaction of Alfred Noyes, who did his best to set the Law on me'.[6] But, however slaughterous, the author's criticisms would have been of a different order than those of Richards and Fuller, and one can even muster some sympathy with Noyes, who wrote verse on some of the same premises and found the 'new poetic', and the critical standards developing with it, threatening, impossibly esoteric and remote, its roots in tradition indecipherable and baffling. By missing the question of belief in this instance, the critics set up an easy target, a kind of writing which expects to be judged by standards which, acceptable or not, are very different from theirs. 'Woodbine Willie's' war verse, for example, is not best considered as an inferior version of the poetry included in Silkin's distinguished anthology. The critical skills Silkin brings to bear on Owen, Rosenberg and a few others would not be fully engaged even on good writing of this kind.[7]

The comments from Richards and Fuller seem to exhaust the critical attention 'Woodbine Willie' has received. Fussell, in a study which claims a generally comprehensive coverage, nowhere mentions him, and is generally weak on directly religious writing.[8] But we can make a more oblique approach, through T. S. Eliot's uneasy attempt at an accommodation with Kipling's verse.[9] Here a major influence on the new sensibility explores the purposes and resources of a 'public poetry' from which his own creative processes were totally detached. Much of Studdert Kennedy's most popular verse was written in direct imitation of Kipling, and Eliot's generalities establish Kipling as a point of reference in the right framework.

Eliot makes his approach to Kipling by focusing on the tradition of the ballad, though not in a narrow formal sense, and very much in terms of the wide and classless availability of what he calls 'ballad attention' to poetry, a limited response which may not extend to more complex forms. The ballad motive is towards the immediately apprehensible, the feeling that can be completely shared, a commonality of response. Such a writer displays his craft in order to act on his readers and if the result rises to the intensity of 'poetry', as, say, in Kipling's 'Danny Deever', that is not because the words have emerged out of some inner imperative, working obscurely towards their right form. Poetry in *that* sense may emerge in spite of deficiencies of craft. Kipling's ballads, however, including the Browningesque monologues, which are 'metrically and intrinsically ballads', are triumphs of applied skill, versatility and variety within clearly defined structures, unobtrusive aptness of phrase displaying energy within an unambiguous and restricted frame of reference. The language departs from prose only in order to heighten, to concentrate and dramatise a content that can be quite fully paraphrased.

There is no comparison in terms of quality, but these generalities identify assumptions behind 'Woodbine Willie's' verse. His most successful poem is a 'ballad', which notes without fuss the primary loyalty of the trenches which came to be invested with so much sacramental significance.

. . . And that night I'd been in trenches,
  Seeking out the sodden dead,
And just dropping them in shell-holes,
  With a service swiftly said.

. . . So I crawled round on my belly,
  And I listened to the roar
Of the guns that hammered Thiepval,
  Like big breakers on the shore.

Then there spoke a dripping sergeant,
  When the time was growing late,
'Would you please to bury this one,
  'Cause 'e used to be my mate?'

So we groped our way in darkness
  To a body lying there,
Just a blacker lump of blackness
  With a red blotch on his hair.

Though we turned him gently over,
  Yet I still can hear the thud,
As the body fell face forward,
  And then settled in the mud.

> . . . There are many kinds of sorrow
> In this world of Love and Hate,
> But there is no sterner sorrow
> Then a soldier's for his mate.
> ('His Mate')

Kipling, Eliot observes, is an intensely impersonal poet, and Richards applies the same word to Studdert Kennedy. Eliot himself, of course, pursues a different kind of impersonality, in writing poetry that is not didactic or 'animated by any other social purpose',[10] but what the ballad motive demands is the impersonality appropriate in an agent of emotional consensus. The elements of imagery, tone and rhythm in 'Woodbine Willie's' verse, though not always disciplined, as they are here, by a defined structure, invariably contribute to this kind of impersonality, even where the verse is apparently confessional self-exposure, as in 'It is not finished' and 'Come unto me: a shell-hole meditation'. Such writing is not compelled to emerge from the obscure cellular differentiation and development of a unique private embryo. It is done with a prior purpose, to shape and fortify widely shared emotions and orientations. Studdert Kennedy wrote with the confidence of representing a special branch of a tradition which, more broadly, included among his contemporaries Kipling, Austin, Watson, Newbolt (at Clifton with Haig, who was the apotheosis of Howarth's 'Newbolt man'),[11] and of course Noyes, a tradition of 'public poets', deeply hostile to 'aesthetes' and writing for readers who were

> not inclined to treat poetry 'as poetry, and not another thing'. It was the 'other thing' that mattered (as Kipling knew); poetry was only another vehicle on which opinion and prejudice could be trundled into the drawing room.[12]

To opinion and prejudice we can add, in 'Woodbine Willie's' case, an immediately accessible sense of consolation. These writers were at the butt-end of a prophetic line, but the broad readership of Kipling and the socially more elevated admirers of Newbolt were a loyal and substantial following. Kipling, loaded with plug tobacco for distribution to the men, and reciting his ballads at smoking concerts during the South African war,[13] had established the part of the soldiers' poet for Studdert Kennedy to take up, with his bag of woodbines and his trench balladry.

The results of such poetic intentions and their implications for the public purposes in which the Messenger was involved can only be indicated by looking at particular texts, and this will again raise issues introduced by Richards and Fuller. But a rough classification of the verse reveals Studdert Kennedy's thorough and perfectly self-conscious application of working assumptions which have been so completely repudiated by poets and critics alike. Virtually every poem is a paraphrase of one of the major or minor themes already discussed in the context of his prose, an attempt to heighten and dramatise, to release a diffuse emotional response and establish an immediate mood. This is most easily seen by examining his use of quotations, often of substantial length, which increasingly crowd his pages, from about one every fifteen in *The Hardest Part* to one every eight in *The Wicket Gate* and one every six in *The Word and the Work*. The discursive argument is reinforced in a stretch of metrical assertion and allusion. The use of quotation to bolster argument was particularly common among clerics of the period, and several supporters of the ICF indulged in it to excess.[14] Almost invariably the result is feeble, shallow currents of thought washing round islands of rented emotion. But the emotional level of the Messenger's rhetoric carries the quotations, from his own work and Browning particularly, whilst his normal indifference to the academic habit of acknowledgement emphasises both the continuity of prose and 'poetry' and the purposive and rhetorical manipulation of the latter. He had developed a rhetoric which riled Bishop Henson: 'Dramatic perorations about "the naked Christ" go a long way with the half-educated enthusiasts who mainly compose the religious public'.[15]

The repudiation of a Napoleonic God and the assertion of God's suffering occupy many poems, such as 'The Comrade God' (quoted *HP*, 199) and 'The Suffering God', written, he records, on an upturned biscuit tin in the gas-polluted air of 'Oxford Street', Havrincourt Wood.[16] (Various stanzas quoted *HP*, 187; *FFU*, 227, 249, 285; *L*, 4; *WW*, 73; *WWC*, 71.)

> . . . Swift to its birth in spite of human scorning
>   Hastens the day, the storm-clouds roll apart;
> Rings o'er the earth the message of the morning.
>   Still on the Cross the Saviour bares his heart.
>
> Passionately fierce the voice of God is pleading,
>   Pleading with men to arm them for the fight;
> See how those hands, majestically bleeding,
>   Call us to rout the armies of the night.
>   ('The Suffering God')

Like Kipling, he often wrote to tunes rather than metres, a hymn tune here but music hall songs on other occasions, the jingles of the latter sometimes at odds with the content, but both of course implying a community of participation. Other poems on this theme include 'Eternal Hope', 'Come unto me', 'High and Lifted Up', 'A

Sermon' (an attack on cant about an Almighty God) and 'Truth'.

Three treatments of the theme of Christ in the trenches have already been quoted, 'The Gift', 'Solomon in all his glory', and 'Dead and Buried'. 'A Mother understands' (quoted *HP*, 137) echoes liturgical cadencies.

> Dear Lord, I hold my hand to take
>   They Body, broken here for me,
> Accept the Sacrifice I make,
>   My body, broken, there, for Thee.
>
> His was my body, born of me,
>   Born of my bitter travail pain,
> And it lies broken on the field,
>   Swept by the wind and the rain.
> *Surely a Mother understands Thy thorn-crowned head,*
> *The mystery of Thy pierced hands—the Broken Bread.*

'Demobilised' and, more ponderously, an extended piece of blank verse, 'Non Angli Sed Angeli', also pick up the associated themes.

> . . . And in that blazing light of Love he saw
> The sin of slavery, the sin supreme,
> That slays the world because it values life
> As death, and dares to use as mere machines,
> For pleasure or for profit, living men.
> This blasphemy against the Holy Ghost . . .
> Yes, I have seen them smile at death, and known,
> By instinct of sure prophecy, the Truth
> That seas of dead tyrannic force would break
> In vain against the rock of British hearts,
> Whereon the love of freedom sits enthroned . . .
>
> The minotaur of Mammon tears the wings
> From new-fledged souls and flings them bleeding down
> To dogs of greed and lust . . .
>
> Shall wealth still grow, and woe increase to breed
> In filthy slums the slaves of poverty?
> Shall senseless pride and vulgar luxury
> By gilding over evil make it good? . . .

The pervasive sacramentalism, associating nature with the human and suffering Christ and the development of God's purpose, is celebrated in a number of poems which echo passages in the prose,

'At the Eucharist', 'At a Harvest Festival', 'Wild Rose Way',
'Judgment', 'Well' (a dialect version of 'Judgment'), 'Indifference',
'So I dream', 'My peace I leave with you'. Belief itself, the problem of
the grand hypothesis, is argued in 'Faith', a Browningesque
monologue, 'If Jesus never lived', 'Come unto me' and 'It is not
finished'.

The more incidental themes are also dealt with, death and life after
death ('Death', 'At a seance'), science ('The truth of May', 'The
Psychologist'), sexuality and love ('Only engaged', 'A Gal of the
Streets', and 'Right is Might', among others). Even the exhortatory
crudities of *Rough Talks* appear in the form of verse:

> . . . For to do more than you can
> Is to be a British man,
> Not a rotten 'also ran'—
> > *Carry on.*
> > > ('The Spirit')

> . . . Damn these blame moonition workers,
> Damn them and their bloomin' strike,
> Thinks its same as Peace conditions,
> They can do just as they like.
> Think o' Jimmy Brown! 'E's earnin'
> Easy four pun ten a week,
> And 'e's struck for better money—
> 'E's the one as oughter speak—
> Been and bought a noo pianer,
> And 'is wife a noo fur coat,
> Gawd, I 'opes 'is Sunday dinner
> Stops and turns round in 'is throat . . .
> > ('No Retaliation')

The dialect poems show the extent to which the verse is the product
of deliberate translation from one form into another. There are
dialect versions of the more important poems. 'The Suffering God' is
transcribed into a common soldier's meditation in 'The Sorrow of
God'. 'Judgment' (quoted in full *FFU* 314–16), with its dream in
which the narrator encounters Christ, loses some amorphous
romantic imagery but retains all the essential details in its dialect
version 'Well?'.

> I saw no thronged angelic court, I saw no great white throne,
> I saw no open Judgment books, I seemed to stand alone.
> I seemed to stand alone beside a solemn sounding sea,
> While, at my feet upon the shore, broke waves of memory . . .

He stood with me beside the sea, and listened to its moan.
I did not dare to raise my eyes, I feared what I might see,
A cold sweat broke and bathed my brow, I longed to turn and
flee,
But could not, rooted there I stood, in shiv'ring shame and fear,
The subtle shadow substance took, and nearer came, and near.
O was it days or was it years, we stood beside that sea,
Or was it aeons, timeless times? It seemed eternity . . .

('Judgment')

    I couldn't see no judgment court,
      Nor yet that great white throne,
    I couldn't see no record books,
      I seemed to stand alone,
    I seemed to stand alone, beside
      A solemn kind 'o sea.
    Its waves they got in my inside
      And touched my memory . . .

    I couldn't speak, I felt as though
      'E 'ad me by the throat,
    'Twere like a drownin' fellah feels,
      Last moment he's afloat.
    And 'E said nowt, 'E just stood still,
      For I dunno 'ow long.
    It seemed to me like years and years,
      But time out there's all wrong . . .

('Well?')

The dialect verse, his most popular and immediately 'public', not
requiring borrowed poetical costumery, clearly exhibits symptoms
indicated in Fuller's diagnostic. 'Woodbine Willie' writes, as in his
prose, realistically about war itself, with sympathy for those engaged
in it and with appreciation of courage and humour. But the issue of
realism at another level can be raised by asking the obvious questions
about the use of a form so inherently patronising as dialect. Who is
speaking to whom and why? Kipling's assumption of the voice of the
common man, despite its stylised proletarian syntax, carries
conviction because of an oddly radical sympathy with the common
fodder of war.[17] Owen's 'The Chances', one of the very few successful
dialect poems of the war, forces attention on to a specific and
ultimate mutilation without condescension or extraneous motive
while the notorious 'pity' in his work is implicated in a less
frequently acknowledged anger, a judgement on specific responses
sustaining the condition of war, civilian acquiescence and official

structures of control and justification.[18] 'Woodbine Willie'
condemns the War, of course:

> Damn the blasted war to 'ell, lass,
>   It's just bloody rotten waste:
> Them as gas on war and glory
>   Oughter come and 'ave a taste.

This piece, however, ends by evoking the facile public conventions
surrounding the conflict.

> But the kids will some day bless us,
>   When they grows up British men,
> 'Cause we tamed the Prussian tyrant,
>   And brought peace to earth again.
>
> ('What's the Good?')

Behind such representative writing lies the theoretical structure that
has been discussed. The evil of war is an enveloping metaphysical
fact, to be redeemed through a certain kind of suffering. The
correspondence with Christ's suffering is explicitly set up in a
number of poems, such as 'It's the pluck' and 'Thy will be done'. But
it is easy to read and react to such verse without paying much
attention to its metaphysical substructure. Its effect then, like much
of the material in *Rough Talks* is at one level to endorse the situation,
while celebrating common decencies and loyalties that appear to
redeem it. For those,—many of them not actively involved in the war
and few of them thinking or speaking in 'dialect'—who were not
seriously engaged by the theological content, such writing was a
wishful travesty of the social world symbolically identified by the
dropped aspirates and rough syntax, and a sentimental rendering of
its predicament.

'Woodbine Willie's' own confusion about the purpose of his
dialect *personae* is exposed in a series of prose contributions in dialect
to a church magazine after the war; not, one would suppose,
common reading in many working-class homes, with titles like 'Old
Bill on Gawd', and 'Them There Bishops'.[19] The absence of metrical
jingle makes them seem more of a departure from the dialect verses
than in fact they were. Both forms project, as a representative being,
the reassuring working-class figure one would like to hear,
advancing a reasonable moral claim on society behind which we can
all unite.

> My old England were a curse.
> It were sleepin', sweatin', starvin',

Wearing boot soles for a job,
 It were sucking up to foremen
 What 'ud sell ye for a bob . . .

It's new England as I fights for,
 It's an England swep' aht clean . . .
('Old England')

The blind veteran of 'Worry' is the prototype.

For I've got my legs and arms, sir,
 And these 'ands is willing still,
I can do my job of work yet;
 I can do it—and I will.

There's just one thing I'm afeard on,
 Will they find me work to do?
That's the thing as makes me worry,
 Same as it would worry you . . .

These are unreal voices.

A reading of Owen's 'Conscious' or his 'Disabled' offers a qualitatively different experience. There the writing makes sustained and particular demands on the attention through an intensely considered use of imagery, association and other verbal resources. The concrete and specific development of the idea leaves no room for a self-indulgent or patronising emotional response: it is pity, precisely, in relation to a representative particular, that Owen establishes. By contrast 'Woodbine Willie's' verse is an invitation to place oneself in a generalised situation, and there to release emotion without encountering any provocative perception or qualitative development of response. Characteristically, the prompt experience of a sense of diffuse uplift, even a degree of self-pity, is the manifest purpose behind the writing. 'Only Engaged', like its dialect variant 'The Pensioner', illustrates this.

I can hear their voices singing as the train steams slowly out,
 I can see their faces still through mists of tears . . .

Then a downy head comes seeking for the pillow of my breast,
 And a gleeful voice calls chuckling for its Dad,
And with two small arms around it my soul sinks back to rest,
 Singing nonsense to the child we never had.
('Only Engaged')

The complete poem was in fact used to shape responses to a

discussion of the moral foundation of the social order in the integrity of family life. In the interests of the larger social purpose, he there argues, the surplus women of a decimated generation must live with and seek to transcend their bitter natural frustration, supported by our compassionate sympathy.[20] The poem bids for that compassion but does so, as it were, on the easy terms of a bulk order.

It was not the dialect verse that Studdert Kennedy most frequently quoted in his prose. In his other work the consequences of writing as an act of will to a theme, but without anything like Kipling's technical dexterity, appear in a variety of ways. For example, there is pastiche Francis Thompson and other late romantic verse, and there are grinding attempts in the Browning manner to produce a dramatic speaking voice.

> I must have God. This life's too dull without,
> Too dull for ought but suicide. What's man
> To live for else? I'd murder someone just
> To see red blood. I'd drink myself blind drunk,
> And see blue snakes if I could not look up
> To see blue skies, and hear God speaking through
> The silence of the stars . . .
> ('Faith' quoted *WG* 60, and a sequence of public speeches
> e.g. *Birmingham Gazette*, 2 March 1926.)

There are casual insertions of literary allusion.

> Yet have I looked into my mother's eyes,
> And seen the light that never was on sea
> Or land . . .
> ('Faith')

There is exhausted whimsy ('If Jesus never lived') and syntactical incoherence ('Set your affections on things above') The incantatory use of rhythm and assonance has been sufficiently illustrated.

In the course of discussing his students' comments on 'Easter', Richards refers to 'an undirected, objectless feeling of pathos that will attach itself to anything that will give it an excuse'. This is indeed both an inevitable quality of the writing itself and characteristic of 'Woodbine Willie's' use of other highly charged lines in quotation. Anything goes, if it helps to maintain the surge of unshaped and hastily marshalled emotion.

> . . . I often see [cows driven to market] pass my window here, and think how like they are to men, staggering in a herd to their death in a state of muddled stupidity, being beaten, first on this side and

then on that, to keep them in the narrow way—always seeking to
get away from that stick, and always running into it. That's what
thousands of men feel like.
  'The years, like great black oxen, tread me down,
  And God the Herdsman goads them on behind,
  And I am trampled by their passing feet.'
                                                (*WG*, 129)

He is misquoting ('tread the world', and 'broken' rather than
'trampled'), the last three lines of Yeats's *Countess Cathleen*. Frequent
revisions of successive editions of the play did not affect these lines.[21]
The sequence of thought is thoroughly obscure, to a moderately
attentive reading, and would be indecipherable if the lines were
correctly transcribed.
  Also in *The Wicket Gate*, writing about faith in immortality:

The shadowy hosts whom Virgil pictured in the underworld like
autumn leaves in the Vale of Vallambrosa [*sic*], crowding by the
river bank, and stretching out their hands in longing for the
farther shore, held out their hands backwards to the life that they
had left, not forward to the life which was to come. But as man
grows, the hands turn round and are stretched out forwards to the
future, not back to the past. We become conscious that the most
perfect things in life like Love, Beauty and Truth, fall short of
perfection. And yet, God has given so much, can we believe that
He will not give more?
                                                (*WG*, 53)

It is possible that he recalled from the classical sixth form at Leeds
Grammar School a scholarly gloss on what Virgil's dead had to
expect, which might make sense of the backward stretching hands.
But he has added effectively to Virgil's

            quam multa in silvis autumni frigore primo
            lapsa cadunt folia,

by including Milton's specific and evocative allusion to Vallombrosa,
from the undercurrent of allusion to Virgil in *Paradise Lost*, Book 1,
which he had been reading, since he quotes from it some pages later.
This is a manipulative overloading of elevated literary allusion,
obviously unconsciously done.
  There is a similar whiff of second-hand classical pathos in the
course of a passage which argues that we all experience intimations
of an encounter with the Face of Christ (*WG*, 62).

Just when we are safest, there's a sunset touch,
A fancy from a flower-bell, someone's death,
A chorus-ending from Euripides . . .

The passage containing these lines from Browning's *Bishop Bloughram's Apology* is enthusiastically discussed by Temple in *Mens Creatrix*.[22] The predilection for Browning was encouraged and possibly initiated by Temple who, like many others, read him as an inspiring commentary on the Bible. There have been, of course, radically different readings of Browning.[23] Studdert Kennedy quotes him frequently, at one point in *Lies* (*L*, 171) misquoting a passage from *Men and Women* which appears again in another version, also wrong, in *The Wicket Gate* (*WG*, 50). Both versions garble the sense. On the latter occasion Studdert Kennedy is closely following Temple's Introductory Lecture in *The Nature of Personality*, where, however, the quotation appears in the correct form.[24]

Intellectually slovenly, but rhetorically effective, writing of this kind survived unmodified from edition to edition, and was quarried for responsive audiences in speech after speech. It is an idiom, taking his output as a whole, which slips away from questions that were also being avoided in public debate, suspending a radical devotional challenge in the medium of a defensive social perspective. A substantial public believed that he was articulating fundamental truths that urgently required practical interpretation. His admirers saw their own applications of principle to political, economic and social relations as attempts to express a vision endorsed by a shared framework of belief. He was seeking by these means to establish its reality in the minds of those who attended to him.

6 The Church Public of the ICF

The public figures identified in Chapter 2 as Members of the Council and Executive of the ICF were acknowledged by grass-roots supporters and activists as guiding lights and practical exponents of the vision of social obligation and commitment which the Messenger and his colleagues were seeking to spread abroad. It is less easy to identify and describe the local activists and supporters themselves. Nonconformist churches and organisations, we shall see, provided a dependable proportion of enthusiastic lay support, but the most clearly identifiable public was to be found within the still substantial active membership of the Church of England. But there is no straightforward record of this lay support. The best that can be done, therefore, is to make an indirect approach through an analysis of parishes and incumbents showing some degree of active involvement in the organisation.

A congregation, of course, may or may not reflect the social composition of a locality, and an incumbent may or may not be in tune with his congregation. We can, nonetheless, draw inferences from consistent patterns of activity in statistically adequate groups, if the limitations of the data are born in mind. The following analysis suggests that the most positive Church of England response to the ICF came from congregations with incumbents whose un-representativeness in a statistical sense reflected a consistent bias in social composition and in the relative importance of distinctive career patterns within the church hierarchy itself.

The Messenger's diary was controlled by Kirk, the ICF Director, who organised a gruelling schedule of engagements, which, it is worth noting, made increasingly heavy demands on the preacher's emotional and physical resources, and, indirectly, on his immediate family. Between 8 October and 17 December 1925, for instance, he made forty-six scheduled appearances, moving within ten days from Eastbourne to York, Accrington, Leeds, York again, London and Swansea. The surviving record covers the last six years of his life. It must include all but a handful of the invitations accepted from individual incumbents, though he often worked in additional targets of opportunity. Many more were disappointed. Kirk's acceptances were obviously determined by tactical and logistic considerations. Apart from regular visits to Devon, Somerset and Dorset, the parochial and other appearances were overwhelmingly concentrated in the urban north west, the industrial midlands and South Wales.

From the ICF Diary we can draw up a list of one hundred and thirty incumbents. A number of these were visited on more than one occasion. An additional hundred sat on the Executive and Council, along with some twenty bishops.

To provide one basis for comparison a random sample of two hundred and fifty incumbents has been taken from *Crockford's Clerical Directory* for 1924.

There is also another, more accidental comparison that can be made. The discussion of political tendencies within the Church has almost invariably been forced into the form of close attention to outstanding or vocal individuals together with the organised fractions associated with them, and more impressionistic generalisation about the broad tendencies they have represented or resisted. There is, however, one substantial yet specific group of clerics which has sometimes been referred to but never analysed, the five hundred or so ordained Anglicans who signed a *Memorial of the Clergy to the Labour Members of Parliament in May 1923*.[1] This was presented to MacDonald by its organiser Lewis Donaldson, a friend and colleague in the Leicester Labour Party. Hardly an expression of radical fervour, it expresses sympathy with 'the recent struggle of Labour to secure more effective representation in Parliament', and looks forward to 'the more serious consideration and more adequate treatment of the pressing problems and difficulties of our time, which such a combination of talent, earnestness and first-hand experience will certainly secure'. A signature was scarcely evidence of a socialistic commitment, but even allowing for fortuitous padding and omission in any such list, it seems reasonable to suppose that this group of MacDonald parsons (some three hundred of them incumbents by 1923) includes most if not all of the more radical. Certainly signing was not the sort of public gesture an Anglican clergyman at that time could afford to make without thought. Canon C. S. Woodward, MC, one of the eleven ICF incumbents who also signed for MacDonald, Vicar of the fashionable church of St Peter's Cranley Gardens, after pre-war slum parish experience in Southwark, lost at least one leading member of his congregation as a result of signing.[2] Others felt obliged to justify themselves in the columns of the *Guardian* and elsewhere.[3] In fact Woodward, like the other ICF signatories, is in significant respects at a distance from the central tendency of Donaldson's collection, which may be more accurately reflected in the small group of clergy associated with Conrad Noel of Thaxted, the Mirfield and Kelham ordinands, the officers of various organisations, and the frankly disaffected labourism of individuals like Hubert Handley, Vicar of St Thomas's Camden Town. His diatribes on the class partiality and 'shocking' deference of the Church included uninhibited *ad hominem* contrasts, that between Lang and Gore, for instance, being very much to Lang's disadvantage.[4]

The data for a comparison between the three groups come from *Crockford's Clerical Directory*. A rich but frustrating and inconsistent source, its limitations impose a number of constraints on the classification and tabulation of data. It provides no information about the stipends attached to curacies, chaplaincies, secretaryships and the like, while a generally exhaustive breakdown of the year's stipend for an individual incumbency may be given in either net or, though much more occasionally, gross figures, and it is never clear how much of a gross stipend may be earmarked for a curacy or some other charge. The year of birth is not given, though the year of ordination is. Pre-university schooling is not given, and academic performance at university may or may not be. However, the classifications employed here should be broad enough to take care of these vagaries and omissions, though individuals drop out of consideration in some tabulations because of gaps in the data.

A further point needs to be made about the significance of some of the most obvious variations in the actual data. The Church of England in this period was still an organisation in which managerial anomaly and incoherence were normal. There was no general correlation between remuneration and the extent or weight of responsibility, and only a weak one between remuneration and length of service. We are concerned with a Trollopian world of patronage and preferment, having a deep structure, so to speak, which has never been systematically charted, the product of inumerable charitable accidents, which shaped careers to their distinctive trajectories by a subtle and selective use of the criteria of energy, ability and, a most elusive composite, suitability.

Two differences between distributions in the three groups obviously reflect the special purposes of Donaldson and Kirk respectively. More than a third of the random sample was ordained by 1890, as against a fifth of each of the other two groups. At the same time a good half of the random sample worked in parishes of fewer than 1000 souls, as against a quarter of the MacDonald incumbents and a mere sixteenth of the ICF incumbents. These differences must be seen against a general drift with advancing age towards the smaller parish. This is reflected in each group, but at significantly different levels (Table 6.1).

TABLE 6.1 Median parish population in 1923, by incumbent's length of service

Ordained by:	−1880	−1890	−1900	−1910	−1920	N
Random sample	479	684	700	2400	3289	299
MacDonald incumbents	938	3860	5240	5000	4045	246
ICF Diary		6250		3680	7017	8500	116

After the war, nearly half of the ICF pre-1890 ordinands were still holding down parishes of over 7000, compared with less than a third of the MacDonald incumbents and a bare tenth of the random sample.

The significance of these differences is made clearer by sampling a proportion of the careers at five-year intervals, starting in 1890 and ending in 1925. Table 6.2 gives the probability of finding a 1923 ICF or MacDonald incumbent in a parish of any given size, either as incumbent or as curate, at one of these quinquennial samplings. These observations find the ICF incumbents engaged in parish work 86 per cent of the time, as against 76 per cent for the MacDonald group. The tabulation refers only to the parochial experience represented by these percentages.

TABLE 6.2 Probability of any pre-1900 ordinand being found as incumbent or curate in a parish of given size. Quinquennial sample, 1890–1925 inclusive

Parish population in '000s	Distribution of parochial experience	
	ICF Diary	MacDonald parsons
Above 16	0.11	0.08
Above 10	0.16	0.16
Above 7	0.17	0.13
Above 4	0.25	0.19
Above 1	0.22	0.19
Below 1	0.09	0.25
	1.00	1.00
N of observations	338	777
N of individuals	57	143
Smirnov two-sample test significant at 0.001 level		

The test is significant at the same level for the pre-1890 ordinands (Total N = 85), and at the 0.01 level for the 1895–1900 ordinands (Total N = 68). It is not significant at this level for the 1890–5 group which, however, only involves fourteen ICF men. It is not surprising that

Kirk tended to concentrate visits on the larger parishes, but to a disproportionate extent he responded to, or, as seems more likely, was approached by, incumbents with extensive and sustained experience of such livings.

More striking differences emerge if we consider variations of income between the three groups. One might, naïvely, have expected a higher proportion of the very poor clergy among the MacDonald incumbents. But most parishes with very low stipends were both small and rural. Allowing for this, the income distribution of the MacDonald incumbents is not out of line with that of the random sample (Table 6.3).

TABLE 6.3   Income distribution (net figures)

	$-£300$	$-£500$	$-£700$	$-£1000$	Over	
Random sample	43%	42	11	3	1	100%
MacDonald incumbents	23%	55	16	4	2	100%
ICF Diary	13%	43	18	15	11	100%
ICF Council/Executive	12%	39	23	17	9	100%

ICF incumbents with low incomes are hardly to be found in large parishes. There are none in parishes with populations in the 7000 to 10,000 range, and only one in twenty of those in still larger parishes earned less than £300. But the random sample turned up no-one earning over £700 in a parish above the 7000 mark. The ICF parishes tend to be disproportionately large, but they tend also to be unusually well-endowed.

Table 6.4 shows the disproportionate occupation of very large parishes by ICF supporters, and at the same time a disproportionate material recognition of their responsibilities.

Once again, a longitudinal analysis consolidates this picture. The ICF people establish a decisive lead in material rewards early in their careers. By 1910, 90 per cent of the ICF incumbents ordained by 1900 had moved from curacies to incumbencies, compared with 64 per cent of the equivalent MacDonald group. In fact only three of the former were still in 1910 strictly speaking curates. By 1915 twice as many ICF as MacDonald incumbents from these cohorts were earning over £500. The median increment to stipend between 1900 and 1910 for ICF incumbents had been £180, as against £19.

We can give some further substance to the variable of parish size by considering the number of curates attached to a living, as a measure of its importance and of the local level of church organisation and activity. It would be astonishing if there were no correlation at all between number of curates and size of parish, or

TABLE 6.4   Income and parish size in parishes with populations over 10,000

Parish population '000s	Income								
	Random sample			MacDonald incumbents			ICF Diary		
	Up to £600	Over £600	Total	Up to £600	Over £600	Total	Up to £600	Over £600	Total
10 to 16	34	7	41	27	7	34	21	10	31
Over 16	10	4	14(25%)	10	1	11(24%)	5	12	17(35%)
Total	44	11 (20%)	55	37	8 (18%)	45	26	22 (46%)	48

between incumbent's income and the number of curates under his direction. But in each case the association is significantly stronger in the ICF group. The relative strength of these correlations is given in Table 6.5.Given the nature of the statistic employed, Kendall's Tau for classified data, the values for the ICF group represent a clear advantage. On the other hand, one should probably not attach any particular significance to the one very low value for the MacDonald incumbents. Numerically identical differences between such coefficients increase in significance as the values move away from zero and approach unity. Values can only approach unity under exceptional circumstances with this measure, and the higher values here represent an indisputable pattern of association, but a test of significance would be problematic and none has been computed.[5]

The number of curates tends to fluctuate slightly from year to year in any given parish, so the calculations are based on a 'normal' complement, derived from figures for 1923–5.

An ICF parish is disproportionately likely, not only to be large and well-endowed, but appropriately staffed, a responsibility rather than a burden.

TABLE 6.5   Number of curates related to parish size and incumbent's income, in parishes with population over 10,000. Kendall's Tau classified

	N	Curates/Population	Curates/Incumbent's income
Random sample	55	0.23	0.25
MacDonald incumbents	45	0.12	0.27
ICF Diary	48	0.38	0.44

The descriptive statistics employed here are for the most part of the simplest kind, distributions based on large categories and an elementary measure of central tendency, the median value rather than the average, since the latter can be misleading when the occasional extreme value, of income or parish size, crops up in a small sub-group. The three main groups have decidedly overlapping distributions on these measures. But the claim that the figures are indirect evidence of a distinctive centre of gravity in the parochial support for the ICF is sustained, firstly, by a general consistency of the patterns in various sub-groups, divided by criteria which might have an independent effect on distributions, and, secondly, by a number of other indications.

Thus, the distribution relating to income in two sub-groups of West Midland clergy follows much the same pattern; 15 per cent of the MacDonald parsons have incomes over £500, as against 35 per cent for the ICF. The MacDonald clergy in the West Midlands, however, an area with some parishes of enormous size, have significantly more experience of the very large parishes. The numbers, 42 and 23, are too small to merit a breakdown by length of service. In a very small sub-group of those ordained before 1890, consisting of those who stayed in the same living for sixteen years or more, none of the half-dozen ICF incumbents started these long tenures at a stipend of less than £250. Half of them started above £350 and all their incomes increase over time. Fourteen, or over half, of the MacDonald incumbents start below £250 and eight of these actually terminate their incumbencies below that figure. Finally, median incomes in a much more substantial sub-group, those who served as Temporary Chaplains during the war, are, controlling for length of service, remarkably close to the median values of their respective parent groups (Table 6.6).

The further details relate to the variable of military service again, to educational background and to promotion into the upper reaches of the church hierarchy.

Overall figures for military service are misleading, since recruitment was obviously affected by age. But, controlling for length of service, it is clear that war experience is of differential importance. In the random sample it is only in the 1900–10 and post-1910 cohorts that there is a sizeable proportion of ex-chaplains, 32 per cent in each case. The MacDonald parsons score the same for the first of these cohorts and 40 per cent for the second. Both MacDonald and ICF parsons ordained before 1900 were more likely to have gone to war than those in the random sample, by 18 per cent and 22 per cent respectively, as against 5 per cent. But over half of the ICF parsons in the 1900–10 cohort, in itself rather large compared with the random sample, were in uniform, whilst more than half of

TABLE 6.6   Median income, 1923

	Entire group	Ex-chaplains
Ordained by 1900		
Random sample	£345	£344
MacDonald incumbents	466	460
ICF Diary	680	676
Ordained by 1910		
Random sample	296	272
MacDonald incumbents	350	344
ICF Diary	430	410
Ordained after 1910		
Random sample	303	325
MacDonald incumbents	340	365
ICF Diary	398	435

the twenty-seven incumbents who were visited more than once by the Messenger had shared his war experience. The beneficiaries of even more frequent visits were ex-chaplains, almost without exception. Military service, at the same time, is not independently correlated with modal parish experience or with material circumstances. Whether as curates or incumbents, and in marked contrast to the random sample, very few ICF recruits to the Army Chaplains' Department either left for the war from small parishes or returned to small parishes, and the income distributions in the sub-group of ex-chaplains, age for age, are indistinguishable from those of their parent groups. So those who turned to the ICF after experience of the war appear to have been typical ICF men in some other significant respects. The ex-chaplains on Donaldson's list were, likewise, representative MacDonald parsons. This prompts a comparison with a particular sub-group. If the war, and the priest's response to it, was of central importance to the ICF, it was no less important to the Community of the Resurrection at Mirfield, as the long letters from Mirfield men at the front, which were published in *The Chronicle of the Community of the Resurrection*, testify. Ten of the two dozen eligible Mirfield ordinands on Donaldson's list saw service in the war. But there are no Mirfield ordinands on the list of ICF incumbents.

Mirfield and Kelham were founded to broaden the social base of recruitment into the Ministry. Despite Gore's links with the ICF, however, this development seems not to have impinged on the organisation, which was overwhelmingly Oxbridge in composition (Table 6.7).

Only 40 per cent of the curates on Donaldson's list were Oxbridge educated. Trinity College Dublin and Durham account for 12 per

TABLE 6.7   Proportion of Oxford and Cambridge graduates by length of service

Ordained by:	− 1890	− 1900	− 1910	− 1920	Total
Random sample	0.68	0.49	0.64	0.58	0.60
MacDonald incumbents	0.65	0.73	0.63	0.55	0.65
ICF Diary	0.83	0.81	0.73	0.65	0.75
ICF Council/Executive	0.90	0.87	0.71	0.60	0.80

cent of his overall total. In the large parishes with population over 10,000, the disparities are even more extreme. Only 30 per cent of the random sample had an Oxbridge background, and 54 per cent of the MacDonald incumbents, but no less than 82 per cent of the ICF incumbents.

Finally, there is the question of promotion into the church hierarchy, which is considered here simply in terms of eventual promotion to bishoprics. Norman's reference to Donaldson's Memorial alludes to the fact that ten of the signatories eventually became bishops, with the apparent implication that this is a further incidental illustration of the tendency, not endorsed in the broad membership of the Church, which he finds deplorable on the part of church leaders of the period, to absorb from secular sources in their own social environment the fashionable political reformism of the day. But eleven prospective bishops (H. Hubbard, Bishop of Whitby was not accounted for on Oliver's list) out of five hundred is not such an impressive score from a list of putative leaders of socially engaged church opinion. Taking the three hundred or so MacDonald parsons already in incumbencies in 1923, seven were installed by 1937 and four more within the next ten years. But C. S. Woodward (Bristol), F. R. Barry (Southwell) and L. S. Hunter (Sheffield) were in the group of eleven signatories who had also invited the Messenger to preach in their pulpits. Despite its diminutive size, this group has the modal characteristics of the ICF group as a whole. They were untypical MacDonald supporters. So were A. W. F. Blunt (Bradford) and F. O. T. Hawkes (Kingston on Thames), both of whom actively supported the ICF. And so also was Hubbard, particularly judging from his book *Social Prayer*. Despite bold talk in an Introduction contributed by C. Cheshire, Editor of Scott Holland's *The Commonwealth*, about a radical reconstruction of the existing industrial order, he reveals a comprehensive familiarity and sympathy with arguments the Messenger was beginning to deploy at this time.[6] Turning to the much shorter list of two hundred and thirty ICF incumbents and Executive and Council members, we find that no less than thirteen of these were advanced to bishoprics as early as 1937, to be joined by another four by 1947. Included among them were C. M. Chavasse, MC, and H. St J. Woollcombe, sub-dean at Coventry, whose name was submitted to Baldwin by Lang for the Bishopric of Whitby on the grounds that he had 'commended his ministry to people of all classes, particularly of the working classes',[7] and there was E. W. Barnes, appointed to Birmingham by MacDonald in 1924, in preference to Lewis Donaldson. E. A. Burroughs, Bishop of Ripon from 1926, made several contributions to the sizeable ephemeral literature touching on ICF themes and produced by leading clerical supporters.

Perhaps we can conclude that the significance of the MacDonald Memorial lies in the blurred glimpse it provides of the existence of relatively uncompromising radical sentiments, having no organisational focus, typically lurking in interstices and pastoral dead-ends, like the interminable curacies of the Rev. A. Bevil Brown, in some, but only some, of the 'rebel' ministries of Anglo-Catholics in Birmingham, and in the labourism of individuals like Handley. Kirk had pre-empted the field with a thoroughly establishment organisation, contentious at times, but run by and most actively supported by clerics who were doing well and likely to do well, in the public and obvious senses, taking on 'important' parishes, occupying prominent positions in superior local establishments, joining the pool of coming men. Among them, of course, were independent and even radical figures, like G. K. A. Bell, later to be Bishop of Chichester, and H. A. Wilson, Bishop of Chelmsford from 1929. Unlike many clerics at the end of the war, for example, Wilson had been unimpressed by the talk of outrages in 'godless Russia', since all revolutions are achieved at a cost which must be set against the generations of exploitation they end, and later he was to be condemned for supporting Republican Spain and suspecting Chamberlain's Munich.[8] But the occasional puff of radical political sulphur released by the ICF itself was palpably a stage effect. The clerics who invited the Messenger to preach to their congregations knew very well what they were doing, and the evidence suggests that these congregations were not disappointed.

Part Two

7 The ICF in Action

ESTABLISHING THE ORGANISATION

A substantial proportion of the activity of the ICF had to be concerned primarily with the survival and maintenance of the organisation itself. Preliminary episcopal endorsement brought with it no guarantee that it would be accepted within the Church as an agent of representative opinion, since many Churchmen were suspicious from the start and fresh criticism was provoked by various incidents, particularly by the intervention with which it was associated in the course of the crisis of 1926. On this occasion Kipling, an intimate friend both of Lady Bathurst, until 1924 Proprietor of the implacably hostile *Morning Post*, and also of H. A. Gwynne, its Editor, noted that 'I see our accursed priests (who can no more keep out of the spotlight than actors) are loose already; and there will be the old dope about "leaving no bitter memories" etc'.[1] On 20 May, shortly after the Archbishop's public appeal to the contestants, which he had discussed on 7 May with Kirk and Bishops Garbett and Burroughs, both employers and unions rejected the Government's terms for a settlement of the Strike. A Standing Conference, consisting of Gore, Temple, Woods, six other Bishops, including Barnes of Birmingham, and eleven nonconformists, then endeavoured to mediate. On 15 July they reached agreement on several points with the miners' leaders, H. Smith, A. J. Cook and W. P. Richardson. Their attempt to communicate and explain this agreement was forestalled by the publication of a rejection by Baldwin of their proposal as he understood it.[2] The recriminations that followed contributed to a widespread scepticism over the ICF's larger claim that it was the vehicle for a non-partisan, interdenominational and impartial social concern, and that it was a public instrument of reconciliation, therefore, for all men of good will.

Within the organisation contention circled round the questions, firstly, of partisanship, in relation to the immediate risk of compromise through some organisational affiliation or expression of policy, and secondly, the problem of providing operational definitions for key elements of rhetoric or principle, such as the 'living wage'. The internal structure, however, was such that attempts to force these issues could be shifted rather easily through irresolution into abeyance. Kirk was in a strong position as Director. The Council and Annual General Meetings, which included some Free Church representation, were filled up by a programme of speeches from leading figures and reports from lay missioners, and were well covered, not only in the church press. Speakers were sometimes criticised for vagueness, and the absence of any obviously working-class attendance in the body of the hall was regularly remarked on, but, at least until the end of the decade, the meetings were presented as occasions dominated by shared fervour and enthusiasm.[3] The Executive, which met about once a month, consisted of the officers and co-opted members, and specialised committees dealing with finance, personnel, policy, women, publicity and crusades. It is clear from the way the Director monitored their activities and himself proposed initiatives that he had a good sense of the shoals and channels confronting the organisation. Invitations to identify with specific groups, such as the Counter Communism Crusade, with which Russell Wakefield, Bishop of Birmingham, was associated, or the League of Empire Settlement, were turned down routinely by the Executive. In January 1924, Kirk expressed the hope that the Publicity Committee would not go ahead with a pamphlet entitled 'Wealth and Class Warfare', on the grounds that it might harm the ICF. A pamphlet by the Messenger on 'Christianity and the right to lay down arms' was turned down by the Committee in June, and another, 'The Sorrow of the Idol', which included a section on 'The Worship of Mars', was held up though eventually published as Crusade Leaflet No 14. The Messenger's anti-war speeches raised questions in the press about his patriotism and integrity.[4] An attempt supported by P. E. T. Widdrington and other associates of Reckitt's to get Douglas's Social Credit scheme on the agenda for serious discussion was allowed to die in polite consideration in the Research Committee under Lascelles. A major dispute at the Council Meeting of June 1927, between Canon Donaldson and Major Birchall, Conservative Member for Leeds North East from 1918 to 1935, was gratefully recorded, and ignored,[5] to the frustration of the protagonists. Birchall's simmering anxieties about political tendencies had boiled over after the public inquest on clerical interest in the General Strike, and he was demanding a stand on principles exclusively, a detachment from specific programmes or policies and an emphasis on the personality of the individual Christian. Donaldson responded in terms of a duty to stand for what is right and the unavoidable obligation to take sides on political questions. Birchall resigned his connection with the ICF exactly a year later, after discussions with Kirk and the Chairman, but seems not to have taken anyone with him from Council or Executive. Donaldson stayed on, valued for his energy and reputation, as an institutionalised 'radical' voice. Earlier, in an Executive meeting on 4 April 1924, Widdrington had demanded a more positive affirmation of agreed principles on the industrial system, and asked what steps the ICF would take to dissociate itself from a statement made by Hichens to the effect that under present conditions interest on capital and not a living wage for the workers must be the first charge on industry. Elvin and Rear-Admiral S. R. Drury-Lowe, an old CSU and Life and Liberty man, proposed a letter to Hichens asking if the report was correct and if he still supported the principle of the Archibishop's Fifth Commission on the Wage Question. Drury-Lowe had run as a Christian Independent for Westminster in 1922 and as a Liberal for Portsmouth South in 1923. In reply to rumours, he was obliged to announce in 1924 that he had not 'as yet' decided to join the Labour Party.[6] But Hichens' wage fund views, as we have seen, were pragmatically expressed and by no means crudely sectional. He was unruffled by this sort of challenge and had no intention of resigning or coming to terms, where no one was capable of persuading him to do so. The living wage and the just price continued as topics for diffuse and increasingly pessimistic discussion, but to a greater extent in Widdrington's diminutive *League of the Kingdom of God* than in the ICF. Ruth Kenyon, also active for the ICF, rehearsed the familiar arguments in a League pamphlet in 1927.[7] She cites the endorsement of principle by the Archbishops in 1918, elaborates on its content in terms of continuity of employment as well as adequate payment during employment, and makes the familiar case for the living wage in terms of efficiency. But, she laments, the rank and file have not followed, and the Church has not obeyed its Archbishops. It is up to the League, the ICF and COPEC to see that these things happen. 'Have they perhaps not happened because we have not prayed enough?' 'To deny that our economic life can be ordered according to moral and spiritual principles is sheer atheism.' But the 'economic realists' were not forced by these immobile polemics to make any such denial, or to dispute the need for 'keen study' of various proposals, from the control of credit and prices to communal production. At the same time there could be no effective initiative from either the ICF or COPEC. A clearer awareness of problems of social structure was to emerge in the research directed by V. A. Demant for the Christian Social Council, which superseded COPEC in 1929,[8] and some of Kenyon's own work for the CSC was more incisive, even discussing political implications of Hobson's High

Wages Policy.[9] But throughout the twenties any possible development in this direction, against the grain of the ICF, was inhibited by the executive's anxieties about a fragmentation of common purpose and a consequent loss of public credibility.

Kirk himself was active in the pursuit of endorsement, publicity and money. He had been careful, when working on the initial appeal for £15,000 in 1920, the year in which Studdert Kennedy was appointed a King's Chaplain, to publicise his visit to Sandringham to explain the ICF aims to the King and Queen and to make known their donation of £30.[10] In 1923 he secured the endorsement of thirty-four bishops, who confirmed the ICF's complete independence of any party, and asserted that it would be disastrous if it were obliged to curtail its activities. The letter was used to justify an appeal for an increase of £6000 to bring the required income up to £18,000.[11] He got the Messenger to make another appeal a year later.

Less successful, though it became the occasion for a special reprint of *Lies* and *Food for the Fed Up*, in half-crown editions, was the decision to take a stand at the Wembley British Empire Exhibition of 1924. The other exhibitors in this section were two hospitals, the Shaftesbury Society, the Glyn Vivian Miners' Mission and the Imperial Settlement League.[12] Of the exhibition as a whole Birmingham's Labour weekly, the *Town Crier*, commented that it might be an imperialist stunt but it was well worth a visit. However, the series of conferences designed for the Messenger, and intended to increase subscriptions as well as spread the message, had to be abandoned because attendances were poor. Lady Kirkpatrick, with her husband an evangelical from the Navvy Mission, complained, as did a number of others on the Executive, that the kiosk was too much geared to the Messenger's works, and the Publicity Director was required to modify this unbalanced presentation.[13]

Bishop Barnes, Bentinck and Hichens, as Trustees, reviewed the decisions of the Finance Committee. Barnes, who took a keen interest in stock market ·movements on his own account,[14] occasionally made recommendations, but most decisions were straightforward. Correspondence on the purchase of securities seldom refers to transactions involving more than a thousand pounds at a time, though there were legacies, more in the thirties than the twenties. A portfolio of securities worth £4737, which came to the ICF in 1948 under the will of the Rev. J. H. Jackson, however, seems to have been very much larger than the normal benefaction. The most positive advice on investment from Bishop Barnes was a recommendation to dispose of a legacy of a small number of shares in Vickers in November 1933. 'As they will stand in my name, I shall find pacifist speakers all over the country asserting that I, like the Bishop of Hereford, am an armament profiteer.'[15] The purchase of about £500 of cumulative preference shares in United Gas Industries, at 7 per cent, and shares to the same value, at 5¼ per cent in the Monsanto Chemical Company, in 1936, was, in the context of the ICF accounts, a substantial investment.

In general, the internal records, such as they are, leave an impression of prudent and successfully centralised management. Financial resources never matched aspirations, and Kirk may have allowed the fact that the vague taint of socialism could scare off possible supporters to affect his approach to policy. But he can be credited with good housekeeping. Most donations were small and the attempt to attract big contributions was never very successful, so insistent demands were made on local resources. After the Derby Crusade of 1921, Canon A. W. F. Blunt told a ruridecanal conference that several firms in the past had paid between £200 and £240 to support a full-time missioner.[16] The firm of Pearson and Dorman Long, which acquired Kent Coal Concessions (see above, p. 20), approached in conjuction with Lady Dorman herself, declined an invitation to support a missioner in the Kent coalfields, but the local rural dean was prevailed on to find £125 for this. In 1928, Terrey asked for a missioner at the Ewden reservoir works, and the Sheffield Corporation offered to pay the full salary, as it had done before. Such demands on local resources involved no loss of control over the lay missioners themselves, through the half-dozen Organising Directors in the regions. Their work appears to have been closely supervised: they were provided with material and expected to send in essays as well as reports, in order to increase their competence with standard questions on the pitch. They were hired and, where occasion demanded, fired or retired by the central organisation.

Kirk's approach to management reflected continuous and contradictory pressures from the environment in which the ICF had to make its way. The treasurer of the Leeds branch, to illustrate one aspect of this, reported in 1929 that there was much indifference to the ICF on the part of local Church Councils, which was due, he suggested, largely to ignorance of the work but in some instances to the fact that the Leeds Missioner was regarded as a socialist. A continuous struggle over the public credibility of the ICF took the form, in the main, of stylised shadow-boxing over the amorphous issue of 'socialism' and also of argument on the question of competence to pass judgement on public issues. The dispute threw no light at all on the concept of socialism itself. The Messenger was accused of it during the coal dispute correspondence in *The Times*, and repudiated the allegation, as he had done often enough before.

Not a single one of the ICF activities has fallen under the control of Socialists. If any of them did, I would sever my connection with the society immediately. I am not a socialist and spend a considerable amount of my time exposing popular Socialist clap-trap, which is a curse to sane thinking, as popular Tory clap-trap is on the other side. Bother them both . . .[17]

The charge was being pressed at this time by Henson, Inge and Bishop Headlam of Gloucester, among others who included laymen, and by the Archdeacon of Chester, who wrote that

The objects of that organisation are excellent, and it was started under promising auspices; but its operations have been conducted in such a partisan way that many of the clergy will now have nothing to do with it.[18]

There is continuous evidence of local criticism along the same lines, after a meeting at Rugby, for instance,[19] and even in the Coventry press after a Crusade that had been very generously treated.[20] Verbal complaints, it was here pointed out, against socialistic aspects of the venture were almost without number. It is probably relevant that Donaldson and Widdrington[21] joined the Messenger and the more regular crusaders on this occasion, and that there was some threat at the time to the further employment of the Coventry Industrial Missioner, the Rev. J. J. R. Armitage, whose 'work in antagonism to socialism' the paper supported.[22]

The contention and ambiguity surrounding the ICF were a matter of concern to Archbishop Davidson from well before the crisis of 1926. He made a careful record of an interview with the Messenger on 2 March 1923, held ostensibly to advise on an invitation to visit South Africa, but in the course of which Davidson was concerned, firstly, to point out that he had not had him instituted at St Edmund's in the previous year 'in order that he might live on its income and spend his time going up and down the world', and, secondly, to discuss the contradictory charges levelled against the ICF, that it was a 'cloak for capitalism to serve as a religious opiate to the downtrodden', and that, alternatively, the Messenger was 'a camouflage for Communism and . . . really a disciple of Marx'. The response recorded to the charge of bolstering capitalism is too condensed to be clear, but on the second charge the Messenger pointed out that he had 'been preaching lately against Marx in order to meet this objection'.[23]

Indeed, he had always done so. His usual theme was reported at length in an account of a meeting at King's College London in 1920.[24] Marx was the father of ignorance, and if *Das Kapital* was the gospel of the working people, it was an unread gospel, because it is intensely difficult, 'unless you have the patience of a German or the determination of a Jew, to get what it really, honestly means'. He himself had tried four times without success. Yet that book had caused the tremendous unrest, setting up the capitalist in the position of the devil and attributing our sin, ignorance and greed to the capitalist system. Unhealthy unrest had spread the gospel of hatred and the sense of service to the community had largely vanished. 'I told a collier the other day that he was a priest of God, and his only reply was "Gor blimey".' The Fellowship, he added, was on the right lines for the curing of the unhealthy part of unrest.

To have any effect, certainly if they were to reach newspaper readers, such arguments had to be presented in crude terms, and reviewing reports over the decade, one can see the relevance of the Archbishop's sympathetic warning against 'becoming a mere oratorical hack with no adequate time for thought and study and devotion'. But even these declarations were insufficient to still the accusations of subversion.

The ICF, however, made what use it could of 'marxist' attacks. *The Torch* even reproduced a crude cartoon circulated with a communist broadside in Yorkshire. It was later claimed that both editor and artist responsible for this production had rejoined the Church.

Kirk certainly worked on his press relations to improve the situation. Attempts to soften *The Patriot* and the *Morning Post*, which printed a succession of attacks,[25] were not successful, quite predictably, perhaps, in the light of the Duke of Northumberland's encounter with the Sankey Commission and his stake in the *Post*. Maurice offered to approach Dawson, and *The Times*, though critical,[26] gave a good deal of space to ICF corrections and disclaimers from Gore, Kempthorne, Temple, Kirk and the Messenger. With the *Spectator*, again predictably, since its versatile former editor and proprietor John St Loe Strachey was actually in Temple's group for the deputation to Baldwin, he was much more successful, securing an editorial which opined that some ICF meetings, it may be, 'have been undistinguishable from socialist meetings. Rumours to that effect are a little too strong to be denied', but went on to say that such an admirable organisation could be kept on the right lines if it were actively supported by the right people.[27] Maurice wrote regularly on military matters for the *Spectator*, and Macassey's more occasional contributions included a major and very respectful review, in two parts, of Milner's *Questions of the Hour*.[29] Strachey himself was the devoted nephew of the Renaissance historian J. A. Symonds and therefore part of the Vaughan–Green family network (see above, p. 76).

Henson's allusions to the 'meddlesome activity' of the ICF entailed another kind of criticism of the organisation's public claims, that of simple incompetence in the face of the complex economic facts of

3 Cartoon from a Communist broadsheet, reproduced in *The Torch*, June 1927

life. Temple's justifications, in a long letter to *The Times*, which was reproduced in full in the *Manchester Diocesan Magazine*, and in public statements, like one made during the Church Congress from a platform shared with the Messenger,[30] suggest that his group's inexperience was reflected in some clumsy communication with the Prime Minister and some insensitivity to the consequences of an appearance of partisanship with was forced on them by the particular circumstances. The group, incidentally, was not, as Kempthorne and Kirk were to explain with questionable formalism, an ICF one. Kirk had merely 'brought together' those involved, and the ICF Executive had not had time to meet before the crisis. But Temple's claim, in essence that they were concerned to show that the conflict had not in fact moved out of a framework of rational and legally manageable adjustment, seems a reasonable one. The group's intention, understandably misperceived in an atmosphere of stress, was not to advance a plan but to confirm the survival, beneath the deadlock and bitterness, of a potential consensus. The miners' leaders in the final anxious discussions with the churchmen seem to have acknowledged the validity of the claim, but the owners did not. So the breakdown, on this view psychological and moral rather than political, was in this instance, on balance, the responsibility more of the capitalists than of the unions. The ICF's partisanship went this far. But from the start it had issued a steady rumble of denunciation of what Woods, Bishop of Winchester, called the 'deplorable exhibition of outlook' by both employers and employees.[31]

It seems unlikely that many critics were disarmed by Temple's disclaimers, which were detailed and called for patient reading, and Headlam went further to develop the theme of incompetence by publishing a pamphlet 'Economics and Christianity'. The ICF reply to this was written by Lindsay, the Master of Balliol.[32] This of course cut no ice with Henson or Headlam, but surely got the better of the argument and effectively marked out the middle ground the ICF was attempting to occupy. It is explicitly anchored in the tradition established by Green.[33] Lindsay spends some time justifying the gamma minus merited by the Bishop's economic thinking, particularly by the archaic rigidity and crudity of his wage fund theory. He acknowledges the complex involvement of moral and technical questions, and argues for the application of an appropriately expert impartial intelligence to questions formulated in the light of collective priorities, the kind of expert impartiality represented by the Samuel Coal Commission, which the churchmen had wished to protect, but which they conceived to be temporarily submerged by a failure of detachment and social obligation.

On the whole the ICF did not do well out of the attempt at mediation, but Kirk could take encouragement from the success of a more routinised initiative, the Industrial Sunday scheme, the idea of which was to promote the holding of special services on the Sunday nearest May Day. This appeal was annually associated with the distribution of a letter with two groups of signatories, one from the Labour Movement, and the other from industrial management. The list of names in each case grew progressively longer. There were seventy-four, including thirty MPs, on the Labour list in 1923, a hundred and seventy-four in 1926, and two hundred and twenty-three in 1930. In that year eighty-one were MPs, seventeen on the TUC General Council, with seventy-two General Secretaries of various unions and fifty local secretaries. The list of businessmen went up from a hundred and fifty in 1926 to two hundred and seventy-six in 1930. Though there are carbons of refusals from Walter Citrine, the General Secretary of the TUC, a signature was eventually, perhaps, easier to give than to refuse, and a refined analysis at an individual level would be unrewarding. The signature of the miners' leader A. J. Cook in 1926 was interpreted by one correspondent to *The Times* as clear evidence of the ICF's communistic affiliations, though it might look, given some of the company he was joining, more like a gesture of defiance on his part. There are obvious uncertainties about individual motives.

But the Industrial Sunday Scheme is a rough measure of Kirk's success in establishing the organisation as a recognised vehicle for the expression of a current of consensual reformism in politics and industry. Well-disposed papers reported the larger services at which trade unions and civic dignitaries were often formally represented. The King sent his Secretary to the Windsor service in 1920. At Southwark Cathedral the following year, the Mayor George Isaacs claimed that practically all the South London labour leaders were present.[34] The institution of the special service was threatened by parochial withdrawals in 1926, and Kirk wrote to all the diocese invoking the authority of the Archbishops in its defence. But over the decade it came to be well established in many parishes, and the ritual associated with these occasions was important to leading local figures on both sides of industry. MacDonald and Sidney Webb signed the letter in 1930. Muspratt signed in that year along with five of the thirty-nine industrialists selected by Mond for the original Conference on Industrial Reorganisation and Industrial Relations, and many of the business signatories came from specific firms and from sections of industry closely interested in the Mond–Turner initiative.

THE ICF, THE BROTHERHOODS AND THE TUC

The organisation's goal of spiritual permeation was pursued most vigorously through the Crusades and mass meetings in relation to a broad public opinion, since links with specific organisations carried the hazard of objectionable programmatic commitments. Meetings with groups of businessmen might be arranged through rotary clubs, particularly during the Crusades, but any direct combination with the world of business was exclusively through individual employers and managers. David Smith became a valued member of the Birmingham Business Club, where he successfully solicited support for ICF activities, but this was personal enterprise on his part. The Club's house journal showed interest in what it liked to describe as a virile and practical approach to the general issue of 'bridging the gulf', through Whitley Councils, exploring the possibilities of profit-sharing and co-partnership, and teaching the workers enough economics to demonstrate the imperatives of industrial unity.[35] It printed an appreciative note in 1921 on a discussion with the Rev. R. R. Hyde, founder of the *Industrial Welfare Society*, an organisation that was actively supported by Hichens, and followed this with eulogistic comments on 'Navvy' Smith, who was present, 'a deeply sincere and delightful man' and 'an immense force for good' in the city.

> . . . honesty always pays in the long run, and Mr 'Navvy' Smith does not speak to the working classes as though they were the salt of the earth; as though they were the most oppressed of all classes (which is far from being true), and as though they were the elect for whom the honours of the future life were waiting.[36]

On the labour side, however, the ICF established a valuable bond with the TUC, which is best considered in connection with another link, involving mutuality of interest rather than permeation, with the Brotherhood Movement.

Considering the numbers it attracted and the variety of its activities, John Blackham's Brotherhood Movement has not yet received much attention from labour historians. It originated in the Ebenezer Congregational Church, West Bromwich, in 1875, and J. W. Tuffley, General Secretary from 1924, claimed that by the 1880s up to a 100,000 men were meeting in classes in a ten-mile radius of West Bromwich. By 1906 its national membership had risen to 250,000 and there was a Sisterhood Movement well under way by 1912.[37] The Movement offered, as Arthur Henderson points out in his Foreword to Tuffley's account, through its Adult Schools and 'Pleasant Sunday Afternoons' (known as PSAs—originally Bible classes, but extending into various forms of self-improvement), a

strong and direct appeal to social classes whose life and thought alike were becoming divorced from the organised activities of religion, the common aspiration towards a new social order, a new world order, in which brotherhood would be practised in the relations of classes as in the relations of nations . . .

. . . it has concerned itself with the duties of citizenship, and with the citizen's social concerns, without becoming a political movement. Its emphasis has been all the time upon the citizen's individual responsibility, but it has interpreted individual responsibility in the light of social needs.

Like the self-improving artisans of the previous century, its members chose a politics of 'virtuous passion',[38] close in rhetoric and content to the redaction of English idealism offered by Anglican exponents of the social gospel. It interpreted the sacrament of service in practical and individual terms, local branches acting informally as employment agencies and benefit societies. The Hampshire branches were particularly active immediately after the war, organising relief and distributing clothing to ex-servicemen and their dependants.

Its output of general moralising on the state of society was substantial and consistent. Ammon's address 'The Road to Jericho' is representative.[39] 'The road to Jericho is the modern competitive system. It is strewn with the dead and dying.' He contrasts an eightpenny breakfast menu for six persons, produced for girls studying cookery at an LCC school, with a menu for a country house breakfast, taken from the Women's Supplement in *The Times*. He asks, 'Why should those who create the bulk of the wealth of the community be kept outside to fight among themselves for the husks that the flame of life be kept flickering for a few years?' The question is rhetorical and his positive recommendation, despite large demands for fundamental change, is a diffusion of samaritanism. *The Brotherhood Outlook* regularly published such reflections, along with reading matter of a generally improving nature and serialisations of work like George Eliot's *Adam Bede*. Henderson, National President from 1914, wrote on the themes of Brotherhood and Public Affairs, a Plea for Better Men, Christianising our Civilisation, and the like. Hodges wrote on Brotherly Service, and Ammon, who also became National President, on Peace in Industry.[40] Dr John Clifford, the Free Church leader, became National President during the war, and, in addition to his own inaugural, the John Clifford Lectures, established by the Brotherhood, included Snowden's 'The way to industrial peace', Baldwin on 'Democracy Old and New' and Stamp on 'Internationalism'.[41]

The ICF had many points of contact with the Movement in addition to the dedicated memberships of Henderson and Ammon.

Bentinck was a member. The Rev. Henry Carter, of the Welfare Department of the Wesleyan Methodists, who was frequently associated with Kirk and Kempthorne and the ICF, ran the Harrow Brotherhood. Dick Sheppard became President in the 1930s and Canon Guy Rogers was President of the Birmingham Federation. ICF figures, including Parmoor, Picton-Turbervill, Spoor, Pym and Moore Ede, spoke to local branches. The ICF Director of Publicity, J. Miller McCormick, went the rounds with a favourite story of representative significance.

> I once met Trotsky . . . In fact I had tea with him in New York. I thought then that he was a fine fellow. He was a man who would give the very shirt off his back to anyone in New York in need of one. I said 'look here, Trotsky, will you come to church with me tonight?' He said, 'No, I don't think I will'. Trotsky was a secular Jew. He went back to Russia not only un-Christian but anti-Christian. Can any of you here this afternoon tell me what it would have meant to Russia if Trotsky and Lenin had been Christian men inspired by Him made visible to them by faith?[42]

The ICF Messenger was a regular speaker to the large audiences at the active Brotherhoods, particularly of West Ham, Croydon North End, Portsmouth and Southampton. The *Outlook* printed enthusiastic reviews of his books—'Get it and let it soak in' was the recommendation on *Lies*—and it printed two columns of extracts from *The Wicket Gate*.[43] This was symptomatic of the generally unqualified appreciation that his ministry enjoyed in the Free Church world.

Tuffley boasted of the role of the Brotherhood Movement in promoting old age pensions as a social expression of Christianity during the early 1900s, and the London Federation provided a setting for the early initiatives that were to develop into the Mond–Turner talks. The Mansion House Conference of 17 October 1927, which was addressed by Sir Thomas Inskip, Mond and Ammon, was allegedly convened in response to Snowden's Clifford Lecture at the suggestion of leading London members.[44] The talks began a few weeks later.

It was through figures in the trade union establishment with strong Brotherhood links that the ICF developed a recognised part of the fringe activities of the annual conference of the TUC, the meetings and services for delegates which would be addressed by the best speakers it could muster. The Congress Report for 1921 records that 'special sermons were preached in eight of the churches of the city, the arrangements being made by The Industrial Christian Fellowship in conjunction with the local clergy'.[45] Henderson chaired

4 R.R. Hyde, of the *Industrial Welfare Society*, C. G. Ammon and J.W. Tuffley at the Peace in Industry discussion of the Brotherhood Parliament, July 1928 (*Sheffield Independent Press*)

a meeting attended by 1200 people, many of them delegates, in Cory Hall, Cardiff, which was also addressed by Carter, Spoor, Miss Knight-Bruce of the ICF and the Messenger. The Messenger expressed doubts about the existence of a religious consciousness within the labour movement, spoke up for union membership as a basis, if rightly interpreted, for community and fellowship, and developed his vision of a lay sacrament of work and service, concluding with a reading of his own ICF hymn.[46] Poulton's Presidential Address to Congress had expressed other aspects of the Fellowship's vision, and attracted the favourable attention of the *Church Times*. He appealed for a long view, a policy of evolutionary revolution and for unity behind the elected leadership. The resolutions finally passed by Conference, however, on minimum wages and the creation of employment particularly, struck many observers as a rejection of rational restraint, and the *South Wales Journal of Commerce* called down the crushing orthodoxies of Hichens's recent address to the British Association[47] and applauded the realism of Frank Hodges in a recent speech in Aberfan, which looked to see an increase in the standard of living among miners from 'the men putting their backs into production and the managerial mind effecting economies in working'.[48]

The *Church Times* was impressed by the development of the ICF programme the following year at Southport. The Messenger preached to a large congregation on the law of combat giving way to mutual service. The Rev. F. E. Mercer, ICF Organiser for the North East and formerly Secretary to the Alberta Labour Party in Canada, preached in two churches on a labour solidarity based on firmer foundations than self-interest, and Henderson again chaired the mass meeting and paid an eloquent tribute to the ICF. The Messenger, according to the report, 'roused the vast audience to the highest pitch of enthusiasm by his great oration on the sacramental value of material things'.[49] He spoke again at Hull in 1924,[50] and at Edinburgh in 1927; ' "Woodbine Willie" trounces agitators', was an *Evening News* announcement.[51] Donaldson gave the TUC Sermon in 1925. He would always represent a perceptible shift in emphasis, a voice from the edge of the ICF coalition, but though more hostile than most parsons to the values of middle-class society and much more willing to contemplate a significant structural rearrangement than the representative ICF figure, he was still Ramsay MacDonald's 'clerical shadow', to echo Henson, a 'socialist' committed to a consensual, organicist paradigm, which he could articulate with surprising intensity, as, for example, in a sermon delivered in Westminster Abbey on the sacramental patriotism represented by the 'socialised' monarchy.[52]

5 Arthur Henderson (*Wesleyan Methodist*)

THE CRUSADES AND MASS MEETINGS

Kirk seldom had occasion to complain of thin coverage of the Crusades in the provincial press, which was still, though no longer overwhelmingly so, liberal in its political sympathies.[53] He did particularly well with the *Barrow Guardian*, the *Coventry Herald*, the *Bristol Evening News* and, a paper with a long radical liberal tradition, the *Staffordshire Sentinel*. At the height of the ten-day Barrow Crusade the *Barrow Guardian* gave the Crusade a hundred and thirty column inches in one issue, and the *News* used ninety on the same day. On 9 June 1928, during the Monmouth Crusade, the *South Wales Gazette* used seventy column inches, and the *Weekly Argus* seventy six. The *Birmingham Post* gave around forty inches a day to the 1930 Crusade, a long story for its particular house style. The tone of these and many other reports ranges from the fulsome to the strongly supportive. There is obvious evidence of editorial engagement with particular aspects of the message, in the anti-socialist preoccupations of the strongly liberal *Coventry Herald* in 1923, for example, but the reports are usually also detailed enough to reveal variations between the different Crusades as well, which in part must reflect decisions arrived at between the diocese, the central Committee for Church Crusades, and the ICF's own Crusade Committee. The number of crusaders brought in and locally recruited varied considerably, a modest handful at Norwich in May 1919 and Hull in October 1920, approximately four score, including a high proportion of nonconformists, in a distinctively evangelical Crusade in Croydon, the suffragan bishopric from which Bishop Pereira of the Old Navvy Mission had just retired, in February 1925. A hundred and twenty were commissioned in Newport for the unusually dispersed Monmouth Crusade of 1928. Coventry and the Potteries, in June and October 1923, were major ventures and regarded as highly successful. Smaller, but still notable operations were mounted in Walthamstow (1922), Northampton (1923), Teeside (1925), Accrington (1925), Mansfield (1926), Sheffield (1926), Battersea (1927), Amman Valley (1927), Clay Cross and Chesterfield (1927), Wolverhampton (1972), and Middleton and Stockport (1929). There appear to have been some more modest affairs as well. ICF people were involved on other occasions, such as the large, evangelical Medway Towns Crusade of September 1927, Luton (1925) and a deanery Crusade on Tyneside (1924), when the Messenger preached in his brother's church in the comfortable residential district of Gosforth.

The Crusades were mounted in response to local initiatives, at Mansfield, for instance, prompted by anxieties about a sudden local increase in population, and there are only scrappy records of any process of selection on the part of the ICF Crusade Committee. But a

number of Crusade sites were notable for very strong liberal
traditions, the Lib–Lab tradition of the Derby railwaymen and the
Chesterfield miners, the small middle-class nonconformity of
Northampton, the long-standing loyalty of Bristol to the Liberals and
the comparative weakness of a labour movement there up to the
Great War, the working class liberalism of Teeside, Accrington and
Mansfield, and above all of the Potteries, Amman Valley and
Monmouth, where the crusades had their most dramatic and lasting
effects. Sites with particularly strong nonconformist traditions
included Northampton, North Bristol, Teeside, Stockport and South
Wales.[54]

On at least one occasion, in Birmingham in 1919, plans for a
Crusade were abandoned. In Birmingham it was partly because of
divisions among the clergy of the diocese, but mainly because of the
'present temper of the working classes', which the experienced
'Navvy' Smith among others judged to be wholly unreceptive.[55]
There were later difficulties in Birmingham, but for contrary
reasons. In October 1926, after a long discussion with Canon Rogers,
Bishop Barnes put off a visit from Kirk, who was looking for financial
support from the diocese for the Birmingham missioner. 'Political
reaction as you know is immensely strong in this area and the Coal
Strike with its serious effect on local industry has practically killed
any sympathy with the point of view which the ICF represents.'[56]
Birmingham in fact experienced a sharp, though short-lived,
political polarisation and a socialist advance up to the 1929 election.[57]
But a local committee was operating in 1927 and planning special
meetings for the Messenger in February 1928. It was possible in 1930,
despite the abstention of most of the fifteen or sixteen 'rebel'
churches which had been at odds with Bishop Barnes over irregular
ritual practices, to mount the largest of the ICF Crusades to date in
Birmingham, as a major interdenominational and civic event, which
was covered at length and in glowing terms by the local press.[58]

Invariably it was the policy to enlist the support of the free
churches, but their actual involvement varied, from expressions of
support for some of the earlier Crusades and the holding of special
services, as in the Alvaston Brotherhood at Derby, which was
addressed by the Rev. S. D. Morris of the ICF,[59] to very active
involvement at Bristol, where Scott Lidgett made a major speech.[60]
He was the Wesleyan Moderator of the Federal Council of the
Evangelical Free Churches, and no friend, it may be added, to the
Labour Party. Nonconformists were heavily involved also at Croydon
and Birmingham.

Newspaper reports obviously call for interpretation, a given
account reflecting in uncertain proportions editorial perceptions
and the shadow of other events affecting the local climate, as well as

the flavour of the Crusade itself, but ICF records and the newspapers trace a clear development in the size and complexity of the Crusades. By the middle of the decade there were large numbers of factory lunch-hour meetings, arranged through the employers, and on occasion involving their spontaneous participation.[61] There were formalised 'debates' between church and labour, and special meetings for businessmen. From early in the period, though with initial caution on the part of the Mayor of Barrow in 1921, civic dignitaries came to be involved as a matter of course. It is worth now looking in some detail at a sample of reports of a group of contrasting Crusades and, in conclusion, at accounts of some of the mass meetings over the decade.

At Derby and Barrow in April and September 1921, the dominant theme of the alienation of labour from the Church reflected the impact both of the war and of the immediate economic crisis. At Derby Mercer spoke for a repentant church, but the presence of Adderley, who was affectionately profiled as the firebrand son of a former Member for North Staffordshire, was a reminder of a more long-standing concern in the church with labour questions.[62] In a formal exchange with Mercer, Councillor W. R. Raynes issued a Labour challenge to the Church to get back to the teaching of its founder.

> When the news came through to Derby that the Triple Alliance was off he saw men with tears of vexation and sorrow in their eyes because they had been told that they must not strike in favour of the miner. That was an exemplification of the spirit of Jesus, as these men were willing to do that in support of a class suppressed. (A voice: 'Very doubtful'). The church needed educating in social matters.[63]

On this contentious issue Studdert Kennedy confined himself to speaking dismissively of those who accused striking miners of unchristian behaviour but who cared little if their wages went below the 'proper level'. Donaldson, in a closing sermon at St Werburgh's, spoke about the slow evolution of human society being 'occasionally hastened by a crisis, which can be likened to a thunderstorm, caused by a creative act of God. Civilisation is today in the throes of a crisis partly revealed, partly created by the War'.[64] But the Labour Movement does not arise from the 'Extremist'; whatever its faults it is on the brink of a new moral consciousness. The confrontation of 'Marx' and Christ had been referred to by other speakers.[65]

With the tenor of these generalities J. H. Thomas, the senior Member for Derby, was in full agreement. In a major speech at the subsequent May Day demonstration, where Raynes carried a motion of faith in the international co-operation of the workers, Thomas defended the NUR leadership's performance over the strike in characteristic terms.

> . . . yet some people say, 'Yes there is one short cut to a removal of these difficulties. We believe that the short way is to immediately have a bloody upheaval. Let us unite in one solid body, and by an industrial upheaval remove the whole system of society as it is today'. My answer to that is this: is it honest, is it logical, is it commonsense to ask you people to strike or engage in a bloody upheaval to obtain something that, by the exercise of your commonsense on the ballot paper, you can achieve in a much more simple manner.[66]

Thomas's message to the Crusade, read out at the main meeting, had spoken of the worker's suspicion of the Church, 'but you will, I know, find a wide response to your message when the workers realise that you stand for the principles of fellowship and justice in every sphere of life'.

C. M. Chavasse, MC, was the Vicar of Barrow, a parish in which the structure of the work force had been drastically affected by the wartime munitions industry. As its advance agent, the ICF sent W. A. Millington, formerly Vice-chairman of the Lancaster Divisional Labour Party,[67] who prepared the way by claiming for the ICF the 'approval and benediction of England's most respected Labour leaders—Arthur Henderson, J. R. Clynes, C. W. Bowerman, E. L. Poulton, George Edwards, Ben Spoor', and brought with him a lengthy appeal from Egerton Wake, National Agent of the Labour Party, which spoke of the distinctly religious character of the Labour Movement, and looked to the ICF to inspire the idealism of Labour.

> In the complex form of modern life, we are compelled to remember that it is necessary not only to convert individuals but also to convert institutions such as our political machinery, our local administration, and all the governmental functions of the state as a means of bringing the Kingdom of Heaven upon earth.[68]

A. Holden, the Rugby missioner fresh from the Derby Crusade, was introduced as a trádes unionist. As J. H. Brown, Chairman of the Barrow Labour Party, pointed out, the Rev. Mercer was there, not to bring labour to the stool of repentance, but with a message for all classes. Mercer, after acknowledging the unfortunate necessity for the strike weapon, argued that Church and Labour had to build an organisation far more powerful than a strike; 'The great ideal of the Labour Party was peace, and whilst that was its ideal it should not carry on class war'. The Rev. E. Harrison, MC, ICF Organiser for the north west, at another meeting, spoke of the transcending ideal of service with reference to the practice of ca'canny, of giving as little and taking as much as one can.[69] But if local labour figures were as concerned as the crusaders with what the Bishop of Carlisle referred to as the attempt 'to achieve some kind of social equilibrium', in a speech entirely concerned with immediate questions of social unity and social trouble, they expected and got something more than generalities. Four resolutions were proposed at a civic reception by G. Basterfield, the Mayor, in conjunction with the Bishops of Carlisle and Barrow, seconded by Harrison and unanimously passed. They all demanded assistance from central funds to meet Barrow's industrial and unemployment problem. This was to act, it might be thought, in the spirit of clerical interventionism that had recently annoyed Lloyd George. His attack on the April Convocation will be discussed below. Bentinck, who came to Barrow to speak about international action as the road back from unemployment, in fact took the opportunity to give his opinion that the Prime Minister had been wrong about church intervention. The *Church Times*, however, made no reference to these details but noted the great impression made at a huge meeting on the final day by the Messenger, who is not referred to in the Barrow press.[70]

The *Barrow Guardian*'s evident sympathy with the move towards a reconciliation between Labour and the national church reflects its own editorial preoccupations. It was devoting a great deal of space to the coverage of local unemployment, carrying verbatim reports on various Council meetings. A few days after the Crusade, an editorial criticising the Government followed a short essay on Liberalism, which reaffirmed the principles of 'the grand old Liberals now dead', and the old watchwords of Peace, Retrenchment and Reform:

> Liberals must wake up to their responsibilities. They have permitted themselves to be overshadowed by the camouflage of the Coalition Party on the one hand, and the various actions by the several sections of the Labour Party on the other ... noisy sections of the Labour Party, who, in their claims for freedom, exceed the bounds of reason and even go so far as to claim that the bloody rule in Russia is preferable to that obtaining in our own country today.[71]

The Crusade, on the evidence of these pages, shared the same central preoccupations. A curious advertisement, inserted in the middle of a couple of columns of local news items, is consistent with the recorded flavour of the week's activities and fairly represents the kind of public response emerging in questions put to the platform after the main speeches at meetings.

> The I.C.F. Crusade.—Alston, the bootmaker, greatly appreciates the I.C.F. Crusade principal [*sic*], and is determined to sell Alston's boots on their conditions—a square deal all round—so please buy from this store, and make yourself known when you try Alston's boots. 170 Dalton road.[72]

Immensely successful in the ICF view, the Potteries Crusade of 1923 involved over sixty imported crusaders, supported by the local clergy. Hughes, Elvin and Slesser, who was announced as Standing Counsel of the Labour Party, were among them. At a debate in Tunstall, W. Tunnicliffe of the Pottery Workers Society observed complacently that

> in the pottery industry they were considerably ahead of many other industries. That was due, perhaps to the fact that many manufacturers 'knocked about' their works all the day. There was nothing better for taking the rough edges off employer or workman than to meet each other.[73]

With potters dispersed among miners in an atmosphere almost of village intimacy, the Labour Party had a hard time developing a base. In Stoke both miners and potters combined behind John Ward, the 'Navvies' M.P.' until his defeat by Cynthia Mosley in 1929. Hostile to the Labour Party and therefore acceptable here both to the working-class and the middle-class Liberal politicians in his district, he has been somewhat misleadingly described as a Labour stalwart. He was first elected as a Liberal–Labour member in 1906, and despite describing himself as Independent Labour in the twenties was, according to Craig, the product of a local Liberal–Conservative pact, with the support of some local trade unions. He was claimed by the Liberals and accepted their whip.[74] The ICF found the climate in which Ward survived congenial and hospitable. There was a civic welcome at Stoke, and at another large civic reception the Mayor of Newcastle welcomed the healthy influences being introduced by the clergy in troublous conditions. Kempthorne responded gracefully with an allusion to St Paul's 'true word, when he said that "the powers that be"—by which he meant the civic powers—"are ordained of God" '. The Rev J. V. Wilson of Sneyd, one of the MacDonald parsons, did return in his contribution to the Crusade to the theme of the repentant church, which 'during the last five or six years' had come to realise the sin of the past.[75] But in general on the ICF side the references are much stronger and less apologetic to the themes of individual obligation, unity, and the 'lie of equality'.[76]

The marked contrast with the Croydon Crusade of February 1925 reflects the very different social composition of a south London suburb where Tory Members were invariably returned with comfortable majorities, but also a strong local evangelical tradition, at St Matthew's and a number of other churches and in the free church congregations. On this occasion the Primate himself launched the Crusade, and Mrs Davidson accompanied him at the opening ceremonies. An occasion of overflowing congregations rather than mass meetings, there is virtually no reference to political stresses and anxieties and the Messenger appears in the role most vividly recollected by regular churchpeople, effectively concentrating the attention of large numbers of individuals on their personal and inward deficiencies of motive, purpose and commitment.[77]

The alliance with nonconformity was more tentative in the Monmouth Crusade of 1928. The Bishop of Woolwich, a veteran leader of Crusades, was obliged to spend time explaining the demands on episcopal salaries in response to questions prompted by a traditional regional hostility, and much was made of the fact that the Bishop of Hereford, accompanied by the Vicar of Blaenavon, attended the induction of a local Baptist Minister.[78] But the Crusade, like many other visits made by the Messenger in the region, seems to have drawn on the distinctive strain of fervent nonconformity which had made local communities in the Welsh mosaic of industrial villages and towns resistant to insurgent socialist appeals.[79] The revivalist idiom was a familiar one and, particularly when the Messenger was involved, there was a reported lack of inhibition, missing from accounts of the most euphoric meetings across the border, about the emotionalism of some of the mass meetings, where hymns were sometimes sung in Welsh and tears flowed. On these occasions the Messenger dwelt on the tragedy of the pockets of atheistic materialism created by the unmitigated harshness of industrial conditions. He is reported addressing an audience of 3000 in the Central Hall of Newport:

> Do you know that there are men in the valleys of Monmouthshire in the nostrils of whom stinks the name of Jesus Christ? They are sick of gentle Jesus, and bishops and parsons. And you can't blame them. Socialism is no use; something more radical has to change the thought of this country. Socialism is rotten, and it is not going to wipe out the slums and poverty you can find any day in Newport.[80]

On this occasion, we are told, 'women wept and men broke down'. During this week Labour debates were held under the auspices of the

6 G. A. Studdert Kennedy (*St Martin-in-the-Fields Review*)

Newport Labour Party, and the Mayor and Councillors were prominent at other meetings as well. A local paper estimated that the Messenger himself had been heard during the Crusade by some 20,000 people.

His state of mind at this time emerges in clear outline from a series of extended reports. The 'something more radical' is being announced with a sense of exhaustion and threat which is reflected in the prominence of themes, which were not, however, new. We must have politics: our hearts must be with God, and our heads with whichever political team we think best serves His ends. At the same time he fiercely denounces the passionate confusions of party and political life. Frequently and at length, and in phraseology that is unmodified across the decade, he confronts his hearers with the lie at the root of such institutionalised expressions of greed.

> Men who knew looked with apprehension over the world. They did not think men were naturally wise, sociable and easily united . . . In this country we were locked and united together and the barriers that arose between us were due very largely to our enormous natural inequalities. The teaching that all the classes have an economic origin—that they were poor because they had never had a chance to be anything else—was only partly true. The fact was that we were not born equal. Nature intended that we should be born unequal, and it was possible to be born of the same parents three fools and one genius. The classes had a biological basis.[81]

He draws attention to the outstanding and exceptional qualities, whatever their failings, of the great leaders of the past.[82]

A solution, or partial solution, which repeatedly appears in an inexplicit connection with the radical religious content of his message is Rationalisation, something that is bound to come as increasingly complex interdependence is forced upon us. The theme was an appropriate one at the time within a few miles of Mond's former political bailiwick and sphere of influence in Swansea, but it seems to have been a consistent thread in the Messenger's speeches into the new year. In Carlisle, after justifying the clerical intervention in the General Strike, as he had been doing earlier in Wales, and after registering his total impatience with 'people who turned economic questions into parliamentary questions', he said;

> Whether they like it or not they were coming to what he would call the rationalistaion of industry. By that was meant a drastic rationalisation of the entire industry of the country. Some of the things that would be done would be to eliminate waste, the costs

of production would be decreased, lower prices would be aimed at, real wages would be increased so that they could buy more with the wages they would get; the demand would be stimulated and the unemployed would be reabsorbed through the increased demand . . . The problem had to be tackled together, with an unwavering hand, and with a co-operative effort.

At a packed reception the Mayor of Falmouth observed that the message they had heard was badly needed. These reports invariably refer to large and enthusiastic audiences.[83]

The crowds and enthusiasm are reported with monotonous regularity in connection with the Messenger, whether during the Crusades or at the large number of meetings addressed by him between these major events. But his personal performance was supplemented by the regular activities of a varied group of speakers, sometimes appearing with him, sometimes following their own schedules. They were all by the standards of the day effective on the platform. There was a rough division of Labour between the more heavily worked of them, with Miss Knight-Bruce, for example, on the sacramental view of life particularly effective at meetings for women and girls, Cash speaking often on the class theme, and the area organisers with their own individual approaches. One of Harrison's themes was a presentation of Temple's argument on competition. These contributions are in general less fully reported and at this distance breathe less in the way of atmosphere or sense of occasion, but one does well to remember that their audiences were not yet habituated to radio as a medium and had a taste and stamina for this kind of mass communication which is now hard to imagine. The ICF Crusade service at Bristol was only the second ever broadcast from the Cathedral, and the main service at Croydon was ruined for one bed-ridden listener by a local 'oscillator' playing with his valve set.[84]

There were in addition the lay missioners, not many with such well-known pitches as the Birmingham Bull Ring, but each reporting scores of meetings every year to surprisingly varied audiences, though these were mostly composed, in the words of one agent's report, of 'artisans with a smattering of the unemployed.'

Like any other roving and overworked public attraction, the Messenger himself was bound to rely on a limited repertoire of themes, at least for a run of meetings, and variations in a series of accounts often seem to reflect selective reporting rather than any substantial departures from the current theme.

Thus, soon after his return early in March 1924 from a four-month trip to the United States, a sequence of speeches in the north west was concerned with the large theme of evolution, the imperatives of co-operation and competition in service, the herd instinct and the hazard of collective retrogression. He speaks, as usual, with compassionate sympathy for those who strike under extreme pressure, but 'fighting never did anything for anybody'.[85] In this week, coincidentally, a threatened lock-out at Birkenhead was reported, the result of unofficial action at Southampton which affected work on HMS *Rodney*, then on the stocks at Cammell Laird's.

A long series was shaped by the row over the clerical intervention, in which he contrasts the 'sentiment' of the 'bishops', as Temple's group was casually referred to, with the passionate sectional hostility behind the final outcome.[86] He also denies the allegations of episcopal incompetence.

> William Temple was a man that any newspaper in the kingdom would be very anxious indeed to get to write any of their beastly articles on economics, or anything else.[87]

He started working the rationalisation theme into prominence from the end of 1927.[88] But there is no modification or development of the message as a whole over the period. Continuously he circles round the implications of the 'higher freedom' (not a phrase he uses), both for ordinary people and for those with the talents and obligations of leadership. 'The worst of it was that the people who were not suffering had the clearest heads and they did not care enough.'[89] At least this was true of some, and we had to, for example, increase the class of benevolent mine-owners.[90] And yet there were others, many more than could be recognised by those nursing a sense of grievance. On this point he is at his most vivid and explicit with the solid and prosperous congregation of the Wesleyan Methodists at Pudsey Trinity United Methodists Church, a community he visited annually in May and with which he had a family connection through his wife.

> ... men talked about employers as big-bellied, bloated fellows, and yet when they came in contact with them they found them very human. John D. Rockefeller was now a friend of his. He thought he knew the picture they would have of Rockefeller. Rockefeller told him that it was a worry to him how to spend his money without hurting anyone ...

He continues with the story of a strike, Rockefeller's visit to see what was going on, and his encounter with a striker, who

> poured his story out, and Rockefeller said 'Yes, it's rotten, it shall be put right. Go to the office and you will get the money'. The man replied, 'I can't believe that you are John D. Rockefeller'.[91]

Two years later, addressing the same community, which had barely been affected by the General Strike, he spoke of God's providential creation of coal, his hope that the miners would sheath the sword and the obligation on society to solve the problem.[92]

Speaking of the miners to a group of midland businessmen:

> They are God's children and your brothers. Stupid? Ah tragically stupid, but men for all that and not to be despaired of ... You cannot let the women and children starve even if the men are fools, and perhaps you feel in your heart that all the fault is not on one side.[93]

But hitting out, herd behaviour, is a powerful temptation in a crowded society, as in a cramped family, and there are fatally attractive justifications for it. There are, he would point out, such a thundering lot of us. It is in this connection that 'Marx' regularly appears, the false prophet of a doctrine of violence. There is very little from ICF speakers in the way of an exposition of this challenge. Within a few days of Baldwin's appeal for a new spirit in industry and for an industrial truce, made before 50,000 Conservatives and Unionists at Welbeck Abbey, we have a bald and representative statement from Kirk, who was introducing the Messenger to an audience at Cromer.

> The Fellowship was faced with an organised movement among the workers who had got hold of the idea of Karl Marx that these things could only be obtained by force. The Fellowship had to prove that this would lead to chaos.[94]

This condensed and personalised source of error was made to sound at once more threatening, and more foolish in the Messenger's addresses, at a Southport meeting chaired by Sir Robert Connell, for instance, and at Birmingham and many other places in the year of the General Strike and thereafter. 'The fact that the British people is becoming political rather than religious is one of the most dangerous things in the world.'[95] Political passion, specifically, fogged any clear and objective view of those who handled substantial resources. There was no such thing as private property, since all property was in trust as a sacrament of fellowship. The capitalist, unlike the parasite, did not consume, he saved. Hostility to the capitalist was the product of blind bitterness against the agent of a process essential to society.[96] It was foolish to complain about the structural consequences of a given social order. He grew, he said, 'sick and tired' of nonsense about capitalism causing unemployment.[97] We had to live, not in a 'system' that was susceptible of a constructive transformation in to any other we could conceive of, but in a social organism in evolution.

Studdert Kennedy never had any illusions about the minute proportion of his listeners who might have been drawn back by him, with any enduring commitment, into the communion of the Church. But when he died, during an intensive series of engagements in Liverpool in March 1929, it is clear that very large numbers of people, ex-servicemen and many others who had been affected by his post-war ministry, were touched by a real sense of loss.[98]

What survives most clearly from his itinerant ministry in the fragmented form of these press reports is a consistent reiteration of themes that compose an orientation to the social order which is familiar in several different versions to the student of British politics. Elements of central importance to the Messenger himself were almost certainly underplayed in the press, however: it is noticeable that direct references to the suffering Christ are relatively infrequent and most likely to register in the form of a particularly striking image, such as the battlefield epiphany he often referred to, when he found himself suddenly looking down on a dead German boy and seeing Christ in this lump of mutilated humanity. This aspect of his message is more adequately represented in some of the homilies appearing regularly in *The Torch*, which had a circulation of about 45,000 by 1926, about 12,000 being parochial subscriptions at this time.

But what calls for attention in this account is less the presence of a familiar combination of beliefs about political and economic relations, than the fact that an anglican parson with an articulate commitment to a sacramental understanding of the world could engage a large and diverse public in relation to these beliefs so very effectively. For numbers of people, it would appear that the loosely recognisable elements of a social theory were, in however crude a form for the majority of them, attached to notions about a supranatural order, a divine, purpose and individual obligations under it. What survives in the record as a highly questionable set of assumptions and prejudices about man in relation to society was conveyed with a conviction of the reality of transcending sanctions, indeed as its natural expression, and it was to this combination of meanings that the ICF public responded in varying degrees.

8   Toward the City of God

The Fellowship could fairly claim to encompass a plurality of perspectives and judgements on major social issues of the day. But an examination of this variety within the organisation, particularly if it is set in the context of the significant public actions of those involved, reveals a central tendency, shared assumptions which cannot, despite the grounds on which they were regularly justified, be simply accounted for in terms of a common commitment to the spirit of the gospels. The ICF promoted a comprehensive ideology which was used by different groups as a means of assessing, relating to and acting upon the political and economic trends of the decade. This found expression in a broad theory of political action, in a theory of economic relations, in a normative model of the social structure and an interpretation of the rationality of social choice in terms of a distinctive social psychology. All these elements can be assessed in terms of the interests and tendencies they promote or restrict, and related to similar contemporary configurations of thought, which avoided justification on any grounds of religious belief. This chapter attempts to illustrate central tendencies and assumptions, which were expressed with a degree of confusion and contradiction, in the public activities of leading ICF figures, and to identify some of their implications.

Speaking in Welsh to an audience of Calvinistic Methodists at Portmadoc in the course of the 1921 Coal Strike, Lloyd George kicked back at 'an important conclave of highly placed divines' who had presumed, at Convocation in April, to comment on the Government's handling of the dispute. He shortly turned his attention to the demands of the Sinn Feiners, but having left no doubt about his annoyance with the Anglican prelates.

> They expressed an opinion on the best method of settling the strike. The particular view had reference exclusively to the best method of distributing the profits of these mines. It was not a question which they were in the least competent to discuss.[1]

This 'won't do', said the Messenger, in a charitable and humourous reference,[2] and the *Church Times* of 1 July complained about the Prime Minister's 'egregious Portmadoc speech', but he had been provoked. The Bishops in question were all ICF supporters, T. Woods of Peterborough, Russell Wakefield of Birmingham, E. S. Talbot of Winchester, and Kempthorne of Lichfield, the ICF Vice-President. In the course of the usual generalities Kempthorne had roundly asserted that it had been 'a great mistake to insist on decontrol taking place at the end of March', and that the miners' proposal for a national 'pool' embodied 'an entirely Christian principle'. Woods had made the standard disclaimers about episcopal claims to authority on the 'economic side', but went on to record his opinion that 'there were few examples in modern days of a Government being so unwise and foolish as the present Government had been in refusing to use to its full and originally intended extent the time available for adjusting the difficulties which now seemed so insoluble'. In his dispassionate view, the industry seemed to be singularly inefficient.[3] At the ICF Annual General Meeting in May, Russell Wakefield, who had spent the previous evening at a meeting of miners, managers and owners, agreed with the Right Rev. H. H. Pereira, Bishop of Croydon and formerly Chairman of the Navvy Mission Society, that it would be 'inopportune' to give the pronouncements on matters of detail that 'our Labour friends' had asked for, but there was a strong mood of support at the meeting for the miners' demands for a 'fair wage'. Lloyd George was not alone in taking a serious view of such clerical interventionism. Sir Lynden Macassey, who was due to chair the AGM, withdraw, a craven decision in Pereira's opinion, on the grounds that he had had a number of representations made to him 'by large employers, and also by other friends in the Trade Union world, who are unanimously of opinion that it would be a great mistake to the cause which we have so much at heart that the meeting should be held at the present juncture'.[4] He anticipated rhetoric outrunning reason.

The miners' strike 'was almost entirely of the Government's own making'[5] and Lloyd George was being characteristically disingenuous in making his point—that it was the Church's function to 'ingerminate a greater spirit of good will between the classes, a greater readiness to look at each other's point of view', and not to embark on an assessment of substantive policies. It was shrewdly made nonetheless, for ICF promoters of the social gospel frequently made it themselves, insisting on the non-partisan stance of the organisation, and on the Church's role in promoting a spiritual context, of informed, disinterested service within which contention might be insensibly tamed, but without claiming the endorsement of religion exclusively for any given position. Many were persuaded that they were relying on a distinction that could be maintained in pratice. Lloyd George was quite reasonably irritated by such simplicity. In this case, of course, his critics were supporting charges which were being made within the Liberal Party and the Labour Movement.

Kempthorne gave much of his attention to the issues of the day,[6] and his various attempts to come to grips with them show the difficulties involved in steering a public path between advocacy and encouragement of a constructive Christian concern. His pastoral letters are cautious and qualified. He does not pretend to expert knowledge; but, he complains, it is not easy to see why the parties cannot come together; it is very difficult to see what each side means by a National Pool for wages, but if the miners are going to use it to secure nationalisation 'by a side wind', then, in his humble opinion, they are choosing the wrong means. The pool in fact, as Garside points out, was 'to be formed by a levy on the tonnage of each undertaking for the purpose of smoothing out the inequalities in the wage rates between the several districts'.[7] Kempthorne was inclined to think, and here he accurately identified a central objective of the miners, that they intended that the more prosperous districts should underwrite the poorer. The strong, he points out, should indeed help the weak. But it is not for the Church as a whole to take sides over nationalisation, though he personally regrets the failure to meet the Sankey Commission's recommendations, whilst acknowledging 'the force of the Prime Minister's contention that this is a question which the whole country ought to decide', perhaps through a referendum. There is a charitable silence here on the Prime Minister's breach of faith over the implementation of the Commission's recommendations, something the miners themselves were not to forget.[8] Kempthorne constantly returns to the established grounds for consensus; the miners are no bolshevists, and the owners' proposals to establish a national board 'are (as Mr Hodges admits) an immense advance on any former plans'. 'The method of "fighting it out" is a bad method.'

The rhetoric of the ICF clerics characteristically follows an uncertain drift from the occasional stand on a substantive issue, through an intermediate area of affirmation on points of principle, such as the 'living wage' as a first charge on industry, to the invocation of standard recipes, such as the expansion of foreign trade as a remedy for unemployment, and to generalised exhortation on behalf of a new spirit in industrial relations. The living wage was a slogan with rather precise and, as one factor precipitating the 1926 crisis, momentous implications for the miners,[9] but it had also a well-established position in the general currency of liberal reform.

Lay churchmen, their perspectives more sharply defined by

professional and group interests, need to be further differentiated. But both groups, because they carried the ICF standard into a public arena which set limiting conditions on their activities, through the priorities and exigencies of newspaper reporting and through the intrinsic limitations of stump and pulpit oratory, were engaged in debate at a level where we encounter the message in significantly truncated forms. All the main themes were there, but inevitably without the sustaining context of tone, philosophical rationalisation and theological justification. But, whilst these themes in their popular expression have a loosened connection with their more elaborate sources, they acquire new emphases and associative affiliations at a more pragmatic level. The conclaves of bishops are less important in this development than the lay public figures, most of them players rather than cheer-leaders at the momentous Twickenham of industrial conflict.

The more vocal ICF captains of industry contrast in tone but complement each other in central emphasis. Everard Hesketh, an ICF Treasurer along with C.W. Bowerman and his successor Frank Hodges, MP, represented the paternalism of the older Navvy Mission engineers who ran, as his own house history puts it, a happy shop with a highly developed *esprit de firm*.[10] Since 1877 the major producer of refrigerating machinery for the merchant marine and the navy, Hall's became a controlled firm during the war, producing motor lorries for the army, bomb-dropping gear and ancillary equipment for field guns. They employed 2500 people in 1920 and had taken on up to 315 women under wartime dilution. A Benefits Trust, based on profits, had been running since 1912. Hesketh spoke of community and purpose in the context of a firm of moderate size with a skilled and stable work force.

Colonel David Carnegie, Hichens' colleague from the Canadian munitions mission, was by contrast obsessed by the aggregative irrationality of contemporary industry and the portent of conflict. He quotes Hichens on irrational organisation, duplication and waste, but lingers on the dangers of social upheaval, bolshevism and syndicalism, low morale and subversive anxieties currently prevalent on the shop floor, in successive paragraphs drawing on the testimony of thirty-five reformed derelicts he had met at the Jerry McAuley Rescue Mission in New York, and Samuel Gompers, President of the AFL, to make the point that socialism has never done anything for labour.[11] George Barnes, MP, lately in the War Cabinet, contributed a foreword to this polemic, which expresses alarm lest labour should 'come under the control of some who look only to materialistic forces as the means by which to achieve their ends'. Barnes, along with Hodge, Roberts and Walsh had refused to follow the decision of the Labour Party Conference of 1918 that the Party should fight the election on its own. Carnegie was a keen advocate of Whitleyism, and commented on the links between Whitley's proposals and the report of Lord Esher's Garton Foundation in 1916. Typically, he overlooks the hints contained in the Garton report on the possible importance of an expansionist policy as an incentive to unions to continue wartime co-operation.[12] He represents the widespread anxiety to reconstitute a pre-war regime, which he equated uncritically with the idea of a Christian western civilisation confronted by its emergent antitheses in the post-war disorders.

A more considerable figure, Sir Max Muspratt, a leading northwest Liberal, MP for Exchange in 1910 and Secretary of the Liverpool Liberal Federal Council, joined the ICF Council in 1925, a year before he left the Party and became President of the CBI. He held a number of directorships including Brunner Mond and ICI, and was a keen member of Temple's Life and Liberty Movement and a COPEC activist. Both he and Tawney, whose brief connection with the ICF ended early in 1924, wrote reviews of the COPEC *Report on Industry and Property* for Temple's *The Pilgrim*.[13] Tawney says practically nothing about the content of the Report, preferring, on the grounds that the Church as an institution is professionally expert on the spiritual needs of men, to expand at a very general level on the theme that 'there is no reason why the churches should slink timidly into the field of social and economic theory, with the apologies of a fisherman caught poaching the squire's waters'. His only declaration of emphasis is some comment on the irrelevance of the kind of economistic objections to redistribution put forward by figures like Mallock and Hichens' Chairman on the LMS Board, Sir Josiah Stamp, who had pointed out to an audience at the LSE in 1921 that if all surplus income above £250 p.a. were divided equally among people with incomes below that figure, the gain per family would not be above 5/- per week.[14] Muspratt provides a generally appreciative summary of the Report, but with a substantial reservation over the section dealing with the Distribution of Wealth, which almost caused him to withold his signature. Quoting his dissenting Conference speech, in which he identified a 'grave fallacy' in the Report, he writes that

> While poverty in every form, material and spiritual, is repugnant to the Christian conscience, to therefore deduce that possession of great wealth should also be repugnant is not justified unless there is evidence to show that the one is caused by the other. There is not a shred of evidence to support such a view: indeed all experience is to the contrary; it is the successful and wealthy industrialist who normally gives the example to the less wealthy in wages and conditions and wide philanthropy, and it is the nations with the

largest numbers of wealthy men which have in practice the highest standard of living all round.

He goes on to suggest that there is an empirical law according to which the total wealth of a country is distributed, and

As total wealth advances the difference between the very rich and the very poor widens, but the standard is higher for both, while the large intermediate class increases in both numbers and standard.

It is precisely to Muspratt's 'grave fallacy' that Tawney seeks to draw a fundamentally different kind of sociological attention.

What keeps British industry in perpetual ferment is not that the product to be divided is too small, however desirable it may be to increase it: for when it has been increased, agitation has not diminished. It is that, to a growing number of those dependent upon it, its organisation appears oppressive and the distribution of its produce inequitable.

Muspratt's apologia was echoed by other businessmen who appeared on ICF platforms, but it had been developed most thoroughly by Lynden Macassey, a director of companies as well as a lawyer, in a major political confrontation with Ernest Bevin, at the Dockers' Court of Inquiry (Shaw Inquiry).[15] This encounter exposes an emphasis on the unfolding theme of industrial co-operation which found strong support within the ICF.

No revolutionary, but incapable of sentimentality about industrial peace, Bevin saw industrial justice emerging in a social democracy out of a new balance of power, created by organised class action, and continuously under negotiation by a representative leadership which worked to its own rather than official or managerial standards of economic realism. The objectives were compatible with those of progressive employers because tactical goals were identified in ultimately negotiable terms, but the general perspective is quite distinct from the consensual reformism of the progressives in industry and the trade unions. In the 1945 Labour Government, like Attlee, he saw taxation as the implement that would more equitably distribute the national cake, however, 'they had no wish to bake another cake: they did not tamper with any revolutionary principle, and did not eagerly look forward to a coming struggle for power'.[16]

Bevin presented the case for the dockers in 1920 in a performance of sustained brilliance. Though Macassey, who was briefed by the owners, was acting in a professional capacity, the case was one he

fully identified with. The book he published two years later is an
attack on a false philosophy of fellowship and brotherhood which
creates an actuality of fratricidal conflict, even within the Labour
Movement itself.[17] The Movement has leaders he is glad to have
served under, Henderson, Barnes, Hodge, Roberts, 'but will they be
allowed to lead?'[18] Society is threatened by a breakdown in human
relationships which at each level represent a failure to come to terms
with the imperatives of rational industrialisation, between capital
and administrative staff, capital and manual workers, and among
manual workers.

> Industry I have defined, in the language of economics, as the
> production of commodities and services for the purpose of
> satisfying the wants and desires of men. On this commonplace
> process, which sounds so dull in definition, and on no other, the
> future well-being of our country and the practicability of further
> social improvements and reforms depend. Production ought,
> therefore, to be regarded as the principal means of advancing the
> happiness, social welfare and material prosperity of the nation,
> and industry the chief instrument in that beneficent work, as the
> highest and noblest form of national service.[19]

He covers some of Hichens' themes in very much the same terms,
negative voluntarism on the part of the State towards management,
but State development of public opinion against anti-social direct
action: industrial welfare and rational management; the freedom to
serve of the exceptional individual. He also dwells on the
development of formal co-operative structures, such as the Joint
Industrial Councils which must be protected from arbitrary
pressures from politicians as well as from anti-social activists.

In a general sense, the idea of a structure, built out of negotiated
detail and sustained by belief in its legitimacy, was one he shared
with Bevin, and of course with ICF experts like E. C. P. Lascelles and
Sir Donald Maclean's Committee on Registration and the
Guaranteed Week, which was set up after the Inquiry. But the
ground of agreement about procedures and forms underlines a tense
counterpoint between the protagonists on the nature and meaning
of heavy labour undertaken for a wage and irregularly available.
Macassey produced Professor A. L. Bowley as an expert witness on
nutrition to provide an objective definition of a living wage. He was
much respected as an authority in socially concerned church circles,
and Macassey uses some of his evidence in the book. There could be
no better illustration than the case he presented through Bowley at
the Inquiry of a classical liberal anxiety about the material leanness
and structural fragility of the organic social order, to protect which

we can only summon up the uncertain quantities of willing service under a prudent dispensation. Bevin took Bowley to pieces, with savage patience translating the talk of calorific values into representative servings for a casual dock worker and his family,[20] and exposing in the process the powerful assumptions underlying this expert objectivism, in its bearing on the economic function of profits and their relation to wages and production. 'In 1916', wrote Macassey, 'the Government met direct action by action more direct, and deported from the Clyde the ringleaders, and the strike collapsed'.[21] The decision, which he had recommended, struck him as merely sensible. The contest with Bevin was of a different order, but it was still for him a critical one, an instance of the drag on social potential created by union militancy beyond the limits of reason.

Some months later, at a meeting chaired by Mr Rigby of the Stockport Labour Party, Bevin launched into an attack on the Church. Maud Royden then spoke critically of the Labour Movement in connection with women in industry, and Dr Orchard talked about fellowship. Studdert Kennedy, the last speaker, rose to his feet saying that it seemed to have been left to him to answer Bevin's challenge. According to the *Church Times* of 11 February 1921, he gave most of his time to 'an impassioned denunciation of war' and an explanation of the human quality in economics. But he answered Bevin with arguments contained in *Democracy and the Dog Collar*, for Bevin was the apotheosis of his Mr Organised Labour, more formidably so than the composite he actually sketches of 'Mr Hodges, Mr Thomas, and Mr Clynes, with a dash of Mr Williams and George Lansbury—but only a dash' (*DDC*, 10). Bevin, he indicated in his speech, sought to reduce complex issues to simple ones which could be settled in a fight, created class hatred, ignored the real movement towards better things through the union of good men of all classes. If the Church went hand in hand with the Labour Party she would 'make one of the greatest mistakes in her history'.

This was a view Lionel Hichens would have endorsed, though it is expressed here with a defensive anxiety that never affected him. However one may regard Hichens' thinking on the ethical bases of industrial order, it has the substantial quality of being an integral component of an active and continuous involvement in public affairs. Society as political economy struck him as intrinsically tending to disorder and obstruction, something to be redeemed only by individual commitment to a life of duty to one's neighbour. By definition, therefore, it is beyond the scope of any organisation, church or party, to pass down salvation in the form of a policy solution that seems, to some, and in some quite general sense, to coincide with 'spiritual' expectations, or, alternatively, with some theoretically complete model of economic or political organisation.

The spirit is constrained to make its presence felt indirectly and uncertainly through the myriad objective capillaries of the social organism, and there can be no evading the complex, painful and contradictory considerations involved in public policy. Unlike some of his ICF business associates he is not overeager to spring to the justification of the existing structures. He has, given his assumptions about social change, as strong a sense as Tawney of

> the bitter antagonism between labour and capital, the extremes of wealth and poverty, the miseries of unemployment, the control that one class has over the lives and fortunes of others, the great opportunities of the few and the blank outlook of the many.[22]

His reading of the implications of living in such a world is, of course, a very different one. He 'conducted the affairs of "big business" as though they had been a branch of the public service', to quote a saintly and earnest exponent of the public school service ideal,[23] seeing a liberal, Christian, professional élite as a necessary fact in a modern society with the potential for regeneration, a social formation capable of redeeming contingent social divisions by realising itself in its commitment to the good of the whole. His Foundation Day address as Chairman of the Governors of Birkbeck College in 1929 expresses this in a treatment of the evolutionary theme which closely parallels Studdert Kennedy's, in which the law of progress applies to human as to natural life, though threatened by retrogression if the function of leadership falls into the wrong hands.[24] The coherent personal involvement behind his interpretation of the relevance of the gospel to industry made him a more formidable figure in the ruck of popular debate than some with greater intellectual pretensions. He was well able to hold his own at heated public meetings in the radical atmosphere of post-war Sheffield, where Cammell Laird was a major employer.[25]

However, the distinction Hichens likes to make between the operation of the spirit of the gospel in public life and the contingent forms and complexities constraining it, is deceptive, because he uses his central categories of good will and duty to underwrite assumptions which beg a number of questions. If the spirit is right, he likes to claim, the system, the form of the organisation, can take care of itself. But he cannot in fact mean this in the large sense which his argument seems to imply, because the ideas of good will and duty to neighbour are used in two specific connections in his references to industry which, taken together, constitute a rather exclusive working definition of a rational and right social order. The most obvious connection is with the dilemmas of labour relations, the inherent limitations of formal machinery for arbitration, historical structures which embody inefficiency, distrust, mutual exploitation through ca'canny and profiteering. Here good will is the means towards a rational structure of co-operation and growth. The other, less obvious, connection is in relation to the role of the State and the nature of the managerial function. As Chairman of the Central Council of the Association of Controlled Firms, he was well aware of the need for economic direction by the State in time of war, and was not dogmatic about a rapid return to the *status quo*, in fact arguing along new liberal lines that it was essential for the State to develop fresh powers of co-ordination in certain areas. But he consistently resisted talk of central planning, because it is self-defeating to remove the stimulus of competition, because official bureaucracies are inefficient and subject to political pressures, but above all because the variety of co-operative associations and federations of industrialists and entrepreneurs already in existence are effective precisely because they are voluntary, based on the individual undertakings of free agents and sustained by good will and a shared recognition of wider responsibilities, duty to neighbour in the hard world of affairs. All the other systems, Guild Socialism, socialism and the rest, in one way or another deny the essential conditions under which good will and duty to neighbour can express themselves on a societal scale, whether by restricting individual development and choice, by substituting mechanical requirements for organic bonds, or by systematically setting consumer against producer or class against class.

The importance of Hichens' arguments to the ICF lies in the frequency with which they appeared in an applied form.[26] He brought a general social theory to bear throughout the decade on the wages problem and strikes based on departures from the hard commonsense of profit and loss, on reparations and German competition, on the price of coal and tenders for new ships, and on rail freights and the elimination of redundant labour on the railways.[27] (He was an LNWR/LMS Director from 1918–40.) He discussed in the same light specific criteria for sliding wage scales in the context of arbitration, and pointed to the systematic inequities produced by co-partnership and profit-sharing schemes, placing them, along with schemes for the democratisation of industry, with other essentially half-baked solutions to the problem of creating a climate in which the complementary functions of labour and capital are accepted in the collective interest.

To the collective interest in effective production he gave a thoroughly operational definition in terms of a number of closely interrelated components. Hichens was one of eleven leading figures, including Snowden, Stamp, Balfour and Lord Melchett (Sir Alfred Mond), whose definitions of 'rationalisation' were collected by Urwick at the end of the decade.[28] His definition is one of the more precise: 'the amalgamation of firms doing a similar kind of business with the object of promoting efficiency and economy'. The advantages of vertical integration were generally appreciated in the industry, but he was working on schemes for horizontal integration from the start of the decade. In January 1928, Vickers, Vickers-Armstrong and Cammell Laird amalgamated to form the English Steel Corporation, with financial assistance engineered by Montagu Norman of the Bank of England. By the end of the year Cammell Laird's Grimsthorpe works were closed and the Penistone works a few weeks later, after only ten years in operation. The consequent strike at Penistone, which was union backed, resulted in notices being posted at federated works throughout the country.[29] Carr and Taplin point out that the closure 'caused great distress among the local workers, but this was the price of adjusting industry to a lower level of demand'.[30] Hichens saw this as an exclusively managerial decision, an occasion on which the part must suffer, though temporarily supported by State aid, in the interests of the whole. On the other hand, his reaction to proposals for a capital levy—that it would have worked immediately after the war—was pragmatic and he took a line of responsible restraint on excess profits, which had been ineffectively controlled by wartime legislation.[31]

However, whilst horizontal amalgamation was fundamental to his approach to industrial rationalisation, the range of his concern is better identified by some of Urwick's looser definitions. He promoted research and scientific management, particularly the introduction of professional accounting methods, a development of fundamental importance to the steel industry in the decade. He was heavily involved in industrial welfare, in a sense that left the old Navvy Mission's concern with basic comforts far behind, stressing education for industry and the humanising of working conditions, in close support of the Rev. Robert Hyde's *Industrial Welfare Society*, whose concern was 'to promote the best uses of human resources in industry'.[32] Hyde's work was predictably attacked in some trade union circles for its insidious promotion of class collaboration, but it was highly regarded by leading churchmen. In 1931 he was able to follow up an Oxford mission to undergraduates conducted by Archbishop Lang, an ex-officio President of the ICF and a close personal friend of the Hichens family. Hichens was particularly concerned to draw on the best public school talent for recruits to management. J. G. Lockhart, Lang's biographer, was one of a number for whom he arranged a pre-university training in industry.[33] As far as the partisan critics of 'welfare' were concerned, Hichens had cause for quiet satisfaction. In the opening address he gave to the fourth annual conference of the *Industrial Welfare Society* at Balliol College, he asked

What is industrial welfare then? I noticed that this question was asked by Mr Frank Hodges when he was down here last year, and I am very sorry that he is not here this year, because all of us, whether we are employers or workers, must recognise that he is a man of great ability and enthusiasm, with high ideals. Now, the answer that he gave to the question was this: he said that 'welfare was merely a means to an end and that end is the greater efficiency of the capitalist method of production' ... I do not believe that there would be any of you present tonight, taking an interest in welfare work, if you thought that it was merely the means of strengthening the capitalist's position.[34]

In 1922 Hodges, along with Cecile Matheson, who on several occasions spoke for the ICF, joined Arthur Henderson on the Council of the *Industrial Welfare Society*.

Hodges, trailing quite striking radical credentials, was a considerable catch for the ICF. Hichens' most cordial and long-standing trade union and working-class connections, however, were of a different kind. Like Milner, he had contacts with Alex Thompson of the pro-war *Clarion* and the Socialist National Defence Committee.[35] Thompson described Hichens as one 'of the most alert and enlightened Captains of Industry', printing his warm message of congratulation on Thompson's own appointment as Editor, and picking him, along with Baldwin, Smillie and William Temple, for his team of four just men to bring peace to industry.[36] Havelock Wilson, men from whose National Sailors' and Firemens' Union were employed during the 1921 coal strike in Belgian ports loading coal for export to Britain, despite initial blacking of this work by Belgians,[37] was introduced by Hichens at the first meeting of the *Industrial Peace Union of the British Empire* as a 'large-hearted leader of sane trade unionism'.[38] Allan Bullock, Bevin's partisan but undeniably sober biographer, describes the NUS under Wilson as a company union working hand in glove with the employers in the Shipping Federation, ruthless towards dissidents and doing little for the seamen.[39] W. A. Appleton, President of the International Federation of Trade Unions, and editor of the *Democrat* for the *General Federation of Trades Unions*, corresponded with effusive respect following comments from Hichens on unemployment in *Lloyds Sunday News* in February 1921. He was sent in return a detailed elaboration with information about the situation on the north side of the Mersey, as background for addresses he was due to give to the Liverpool and Manchester Chambers of Commerce.[40] Appleton, who was also Secretary of the GFTU, had come under heavy attack at the 1920 Trade Union Congress for his criticisms of the Triple Alliance and its policy of Direct Action, and for his denigration of the miners. Roberts remarks on the *Democrat*'s fondness for the Liberals and the respect it paid to the middle classes.[41]

However, whilst these associations are illuminating, Hichens' connection with central ICF figures in the world of labour represented a more significant convergence in the post-war organisation and rhetoric of industrial co-operation. Henderson, never on the ICF Council but very willing to appear on its platforms, was committed, like Hughes, Poulton, Bowerman and Elvin, to a programme of co-operative reconstruction the early promise of which formally terminated when the Provisional Joint Committee of the National Industrial Conference 'resigned amidst bitter recriminations' on 19 July 1921, some two and a half years after it had been summoned.[42] Though, as Lowe points out, there was a structural contradiction between this grandiose national scheme established by Lloyd George and the Joint Industrial Councils of the Whitley scheme, this was not clearly recognised and there was considerable overlap of membership between these two structures,[43] and also of the Industrial Council of 1911. Of the ICF figures, Bowerman, then Secretary of the Parliamentary Committee of the TUC, Henderson and Poulton were on the 1911 Council. Henderson, Poulton and Ammon were at the Conference.

At a dinner for the printing trades delegates, during the TUC Conference week at Cardiff in 1921, Bowerman responded to a toast to their JIC by expressing himself 'more than delighted' with its work 'because of the goodwill of the employers'.[44] The Whitley scheme had developed with some success by the end of the war, though not in mining and engineering, where the major post-war problems occurred, and where there was a labour disposition to replace rather than improve the existing system, and also not in other areas where employers were recalcitrant, since the Government showed no disposition to enforce recommendations.[45] Lowe suggests that the National Industrial Conference was 'a political betrayal of Whitleyism, from which the movement never recovered'.[46] This came about because the structure of the Conference itself mobilised a broad current of opposition, articulated by Bevin and Thomas particularly, which tended to submerge areas of potential local consensus. However, support for the Conference and support for the federal development of the JICs came from the same ethos, endorsed on all sides by the ICF. All the more active ICF trade unionists, apart from Hodges, came from sectors of employment in which Whitleyism had taken on. Of particular importance were the 'socially amphibious' clerical occupations, moving between working and middle class, which had produced an upsurge of unionism between 1915 and 1920.[47] Hughes, President of the National Union of Clerks from 1907, and Assistant General Secretary of the National

Union of Clerical and Administrative Workers from 1913, with his close associate Elvin, General Secretary of the NUC, was involved in the extension of Whitleyism.[48] Elvin was Vice-Chairman of the Middlesex Joint Industrial Council, Chairman of the Middlesex Whitley Council and a Staff member of the National Whitley Council. But employers had seen advantages too in the JICs, in the Boot and Shoe Industry represented by Poulton who, along with George Isaacs, General Secretary of NATSOPA and another promoter of the ICF, was backing an Industrial Councils Bill at the TUC in 1923 and 1924 to give them statutory support.[49] Bowerman's Society of Compositors gave general support to the Whitley proposals, as did Ammon's postal workers and the Civil Service Union of which he was the organising secretary.

This trade union commitment to Whitleyism was aptly balanced by the presence of Miss M. P. Whitley on the ICF Council from 1920-4. She was the Rt. Hon. J. H. Whitley's eldest daughter, becoming a Director of the family cotton-spinning firm when he became Liberal Member for Halifax, after herself working in a munitions factory during the war. The Whitleys were keen Congregationalists, and saw the firm's development of co-partnership and profit-sharing as a direct expression of Christian and Liberal ideals.[50]

The trade union figures represent, of course, a craft and clerical interest by contrast with the opposition to the Conference in transport and heavy industry. They were traditionally inclined to think in terms of union interests, rather than those of political labour, the agents of a disengagement, not at the time seen as irretrievable, from close historical links with the Liberal Party. This defection was encouraged by a variety of factors which did not include a programmatic or ideological development representing any significant departure from a radical Liberal perspective. Labour Party rhetoric in the early 1920s was a 'careful concoction' which made the Party plausible, recognisable and distinguishable from the Asquithian Liberals, but to an extent fully compatible with deliberate 'similarities of manner and reasoning'.[51] The ICF trade unionists were spontaneously on the course Clynes was setting for the party, claiming to represent a national average and an obvious commonsense for an entire community in a phase of rapid evolution. Ammon, for instance, articulated the Party norm that set 'human life before property' and softened sectional appeals:

Its aim will be directed to the gradual suppression of the capitalist system, and to this end it will doubtless begin with such services as are necessary to the common weal, which other political parties have admitted should be state owned, such as railways and mines.

The coordinating of such services under one control will avoid much of the wastefulness and overlapping that now obtains, reduce accidents to a minimum and afford a constantly better standard of life to those engaged in the industry.[52]

The gently ameliorative tone of this piece was entirely appropriate in the *Wesleyan Methodist*, an organ of nonconformist opinion appealing to a stratum of the middle and respectable working class, in which the process of partisan polarisation was in a critical state. Ammon spoke, on behalf of Labour, for methodism rather than Marx, as did Frank Hodges.[53]

The National Industrial Conference failed for a number of reasons. Henderson, as have others since, blamed the premeditated duplicity of Lloyd George and the Coalition,[54] but the evidence suggests less calculated failures of legislative preparation and support,[55] whilst bringing into prominent relief a myopia, integral to the ideology of Reconstruction, towards deeply rooted social conflicts, which were the more fundamental causes of failure. An 'unwillingness to come to grips with the structure of British society' was

typical of the whole group of radical politicians who made the major policy decisions about social reform in the war years. It was not just that their greatest desire was 'social harmony' or that they thought of harmony as the natural condition of society. The peculiar ideology of the war effort, of 'all pulling together' . . . led them to believe in the *immediate reality of harmony* between interests and classes in the society which it was their job to 'ameliorate'. To this extent they were effectively disqualified from seeing the need to constrain groups to work together.[56]

The destruction of the Conference ended the more extravagant progressive expectations about co-operative Reconstruction. It did not, however, portend the emergence of a radical alternative view in the labour movement. Reconstruction failed because economic crisis destroyed the conditions in which the ideology of the war effort could lead to further plausible implementation. But its ideology survived, infecting elements in all three parties, whilst playing a critically important part in the Labour Movement, which combined a degree of muted class rhetoric with an orthodox political economy consonant with the intentions of industrialists who entertained beliefs about the harmonics of production or the Liberal paternalism of business as a trust. Its resilience was in part the product of a theoretical vacuum created by tactical errors and mismanagement on the left. Though Hinton and others have claimed that the shop stewards' movement was, despite certain structural weaknesses, a genuinely revolutionary force, which was defeated by a ruthless and carefully planned Ministry campaign to which Beveridge and Macassey were parties, this claim is not convincing and there are better grounds for Barry's conclusion that, by isolating themselves from the trade union movement, large numbers of the most experienced militants in industry had 'stepped aside into a blind alley'.[57] The Clyde fiasco demonstrated that the British socialist movement, with its gradualist expectations, 'had no ideological scheme for dealing with the type of disjointed development which did in fact take place at the end of the war'.[58] ' "MacDonaldism" ', according to Barry, who writes as a partisan lamenting lost historical opportunities, 'was a weed that grew on a plot left vacant.'[59] MacDonaldism, however, was but one variant of a successful and widely distributed species, one closely related to the general social theory subscribed to, with trivial variations of style and tone, by the ICF trade unionists and Labour politicians.

A high proportion of them were lay preachers. Ammon was a methodist who had almost entered the ministry,[60] one of the many untheoretical ILP churchmen, of whom several, like Bennett and Ben Spoor, who was placed by Beatrice Webb among the 'typical aristocratic recruits to the most popular of the Socialist Societies',[61] also joined the ICF. Elvin started preaching at the age of fifteen. Hughes and Hodges were lay preachers. The contribution of nonconformity to the British Labour Movement is, as Bullock says, a commonplace,[62] and Ernest Bevin's Baptist upbringing was doubtless no less important in the formation of his political personality, but the Wesleyanism in particular, that produced figures like Henderson and Ammon, incorporated historical links with Liberalism and its vision of the social structure which were only eroded gradually over the decade.[63] It was entirely compatible, in its social applications, with the Anglican component in ICF thinking.

Fred Hughes' statement of faith, published in 1931, is impossible to read after reviewing Studdert Kennedy's publications without concluding at least that his own perspective had found the strongest confirmation in the preacher's ministry.[64] Though socialism is a word that Studdert Kennedy uses in a negative sense, Hughes' Socialism is indistinguishable from Studdert Kennedy's Democracy. Socialism, we are told, is the expression of a religious faith, that is to say of the growing consciousness of organic unity in society, an extension of the sphere of mutual aid, an identification with the process in which all things work together for good to those who love. History is a record of the process by which men, learning in the hard school of experience, have increasingly substituted co-operation for competition, the law of life for the law of death. Each individual is necessary to the completeness of the whole, and the whole is necessary to the completeness of the one, but at the same time, this liberty of self-development, through service, becomes possible only when society assures the basic primary rights of Food, Freedom and Fellowship. The function of the more able man is to serve more abundantly and effectively than his less gifted brethren, and where he fails to do so he produces inequity instead of harmony. The war, however, made an anachronism of the authoritarian employer, 'an excellent man [but] he had no power to evoke the team spirit. His to *think*, theirs to *obey* . . . The team spirit is the spirit of Democracy', which achieved an increment during the war in the spontaneous development of a vast machinery of consultation, which on the whole worked well.

> Production, wages, profits, all were at a high level, and the workman tasted an independence limited only by a sense of duty to his country. The Devil was sick! Or perhaps he was too busy in other directions to attend to industry.

He canvasses alternatives to the irrationalism of the present system. 'The influence of Karl Marx has undoubtedly been great, but the current habit is to exaggerate its extent and overrate its importance.' Collectivism and economic communism merely meet an economic difficulty. Guild Socialism cannot deal with the system's insecurities. Profit-sharing and co-partnership tend to be delusive, and even where they may not be they involve a selfish localisation of fellowship. He proposes, to forestall a cataclysm, a measure of collectivism (land, banking, minerals, transport, light and power), that would leave capitalist structures undisturbed—this points toward the Liberal public corporation idea and the Conservative Party's Central Electricity Board—and internationally centralised control of finance. Within this framework he sees some expansion of Guild enterprises and of co-operative ownership and production, and 'a bold application of the principles of Communism in Service'. His comments on the 'inevitability of gradualness', with a passing warning on exhausting the people's patience, subside into eighteen lines from James Russell Lowell's 'A Glance Behind the Curtain':

> . . . He who would win the name of truly great
> Must understand his own age and the next,
> And make the present ready to fulfill
> Its prophecy, and with the future merge
> Gently and peacefully, as wave with wave.

On direct action he is at one with Studdert Kennedy.

A passive rebellion, with a positive purpose that is not our own but God's, is one thing. The endeavour to impose our own will by force or fraud upon our fellows in another and a different thing; and woe betide us if we mistake the second for the first. To revolutions so effected the proverb of the Frenchman always applies: 'The more it changes, the more it is the same old thing'.

Hodges, who had more experience of the harsh urgencies of political organisation than the clerical representatives, has been represented as a backslider from a youth of radical promise, but it is hard to believe in his early syndicalist promise. He acquired a reputation for militancy as a miners' agent inevitably involved in local strikes, and through his membership of the Coal Industry Commission (Sankey Commission), where he, Herbert Smith and the outstanding Smillie 'successfully kept "private enterprise" on its trial before the Commission, and compelled the mine owners to remain throughout on the defensive'.[65] But, as he indicates in his autobiography, his reputation as a rebel was in good measure a function of the obduracy of the mine-owners.[66] His defeat of the marxist Ablett, the 'most outstanding in grasp of theory' among the Ruskin College rebels,[67] for the Secretaryship of the Miners' Federation of Great Britain was brought about by the right-wing vote.[68] He held a general view of the Labour Movement as a religious struggle on behalf of the poor and oppressed, but in relation to the specific issue of control of the industry he had vague expectations of a Guild Socialist nature which were not shared by Smillie and probably not by the miners. After the Government's rejection of nationalisation, which Sankey himself proposed, there was little connection between Hodges's 'fine words' about unconstitutional action and the modest course actually followed by the miners' leaders at the 1919 TUC,[69] and on 'Black Friday', 15 April 1921, at an improvised press conference with back bench MPs, he abandoned a central point, national wage determination, for which the miners were fighting. Admittedly confusion surrounded that meeting,[70] but the *débâcle* of the Triple Alliance exposed an infirmity of purpose and organisation for which he shared responsibility, and also personal uncertainty about his political support and the grounds on which he was acting. In contrast to Thomas, who pulled his men away on a realistic assessment of the situation, Hodges seems to have been caught in the 'romantic notion that the Labour movement, through its own solidarity, could challenge economic facts without challenging the Government and the society of which these economic facts were a part'.[71] In company with Smillie and Thomas, he was influenced by 'the belief in the imminence of a Labour electoral victory and a desire not to queer the pitch of growing

middle class support by over-hasty industrial action . . . The scent of
cabinet office was in the air'.[72] To what extent the glamour of
eminence attracted him is not clear, though there was gossip, which
greatly shocked the Liberal politician Angus McCallum Scott, about
a champagne luncheon in Lord Howard de Walden's box at the
Derby during the coal dispute, and Beatrice Webb described him
later as a 'hanger-on of the directors of capitalist industry'.[73] But his
subsequent membership of the Central Electricity Board was entirely
consistent with his emphasis years before in publicising the Coal
Commission's findings. He had stressed wastefulness, lack of
planning and the potential for a rationalised and commercially
successful coal industry. Get the owner off the technical manager's
back and the manual worker will see his function in a new light, co-
operating with him to improve production.[74] Hichens' judgement
was shrewd; Hodges was an ally, more concerned with the potential
for co-operative organisation demonstrated in the war, than with
any larger political implications of the miners' defeat, whilst an
intermittently radical rhetoric was at odds with a negotiator's
pragmatism. Characteristically, he justified his rejection of the terms
offered in 1915 by Runciman, which precipitated Lloyd George's
intervention and a 'political' settlement, by pointing to the three
years of peace that followed in the South Wales coalfields. Snowden,
the architect of Labour's first, Cobdenite budget, applauded by Party
members in the prevailing atmosphere of confusion over economic
theory and the varieties of 'socialism',[75] was for Hodges the greatest
man in the Labour movement.

   This evangelical tendency in the Labour Movement had, to
borrow Cowling's phrase, other atmospheric allies in corners of the
Conservative Party and elsewhere. They converged naturally under
the auspices of the ICF. Lord Henry Bentinck, with one break MP for
South Nottingham since 1895, was not himself a figure of much
consequence, but, in his association with Lord Robert Cecil in 1922,
along lines that were sympathetically viewed by Asquithian leaders
like Maclean, Cowdray and Gladstone, he represented a Tory back
bench interest of some significance.[76] He left the Party in 1918, and
his book *Tory Democracy*, published that year, is an elegy to the
neglected conservatism of Disraeli, Randolph Churchill and
Salisbury, when the Party was above the mere interests of class and
retained a vision of the organic society with roots in the Thomist
hierarchy of the middle ages. He celebrates the Party's achievements
in rational adminstration, treating Hill's Party Committee on the
Poor Law, which covered the same ground as Sir Donald Maclean's
subsequent committee and in the main agreed with it, as a modern
application of the general principle of the just price, and comments
on the Joint Industrial Councils, referring to the pottery trade

specifically, because they institutionalise the principle of treating workmen as human beings. He quotes Hichens, 'a great captain of industry', at considerable length on the subject of industry as National Service for the good of the community.[77] In 1918 he led a delegation on behalf of miners in trouble with the police for strike activity.

In 1922 General Maurice became Principal of the Working Men's College. Its historian notes that

> It was not only to the critics on the left, like G. D. H. Cole, that the College appeared as 'conservative in tradition and hampered by its undemocratic constitution'. *The Times*, in a series of articles in 1921 on the revolutionary movement in the country, assured its readers that the Working Men's College, unlike such bodies as the Labour College, was quite harmless.[78]

To the College where, in the new Principal's epigram, 'we have plenty of classes but no division of class', came a succession of representative figures, George Barnes, Asquith, Sir William Robertson, H. A. L. Fisher, Mr Amery, Lord Balfour of Burleigh, Haldane, and, for the Founder's Day Address in 1925, Asquith again, now Lord Oxford. Whatever impact the College may have had on the Labour Movement over the decade, its records are full of the familiar moralism in a suitably high-minded distillation. Maurice himself regularly invoked the founders' tradition, from the genesis of Christian Socialism when Kingsley and his friends confronted the honest Chartists, marching to London under the influence of evil-minded and crack-brained men. In 1924 Haldane spoke on mass education and the dependency of modern industry on science. The College took an early interest in the scientific study of management, especially in relation to the study of the psychology of fatigue and motivation, and the Principal reported to its Council in 1923 that 'in approaching the big business interests we have tapped a new source, and it is evident that business recognises its debt to the College'.[79] Here was the prospect of a rationally exploited moral victory, over the crude inhumanities of supply and demand schedules on the one hand, and the social warfare of class solidarity on the other.

The growing concern, reflected here, with industrial rationalisation and scientific management, which 'sought to combine the production, accounting and personnel aspects of its job within one comprehensive philosophy which embraced planning, co-ordination and control', informed initiatives from both sides behind the Conference on Industrial Reorganisation and Industrial Relations of 1928–9 (Mond–Turner talks).[80] Bentinck and Ammon were among the leading early promoters of a Conference. After the trauma of 1926, there was widespread support from pulpit and press and appeals for an industrial Locarno became a commonplace in ICF circles. But characteristically, the appeals were generalised in the promotional rhetoric, and specific structural tensions were ignored. The Mond–Turner discussions took place in a complex situation and could bring the two sides together only in some areas. Most of the Mond–Turner employers, like Muspratt of ICI, 'represented large-scale science based industries such as chemicals, rubber and oil, and the newer domestically oriented and capital-intensive industries', whilst the employers most hostile to the suppositions on which the talks were based, in the FBI and the National Confederation of Employers' Organisations, were in basic industries, and for that reason 'particularly conscious of costs and, in important instances, of the objective of preserving managerial authority'.[81] There was hostility where convenient special relationships were threatened, such as the one between Havelock Wilson and the shipowners, for example.[82] Hichens himself had always been sceptical about arbitration in practice, and, though he commended the general orientation of the talks from a platform shared by Thomas, was always ready to draw attention to the critical point at which exhortation and conciliation must be superseded by harsher constraints.[83]

The consensual ideology was of course projected on to an international plane where, indeed, radical solutions to some domestic problems were taken to lie. The ICF itself was not in any degree to concentrate on international issues, but they were a major preoccupation for many of its leading figures. Support for the League of Nations was generally taken for granted within the organisation, though there were sceptics like Hichens and outright imperialists like the Right Rev. G. H. Frodsham, Vicar of Halifax and formerly Bishop of Queensland, who put more confidence in Empire and Commonwealth.[84] Henderson and Parmoor collaborated actively with Benes and Politis in producing the 'Protocol for the Pacific Settlement of International Disputes' (Geneva Protocol), which was not, however, ratified by the Conservative Government and might not have been by MacDonald's had he stayed in power.[85] Bentinck was active in establishing the League of Nations Union, and Elvin was on its Executive and a Vice-President of the International Arbitration League. At the more pragmatic level of attempts to rationalise post-war commodity and labour markets, Hichens was involved, as were Bowerman, Poulton, Tuckwell and Constance Smith.[86]

The ICF's rhetoric on war, conflict and co-operation surely fed into the appeasement climate of the following decade. Until September 1938, appeasement was a confident and unapologetic doctrine, part of conservative orthodoxy, but sustained more widely by guilt over Versailles and over responsibility for the war, and also by Christian sentiments of fair play, forgiveness and reconciliation.[87] Late in the day Dick Sheppard was proposing a prayer mission to Berchtesgaden and his and Studdert Kennedy's anti-war sermons in the twenties affected a great many people. Many saw in them a reaffirmation of principles which nonconformity had painfully abandoned during the war.[88] In 1938, on the other hand, a year after taking over from Bevin as Chairman of the TUC, Elvin was criticising the Church's contribution to appeasement. Hichens at this level was a Hobbesian realist in an unregenerate world, despite his close personal connections with Geoffrey Dawson, Editor of *The Times*, Lionel Curtis and Philip Kerr (Lord Lothian), leading *Round Table* figures among the appeasers castigated by A. L. Rowse.[89]

General Maurice's commitment to the doctrine, however, continued into the final period of nervous submission to threats. Maurice had undergone a conversion in 1919 'to the conclusion that preparation for war, carried to the point to which it had been carried in 1914, was a direct cause of war', and he made this 'confession of faith' to Lord Robert Cecil, promising him what help he could.[90] From around 1935, three years after taking over as President of the British Legion, he was promoting friendly contacts with German ex-servicemen's associations, and at the end of September 1938, perhaps as part of Chamberlain's attempt to keep in touch with Hitler in case 'he needed help in getting off the hook his bluff had put him on',[91] he personally visited Hitler to propose that the Legion should provide up to 10,000 ex-servicemen to supervise the transfer of the Czech territories to Germany. Hitler refused, but by some error the men embarked at Tilbury.[92] Maurice's support for international co-operation had not always been so misplaced. He was drawing attention to starvation and malnutrition in Europe shortly after the war, in Temple's *Pilgrim*, when this was not a popular theme.[93]

The leading lay supporters of the ICF were influential in a variety of contexts and their orientation was expressed in a corresponding variety of ways, ranging from windy educational rhetoric, through life-long involvement in trade union activities and labour law, to successful and widely admired careers in management. In every case they saw their public lives as attempts to realise social potentialities assured by the reality and authority of a transcending purpose, and they accepted that, in their most general and comprehensive form, the values, judgements and commitments truly emerging from a shared, underlying and illuminating structure of beliefs were clarified and promoted by the activities of the Industrial Christian Fellowship.

9 Conclusion

It so happens that one individual who appears in this account, R. H. Tawney, made a major contribution to a debate, which has been of great importance to the social and historical sciences, about the relationship between religious beliefs and other kinds of value and behaviour. Max Weber and Tawney developed closely related explanations, which are all too easy to oversimplify, of the dynamics of crucial developments in Europe by proposing a determining relationship between Puritan doctrine and Capitalism.[1] The complex of beliefs in the Puritan doctrinal code, if their accounts are to be followed, on a straightforward reading provided bearings for conduct pointing in one direction which, however, proved vulnerable to a polar distortion in a particular psychological field of force, and led to contradictory and puzzling historical consequences. The classical debate they initiated raised issues that have a bearing even on investigations as limited as this. A fundamental methodological problem pointed out by their critics is the extraordinary difficulty of either specifying, or establishing any correlation between, such vague and broad concepts as Protestantism and Capitalism. There is another difficulty in the implicit and necessarily contentious claim on their part to a privileged access, through the insights of a theory, to the hidden and truly significant meaning of the values they were concerned with.

The vagueness and broadness of these concepts of Protestantism and Capitalism have been taken to reflect a theoretical weakness in their explanations. But Ernest Gellner, in the course of discussing a contribution to this debate, has pointed out that the 'Puritan' and 'Capitalist' notions that have been historically entertained are imprecise in themselves, and that

> it would be an absurd requirement to restrict sociological interpretation to clear and distinct concepts; these are historically a rarity, and there is nothing to make one suppose that vague and broad notions, whose logical implications for conduct are ill-

determined, do not in fact have a powerful and specific impact on actual behaviour.[2]

This comment can surely be applied to the notions with which this study has been concerned, though they are not at the same level of comprehensive historical generality as the central categories explored by Weber and Tawney. There can be no question about their vagueness and broadness, and if at many points different categories of belief and value, religious, political, economic, have leaked incontinently into each other, it can be argued that that is precisely what they tended to do in this particular arena. Ideas with various and complex historical roots, in no sense, of course, the monopoly of the organisation, were being used by it at different levels of development and articulation, exchanged in moderately elaborate but nonetheless diffuse versions among the members of a somewhat heterogeneous élite, reduced to crude outlines in a public forum, but at every level hinting at sleeping assumptions and implications which are not explicitly formulated and explored. This ideology guided those who were most actively engaged by it, and appears also to have met the inarticulate expectations of a wider public. The material for this account constitutes a valid problem for interpretation in Gellner's terms.

Gellner goes on to point out that what faces the social scientist, whatever the specific nature of the problem he is addressing, is 'the unfortunate need to *interpret* just what the concepts in question meant to the participants'. This calls for caution since the course one must necessarily follow is to examine the uses these concepts are put to in a relevant context. But 'context' is itself a theoretical construct, deriving from an interpretation of a particular social structure: facts that are taken to have contextual relevance are recognised from a particular perspective, while those that are not are ignored.

At one level this has not been an intractable problem, because the more articulate individuals have elaborated on their beliefs in relation to their various activities, and one becomes aware of a series of durable systems of belief, each with distinctive priorities and applications, but sharing certain pervasive characteristics. It does not seem worth asking in general terms the difficult psychological question about the relative dominance of one category of value or belief over another, but a shifting blend of notions, incorporating assumptions about the social structure, the economy, the political system and the claims of religious faith can be understood as far as the participants themselves are concerned in terms of the patterns exposed in this ideological activity and the variety of public activities rationalised by it. A consideration that goes no further than this at least demonstrates the existence in Tawney's own environment of a complex interpenetration of religion and capitalism, though it is not directly illuminated by his own treatment of these ideas.

But as interpretation moves on to the impact of these developments, the question of a relevant context becomes more problematic, because a theme has been developed which suggests that the general undesigned effect of the activities of the ICF and its supporters in this period was to obscure and distract attention from structural conflicts in post-war British society, to encourage an inadequate and tendentious understanding of them in terms that were consistent with some interests and possibilities but not others. This interpretation places the organisation in the context of assumptions about the social structure which its supporters would not recognise and in relation to purposes whose legitimacy they would not accept.

Occasional judgements passed on the ICF within the main stream of Anglican social thought assess it in relation to its own explicit intentions. In that perspective, its failure—for industry manifestly had no inclination to proclaim Christ as the Lord of all Life—is accounted for either on the unanswerable grounds naturally employed by the Messenger,

> When Jesus came to Birmingham they simply passed Him by,
> They never hurt a hair of Him, they only let Him die;
> ('Indifference')

or else it is accounted for in terms of some inadequacy of approach, along the lines of Vidler's Foreword to Oliver's study of the Church and social order in the interwar period, when there was, he says, 'an awful lot of amateurishness and lack of expertise', people *saying* things rather than *doing* things.[3] The ICF, in short, was another tactical failure, containing useful lessons, presumably, for subsequent industrial mission work, but at that time misconceiving its role.

But from the perspective implicit in the present account this is a puzzling conclusion. If the historical evidence suggests anything, it is that for an organisation with diffuse promotional objectives, the ICF was successful with a substantial proportion of the people it had the resources to reach. It attracted support and enthusiastic attention. Its leading speaker became a household name, while its most eminent promoters publicly endorsed and participated in its activities. In the light of an extended analysis of the content and composition of its message, this evidence of success is not so difficult to understand, because what comes into view is a composite message, incorporating elements that have little direct and necessary connection with anything that can be located in the gospels, a lattice-work of broadly developed but powerful organising ideas, which were rooted in the expectations and needs of specific social groups. They can be placed, in fact, in a historical context of some depth. Guiding assumptions about the 'economic system' have been described here in relation to immediate anxieties about post-war destabilisation. But, as Albert Hirschman points out, the capitalistic structural developments which, according to Weber, derived from a desperate search for individual salvation, were accepted by the intellectual, managerial and administrative élites of the period he was concerned with in 'an equally desperate search for a way of avoiding society's ruin'.[4] The 'economic realism', the dogma about a structure of productive relations that is simultaneously fragile and potent, vulnerable to appetitive social energies but the only means of shaping them to harmoniously productive ends, has a secular history which is only intelligible in relation to continuously precarious and inherently unstable relations of power in industrial society. The movement of general ideas to which the ICF contributed was at best equivocal and at worst wilfully indifferent to the implications of this instability. It took for granted the establishment's characterisation of social ruin and of the activities most likely to precipitate it.

A striking symptom of this in relation to the ICF itself is to be found in the ways in which the enemy or opposition is represented. Surprisingly little reference is made to the question of unbelief. The challenge is represented by a network of notions, all taken in unspecified ways to be correlates of unbelief, but all primarily invoking a threat to imperfect but subsisting social arrangements, or, and this is as important, to what are taken to be the possibilities for their logical and rational consolidation and extension. It is much too simple to say that what seemed to be at risk was a mere *status quo*, for there was a pervasive commitment to the notion of a progressive evolution. But some possible developments in the public domain were seen as consistent with that vague notion and others were not. Those that were not were quite inadequately characterised. To have treated them in any other way would have opened up substantive arguments about inadmissible possibilities. So we hear a great deal about 'Marx' at every level, from the Messenger and his colleagues, and from the local agents who dutifully referred to their endeavours in areas 'infested with subversive propaganda'.[5] In the Messenger's vocabulary particularly there is the virtually interchangeable term of socialism. But neither alternative is permitted reasonable access to its own conceptual structure. Both are thus kept at the level of caricature.

The effect is to suggest that there is a radical polarisation of alternatives, an apocalypse on the one hand, and, on the other, hope and reason, which is given a much more differentiated treatment, an organic social structure, capable of responding to a natural leadership of guardian experts, who have outgrown the competitive motives of the political market place, functionally integrated norms, a dynamic entrepreneurial structure, and so on.

The threat from a thorough-going radicalism was, it is true, generally and wildly overplayed at the time, and there was in reality no serious prospect of the horrors kept in view throughout the decade by the crusaders. To a more perceptive observer, G. D. H. Cole, the socialist political scene at the end of the war in fact 'seemed already polarised between an irrelevant "revolutionary" Communism and a tepid parliamentary Labourism'.[6] For a number of reasons, developed in Wright's study, Cole's own concern with 'the demand for access *to* social power', which was in any case marxist only in a qualified sense, entered a quiescent phase in the 1920s. The Guild Movement had subsided and many of the more radical militants had moved elsewhere. Economic circumstances were unpropitious and the organised Labour Movement unreceptive. Cole's own position as a theorist, simultaneously gradualist and revolutionary, was in itself ambivalent.[7] But quite generally at the time, the impulse to develop even a muted radicalism into effective political activity was weak and confused. Such as it was, however, it confronted a public consciousness inhospitable to its appeal. The significance of the ICF in this period, whatever its explicit intentions, was in its sustained contribution to this amorphous public opinion.

> It was . . . a radical view of power which Cole sought to inject into the British socialist tradition—a tradition which, as Samuel Beer has nicely demonstrated, had embraced a paternal governmentalism rooted in a view of power common to much of British life.[8]

It was the tradition of paternal governmentalism that reasserted its dominance between the wars, consolidating round an emerging structure of relationships between the State and new formations of economic power and social control.[9] It was served by new theories of management, industrial relations and rationalisation. It called on the bureaucratic expertise of the post-war Fabians. It promised to institutionalise organised Labour as a collective interest. It further diminished the significance of the parliamentary parties, and secured their complicity. Representative elements from all these interests saw the ICF as a constructive adjunct in the education of the public.

The application of a radical critique to this trend was an esoteric minority affair, quite unable to compete with the rhetorical and ideological resources at the disposal of Baldwin, for example, as he presided over the successful reconstitution of the post-war political order. The figure of Baldwin in the twenties is perhaps the best Epilogue to this account. He was annoyed with the 'bishops' in 1926 simply because they were getting in the way. But his tenacious pursuit of a strategy of conciliation, moulded by the strikes of 1910–12, was made that much easier by a climate of opinion receptive to his own characteristically limpid rhetoric, which effectively conveyed a gentlemanly confidence in the modest and moderate Christianity which he believed would stimulate national solidarity and avoid class conflict. Important figures in each of the main parties also held to that belief. Baldwin's motives as a healer of national divisions were far from straightforward; the process of conciliation that enabled Labour to form its first government also 'dished' Lloyd George and the Liberals and simultaneously weakened the position of the more radical elements in the Labour Movement. But he demonstrated convincingly his commitment to an organic vision of the society, which was integral to his own faith as a churchman. Perhaps exceptionally for a politician, daily prayer, with its commitment to work 'for the country and God's sake', was a sustaining reality for him. In the famous Edinburgh speech of July 1923, in which he took up the challenge of 'those who want to fight the class war' and offered to 'beat them by the hardness of our heads and the largeness of our hearts', he was speaking directly for the 'Mind of the Age', as it was optimistically identified by Temple and more anxiously served by *the Industrial Christian Fellowship*.[10]

Notes

CHAPTER 1. INTRODUCTION

1. Robert Currie, Alan Gilbert, Lee Horsley, *Churches and Churchgoers: patterns of church growth in the British Isles since 1700* (OUP, 1977) p. 112.
2. K. Middlemas and J. Barnes, *Baldwin: a biography* (Weidenfeld and Nicolson, 1969) p. 433.
3. P. d'A Jones, *The Christian Socialist Revival, 1877–1914* (Princeton, 1968) pp. 165–224.
4. David Butler and Donald Stokes, *Political Change in Britain* (Macmillan, 1969) pp. 123–34.
5. M. Freeden, *The New Liberalism* (OUP, 1978) p. 50.
6. Edward Norman, *Christianity and the World Order* (OUP, 1979).
7. E. R. Norman, *Church and Society in England, 1770–1970* (OUP, 1976).
8. S. Mayor, *The Churches and the Labour Movement* (Independent Press, 1967).
9. Robert Moore, *Pit-Men, Preachers and Politics: the effects of Methodism in a Durham mining community* (CUP, 1974) p. 228.
10. Clifford Geertz, 'Religion as a Cultural System', in Michael Banton (ed.), *Anthropological Approaches to the Study of Religion* (Tavistock, 1966) p. 39.
11. *Ibid*, p. 4.
12. E.g. the Rev. the Hon E. Lyttelton, *The Mind and Character of Henry Scott Holland* (Mowbray, 1926) Ch VI, 'Zeal for Social Reform'.
13. G. L. Prestige, *The Life of Charles Gore* (Heinemann, 1935) p. 99.
14. E.g. C. Gore, *The Sermon on the Mount* (Murray, 1896).
15. Norman, *Church and Society, op cit*, pp. 339–40; Robert Craig, *Social Concern in the Thought of William Temple* (Gollancz, 1963) p. 139.
16. H. Henson, *Diaries*, 17 Feb 1925, Chapter Library, Durham.
17. Geertz, *op cit*, p. 39.
18. Freeden, *op cit*, p. 145.
19. Craig, *op cit*.

CHAPTER 2. THE FOUNDATION OF THE ICF

1. W. R. Inge, *All Saints Sermons* (London, 1907) p. 71. Quoted in Norman, *Church and Society, op cit*, p. 260.
2. *Ibid*, Ch 6–8.
3. Jones, *op cit*, p. 177.

4. G. C. Binyon, *The Christian Socialist Movement in England* (SPCK, 1931) p. 162.
5. Quoted in Jones, *op cit*, p. 213.
6. Jones, *op cit*, p. 185; W. Tuckwell, *Christian Socialism and other lectures* (Simpkin and Marshall, 1891).
7. Ross McKibbin, *The Evolution of the Labour Party, 1910–1924* (OUP, 1974).
8. *Society for the Study of Labour History, Bulletin*, 34, 1977, p. 3.
9. Freeden, *op cit*, p. 197.
10. Stuart MacIntyre, Review of McKibbin, *SSLH Bulletin*, 31, Autumn, 1975.
11. Jones, *op cit*, pp. 186–8; R. Barnes, 'Canon Donaldson and Leicester unemployed, 1905', *SSLH Bulletin*, 5, Autumn, 1962.
12. Jones, *op cit*, pp. 177 ff.
13. *Ibid*, p. 255.
14. *Ibid*, p. 164.
15. *Church Socialist*, 1, No 1, 1912, p. 5; Jones, *op cit*, pp. 225–301.
16. D. A. Wagner, *The Church of England and Social Reform since 1854* (Columbia, 1930) p. 306.
17. Memorandum of interview with G. A. Studdert Kennedy, 2 Mar 1923, *Archbishop Davidson Papers*, Lambeth Palace Library.
18. M. Reckitt, *Faith and Society* (Longmans, 1932) pp. 116–21.
19. Wagner, *loc cit*, pp. 306–9.
20. Roger Lloyd, *The Church of England, 1900–1965* (London, 1966).
21. W. Purcell, *Woodbine Willie: an Anglican Incident* (Hodder and Stoughton, 1962).
22. J. Oliver, *The Church and Social Order: Social Thought in the Church of England, 1918–1939* (London, 1968), pp. 65 ff.
23. Norman, *Church and Society*, *op cit*, p. 228.
24. Jones, *op cit*, p. 213.
25. T. Coleman, *The Railway Navvies* (Hutchinson, 1965) Ch 10, 'Sin and Sanctity'.
26. E. H. Lurkings, 'The Navvy Mission Society; its founding and ministry, 1877–1920', *ICF Quarterly*, Centenary Number, July 1977.
27. *Quarterly Report and Trade Journal of the Navvies, Builders' Labourers and General Labourers Union*, Vol 2, No 97, May 1914.
28. *Birmingham Post*, 26 Apr 1916.
29. *The Thirty Eighth Annual Report of the Navvy Mission Society*, Apr 1915–Mar 1916.
30. H. K. Hawson, *Sheffield: the growth of a city* (Sheffield, 1968), p. 215.
31. *History of the Ministry of Munitions*, Vol VIII, Part II, The National Factories, p. 143.
32. W. Johnson, *The Development of the Kent Coalfields, 1896–1946*, Ph.D. Thesis, University of Kent, 1972, pp. 62, 86; *The Times*, 24 Jan, 13 Feb, 2, 9, 17 Apr, 7 May, 28 June 1924.
33. Coal Industry Commission, Vol II, *Reports and minutes of evidence on the second stage of the Inquiry*, P.P. 1919 (Cd 360) XII, pp. 705–6.
34. S. Pollard, *The Development of the British Economy, 1914–1967* (Arnold, 1969) p. 270; Eric Wigham, *The Power to Manage: a history of the Engineering Employers Federation* (Macmillan, 1973), p. 1.
35. Michael Bentley, *The Liberal Mind, 1914–1929* (CUP, 1977).

36. *History of the Ministry of Munitions*, Vol II, General Organisation of Munitions Supply, Part IV, Munitions Organisation in Canada, pp. 14 ff.
37. D. Carnegie, *Can Church and Industry Unite?* (London, 1920).
38. C. Dilke, *Dr Moberly's Mint Mark* (Heinemann, 1965).
39. *Lionel Hichens*, n.d.
40. Walter Nimocks, *Milner's Young Men: the 'kindergarten' in Edwardian Imperial Affairs* (Durham, NC, 1968) p. 44.
41. *Ibid*, p. 69.
42. Robert J. Scally, *The Origins of the Lloyd George Coalition: the politics of social imperialism, 1900–1918* (Princeton, 1975) p. 158; Lord Riddell, *Diary of the Peace Conference and after, 1918–1923* (Gollancz, 1933) p. 329.
43. J. E. Kendle, 'The Round Table Movement and "Home Rule all round" ', *Historical Journal*, XI, 3, 1968, 332–53.
44. Lucy Masterman, *C. F. G. Masterman: a Biography* (Frank Cass, 1969. First edn., 1939).
45. Charles Hobhouse, *Inside Asquith's Cabinet* (Murray, 1977) E. David (ed.), p. 60.
46. Lord Milner, *The Nation and the Empire*, p. 161, cited in B. Semmel, *Imperialism and Social Reform: English Social-imperialist thought; 1895–1914* (Allen and Unwin, 1960) p. 184.
47. Scally, *op cit*, p. 159. He cites a letter from Milner to Sir Clinton Dawkins.
48. *Vide* e.g. *History of the Ministry of Munitions*, Vol V, Part II, The control of women's wages, p. 69.
49. W. L. Hichens, 'Some problems of modern industry', *Papers of the Greenock Philosophical Society* (London, 1918).
50. Scally, *op cit*, p. 311.
51. *Ibid*, p. 311.
52. P. F. Clarke, *Lancashire and the New Liberalism* (CUP, 1971) p. 207.
53. H. Slesser, *Judgment Reserved* (Hutchinson, 1941) pp. 138, 88.
54. *Ibid*, p. 122.
55. *Ibid*, p. 25.
56. William Gallacher, *Revolt on the Clyde* (Lawrence and Wishart, 1978. First edn., 1936) p. 184.
57. *History of the Ministry of Munitions*, Vol IV, The Supply and Control of Labour, Part ii, Labour Regulation and the Munitions of War (Amendment) Act, 1916, pp. 56 ff.
58. C. Wrigley, *David Lloyd George and the British Labour Movement* (Harvester, 1976) p. 159.
59. Gallacher, *op cit*, p. 105.
60. Lynden Macassey, *Labour Policy False and True* (Thornton Butterworth, 1922) p. 76.
61. Slesser, *op cit*, p. 57.
62. Lord Askwith, *Industrial Problems and Disputes* (Murray, 1920) p. 352.
63. *Ibid*, p. 320.
64. H. Slesser, *A History of the Liberal Party* (Hutchinson, 1944) p. 148.
65. M. Cowling, *The Impact of Labour: 1920–1924* (CUP, 1971) p. 97; Bentley, *op cit*, p. 67.

66. *Bath Herald*, 20 Apr 1907.
67. *Scotsman*, 28 Apr 1923.
68. C. A. Cline, *Recruits to Labour: the British Labour Party, 1914–1931* (Syracuse, 1963).
69. Maclean to H. Gladstone, 14 June 1929, cited by Bentley, *op cit*.
70. Bentley, *op cit*, p. 67; Cowling, *op cit*, p. 69.
71. Bentley, *op cit*, p. 80.
72. *Ibid*, p. 86.
73. Robert Blake (ed.), *The Private Papers of Douglas Haig, 1914–1919* (Eyre and Spottiswood, 1954) p. 50.
74. Nancy Maurice (ed.), *The Maurice Case* (Leo Cooper, 1972).
75. Peter Rowland, *Lloyd George* (Barrie and Jenkins, 1975) pp. 440–5.
76. Paul Guinn, *British Strategy and Politics, 1914 to 1918* (OUP, 1965).
77. Lord Hankey, *The Supreme Command, 1914–1918*, Vol 2 (Allen and Unwin, 1961) p. 446.
78. Nancy Maurice, *op cit*, p. 60.
79. The *Church Times*, 14 Nov 1919.
80. Asquith to Maclean, n.d. *Maclean Papers*, Bodleian Library.
81. G. A. Studdert Kennedy, *Democracy and the Dog Collar* (Hodder and Stoughton, 1921), p. 221. Hereafter cited as *DDC*.
82. G. Tuckwell and C. Smith, *The Workers Handbook* (Duckworth, 1908).
83. S. S. Bullock and E. C. P. Lascelles, *Dock Labour and Decasualisation* (P. S. King, 1926).
84. G. Tuckwell, 'The human interest in industry', *Fortnightly Review*, 91, July 1919; *A Short Life of Sir Charles Dilke* (London, 1925).
85. G. Tuckwell, 'The State and its Children', in H. de B. Gibbins (ed.), *Social Questions of Today* (Methuen, 1891) p. 16.
86. Roy Jenkins, *Sir Charles Dilke: a Victorian tragedy* (Collins, 1965).
87. *Trades Union Congress Report*, 1921, pp. 224–7.
88. Cowling, *op cit*, p. 55.
89. E. N. Bennett, *Apollonius: or the future of psychical research* (Kegan Paul, 1927); 'Ghosts and haunted houses', in T. Besterman (ed.), *Inquiry into the unknown: a BBC Symposium* (Methuen, 1934).
90. W. Citrine, *Men and Work* (Hutchinson, 1964) p. 74.
91. Paul Thompson, *Socialists, Liberals and Labour: the struggle for London, 1885–1914* (Routledge and Kegan Paul, 1966) p. 171.
92. Bentley B. Gilbert, *The Evolution of National Insurance in Great Britain* (London, 1966), p. 119.
93. George Edwards, *From Crow-scaring to Westminster: an autobiography* (London, 1922) Ch XVII; Reg Groves, *Sharpen the Sickle: the history of the Farm Workers Union* (London, 1949).
94. M. A. Hamilton, *Arthur Henderson* (Heinemann, 1938) p. 218.
95. Margaret Cole (ed.), *The Diaries of Beatrice Webb, 1912–1924* (Longmans, 1952), pp. 163–4.
96. F. R. Barry, *Period of My Life* (Hodder and Stoughton, 1970) p. 114.

CHAPTER 3. THE WAR AND 'WOODBINE WILLIE'

1. Bentley B. Gilbert, *British Social Policy, 1914–1939* (Batsford, 1970) pp. 75–8.

2. C. L. Mowat, *Britain Between the Wars* (Methuen, 1955) p. 127.
3. D. Marquand, *Ramsay MacDonald* (Jonathan Cape, 1977) p. 271.
4. Pollard, *op cit*, p. 210.
5. J. Harris, *Unemployment and Politics: a study of English Social Policy, 1880–1914* (OUP, 1972) Ch 3.
6. Pollard, *op cit*, p. 217.
7. *Financier*, 2 Feb 1921.
8. *Weekly Dispatch*, 6 Feb 1921, 'Getting Trade Back'; *Daily Sketch*, 22 Jan, 5 Feb; *Sheffield Telegraph*, 19 Feb; *Evening News*, 18 March; *Journal of Commerce*, 29 Apr, 'High Wages and Industrial Depression'; *National News*, 8 May, 'The only road to prosperity'; *Evening Standard*, 10 May; *Evening Standard*, 26 May, 'Where are we going?'; *Sunday Herald*, 5 June; *Liverpool Echo*, 11 July; *Evening Standard*, 22 July, 'Watch the German Workman'; *The Times*, 5 Oct; *Westminster Gazette*, 10 Dec, 'World Financial Crisis'; Cammell Laird and Co, *Report of the Proceedings of the 57th Ordinary General Meeting*, Apr 1921.
9. *Evening Standard*, 24 Oct 1921.
10 Hichens to the Bishop of Barking, 19 July 1920, in response to a request for comment on the draft of the *Report of the Industrial and Social Questions Committee* of the Lambeth Conference.
11. L. T. Hobhouse, 'The Right to a Living Wage', in W. Temple (ed.), *The Industrial Unrest and the Living Wage* (The Collegium, 1913) p. 73.
12. Jones, *op cit*, pp. 198 ff.
13. P. F. Clarke, *Liberals and Social Democrats* (CUP, 1978) p. 49.
14. *The Official Report of the Poor Law Conference, 1920–1* (London, 1921) p. 13.
15. Mowat, *op cit*, p. 124.
16. Cd 8197, '*Report on Transfer of Functions of Poor Law Authorities in England and Wales*', Local Government Committee, Ministry of Reconstruction, 15 July 1918; Gilbert, *op cit*, p. 117; Pollard, *op cit*, p. 261.
17. Mowatt, *op cit*, p. 121.
18. Robert Graves, *Goodbye to All That* (Penguin, 1960) pp. 157–9.
19. Army Chaplains' Department Museum, Bagshot Park.
20. K. A. Thompson, *Bureaucracy and Church Reform* (OUP, 1970); S. Mews, *Religion and English Society in the First World War*, Ph. D.Thesis, Cambridge University, 1973; A. Marrin, *The Last Crusade* (Duke University, 1974); Alan Wilkinson, *The Church of England and the First World War* (SPCK, 1978).
21. Harry W. Blackburne, DSO, MC, *This Also Happened on the Western Front* (Hodder and Stoughton, 1932) p. 115.
22. S. C. Carpenter, *Winnington-Ingram* (Hodder and Stoughton, 1949) p. 279.
23. Marrin, *op cit*, p. 179.
24. L. Masterman, *op cit*, p. 290.
25. G. Coppard, *With a Machine Gun to Cambrai* (HMSO, 1969) p. 73; G. A. Studdert Kennedy, *Rough Talks by a Padre* (Hodder and Stoughton, 1918). Hereafter cited as *RT*.
26. Major R. S. Cockburn, MC, *First War Papers, 1916–18*, MSS, Imperial War Museum.
27. E.g. Neville S. Talbot, *Thoughts on Religion at the Front* (Macmillan, 1917);

Religion Behind the Front and after the War (Macmillan, 1918); A. Herbert Gray, *As Tommy Sees Us* (Edward Arnold, 1918); E. V. Tanner, MC and Bar, MSS *Diary*, Imperial War Museum; T. Pym and G. Gordon, *Papers from Picardy* (Constable, 1917).

28. D. Hankey, *A Student in Arms* (London, seven edns in 1916).
29. The Rev. J. H. Ellison, 'The epiphanies of the War', Sermon in St Paul's, *Guardian*, 15 Jan 1920.
30. Dennis Jones, *The Diary of a Padre at Suvla Bay* (The Faith Press, n.d.).
31. Gray, *op cit*, p. 3; Guy T. Rogers, MC, *Rebel at Heart* (Longmans, 1956) p. 121.
32. Pym, *op cit*, p. 75.
33. Dora Pym, *Tom Pym: a portrait* (Cambridge, 1952).
34. *The Commonwealth*, XXII, Mar 1919, p. 279, cited in K. A. Thompson, *op cit*, p. 153.
35. D. Eyre, *Reform in the Church of England* (Murray, 1915).
36. J. G. Lockhart, *Cosmo Gordon Lang* (Hodder and Stoughton, 1949), p. 256.
37. K. A. Thompson, *op cit*, p. 169.
38. Norman, *Church and Society*, *op cit*, p. 240.
39. F. R. Barry, *op cit*, p. 61.
40. F. B. Macnutt, *The Church in the Furnace* (Macmillan, 1917).
41. A. Vidler, *The Church in an Age of Revolution* (Penguin, 1961) Ch 19.
42. A. M. Ramsey, *From Gore to Temple* (Longmans, 1960) p. 102.
43. E. G. Selwyn (ed.), *Essays Catholic and Critical* (SPCK, 1926) p. 331.
44. J. K. Mozley, *The Heart of the Gospel* (SPCK, 1925) pp. 34–43.
45. Ramsey, *op cit*, pp. 92, 58; G. A. Studdert Kennedy, *The Hardest Part* (Hodder and Stoughton, 1919). Hereafter cited as *HP*.
46. Wilkinson, *op cit*; Paul Fussell, *The Great War and Modern Memory* (OUP, 1975).
47. Wilkinson, *op cit*, p. 116.
48. G. A. Studdert Kennedy, *Why aren't all the best chaps Christians?* R. S. Wright (ed.) (Hodder and Stoughton, 1939).
49. *Royal Army Chaplains' Department Quarterly*, 1, No 1, Jan 1922, p. 6.
50. Marrin, *op cit*, p. 196.
51. Interdenominational Advisory Committee on Army Chaplaincy Service, *Minutes*, 10.1.18 and 14.2.18, Army Chaplains' Department, Bagshot.
52. *S. Sassoon Papers*, Imperial War Museum, 17 May 1917.
53. D. F. Carey, 'Studdert Kennedy: War Padre', in J. K. Mozley (ed.), *Studdert Kennedy by his Friends* (Hodder and Stoughton, 1929) pp. 137–8.
54. Noel Chavasse was in the RAMC. J. B. Lancelot, *Francis James Chavasse* (Blackwell, 1929); G. Selwyn, *The Chavasse Twins* (Hodder and Stoughton, 1963).
55. Wilkinson, *op cit*, pp. 298–300.
56. The Bishop's Letter to his Diocese, *Guardian*, 23 Jan 1919.
57. W. Moore Ede, 'His Life in Worcester', in Mozley (ed.), *op cit*; C. M. Blagden, *Well Remembered* (Hodder and Stoughton, 1953) p. 170.
58. A. V. Baillie, *My First Eighty Years* (Murray, 1951) p. 142.
59. Carey, *loc cit*.
60. Wilkinson, *op cit*, pp. 76–89.

61. Quoted in Carey, *loc cit*, p. 124.

62. E. H. Jeffs, *Princes of the Modern Pulpit in England; religious leaders of a generation* (Cokesbury Press, 1931) pp. 155 ff., cited in Horton Davies, *Worship and Theology in England: the Ecumenical Century, 1900–65* (Princeton, 1965).

63. G. A. Studdert Kennedy, *Lies* (Hodder and Stoughton, 1921). Hereafter cited as *L*.

64. *HP*, p. 126.

65. *Private Papers of Douglas Haig*, *op cit*, p. 143.

66. Malcolm Muggeridge, *The Green Stick: Chronicles of Wasted Time*, Vol I (Fontana, 1975) p. 83.

67. Carolyn Smith, *Dick Sheppard* (Hodder and Stoughton, 1977).

68. Marrin, *op cit*, pp. 93–4; Wilkinson, *op cit*, p. 210.

69. H. W. Koch (ed.), *The Origins of the First World War* (Macmillan, 1972) pp. 2, 11; Fritz Fischer, *War of Illusions: German policies from 1911–1914* (Chatto and Windus, 1972) pp. 28–9.

70. N. Angell, *Prussianism and its destruction, with which is reprinted part 2 of The Great Illusion* (Heinemann, 1914); J. A. Cramb, *Germany and England* (Murray, 1914); *Treitschke: his life and works* translated into English for the first time (Jarrold, 1914); H. W. C. Davis, *The Political Thought of Heinrich von Treitschke* (Constable, 1914).

71. Cramb, *op cit*, p. 118.

72. C. Dilke, *The Present Position of European Politics* (London, 1887).

73. F. Maurice, *Life and Letters of Frederick Denison Maurice* (Macmillan, 1884).

74. Major General F. Maurice, CB, *National Defences* (Macmillan, 1897).

75. G. R. Searle, *The Quest for National Efficiency: a study in British politics and British political thought, 1899–1914* (Blackwell, 1970) p. 98; B. Semmel, *op cit*; Major General Sir Frederick Maurice, *Life of Lord Haldane* (Faber, 1937 and 1938).

76. *Church Times*, 11, 25 Feb 1921; R. T. Shannon, 'John Robert Seeley and the idea of a National Church', in R. Robson (ed.), *Ideas and Institutions in Victorian Britain* (Bell, 1967).

77. G. A. Studdert Kennedy, *The Wicket Gate* (Hodder and Stoughton, 1923), p. 83; *The Woman, the Warrior and the Christ* (Hodder and Stoughton, 1928) p. 150. Hereafter cited as *WG* and *WWC*.

78. Quoted in Carey, *loc cit*, pp. 127–9.

79. Purcell, *op cit*, p. 144.

80. *Guardian* and *Birmingham Town Crier*, 18 Nov 1921.

81. Review of *WWC* by C.E.R., *Liverpool Review*, IV, No 3, Mar 1929.

82. C. E. Raven, *Christian Socialism, 1848–54* (Macmillan, 1920).

83. L. T. Hobhouse, *The Metaphysical Theory of the State* (Allen and Unwin, 1918).

84. Jones, *op cit*, pp. 202–5.

85. Hobhouse, *op cit*, p. 43.

86. *Ibid*, p. 118.

87. *Ibid*, pp. 78–9.

88. *Ibid*, p. 125.

89. Rodney Barker, *Political Ideas in Modern Britain* (Methuen, 1928) p. 18.

90. Melvin Richter, *The Politics of Conscience: T. H. Green and his Age* (Weidenfeld and Nicolson, 1964) p. 212.
91. *Ibid*, pp. 194, 202.
92. P. Weiler, 'The New Liberalism of L. T. Hobhouse', *Victorian Studies*, Vol 16, 2, 1972–3; M. Richter, 'T. H. Green and his audience: Liberalism as a surrogate faith', *Review of Politics*, XVIII, Oct 1954.
93. Fussell, *op cit*, p. 118.
94. Owen to Osbert Sitwell, 4 July 1918, quoted in C. Day Lewis (ed.), *The Collected Poems of Wilfred Owen* (Chatto and Windus, 1963), p. 23.
95. Hobhouse, *op cit*, pp. 2–6.

CHAPTER 4.   ANGLICAN SOCIAL GOSPELS

1. F. A. Iremonger, *William Temple: Archbishop of Canterbury* (OUP, 1948).
2. Ross Terrill, *R. H. Tawney: Socialism as Fellowship* (Harvard, 1973) p. 57.
3. Freeden, *op cit*, p. 16.
4. *Ibid*, p. 50.
5. *Ibid*, p. 17.
6. Graeme Greene, *A Kind of Life* (Penguin, 1972) p. 50.
7. Richter, *op cit*.
8. *Ibid*, p. 116.
9. *Ibid*, p. 202.
10. Freeden, *op cit*, pp. 66–70; Stefan Collini, *Liberalism and Sociology: L. T. Hobhouse and Political Argument, 1880–1914* (CUP, 1979) pp. 164–5.
11. D. G. Ritchie, *Darwinism and Politics* (Swan Sonnenschein, 1889).
12. Terrill, *op cit*, pp. 24, 57 ff.
13. David Edwards, *Leaders of the Church of England, 1828–1944* (OUP, 1971) p. 266.
14. R. Tawney, *The Acquisitive Society* (London, 1921) p. 96.
15. *Ibid*, p. 43.
16. *Ibid*, p. 111.
17. *Ibid*, p. 226.
18. Terrill, *op cit*, p. 202.
19. *Ibid*, p. 205.
20. *Ibid*, p. 143.
21. R. Tawney, *The Attack and other Papers* (Allen and Unwin, 1953).
22. Terrill, *op cit*, pp. 32, 48.
23. Audrey Cunningham, *William Cunningham, Teacher and Priest* (SPCK, 1950) p. 50.
24. John Maloney, 'Marshall, Cunningham, and the emerging economics profession', *The Economic History Review*, XXIX, 3, Aug 1976, 440–51.
25. W. Cunningham, *Christianity and Social Questions* (London, 1910) pp. 14–16.
26. W. Cunningham, *British Citizens and their Responsibilities to God (SPCK, 1916); The Secret of Progress* (CUP, 1918); *Personal Ideals and Social Principles* (SPCK, 1919) p. 25.
27. W. Cunningham, *The Growth of English Industry and Commerce* (CUP, 1882) p. 418; *Strikes; an address delivered during the recent strike at Leicester, England* (Church Social Union, 1895); The Gospel of Work (CUP, 1902).
28. Cunningham, *Christianity and Social Questions, op cit*, p. 166.

29. W. Cunningham, *Socialism and Christianity* (SPCK, 1909) p. 13.
30. A. Vidler, *F. D. Maurice and Company* (SCM, 1966) p. 171.
31. Cunningham, *Christianity and Social Questions, op cit,* p. 75.
32. *Ibid,* p. 11.
33. *Ibid,* p. 112.
34. *Ibid,* p. 187.
35. *Ibid,* p. 89.
36. *Ibid,* p. 211.
37. *Ibid,* p. 105.
38. Cunningham, *Socialism and Christianity, op cit,* p. 19.
39. Cunningham, *Christianity and Social Questions, op cit,* p. 103.
40. *Ibid,* p. 26.
41. *Ibid,* pp. 51–2.
42. Norman, *Church and Society, op cit,* pp. 242–4; Cunningham, *Personal Ideals, op cit.*
43. W. R. Garside, 'Wage determination and the Miners' lock-out in 1892', in Norman McCord (ed.), *Essays in Tyneside Labour History,* Mimeo (Newcastle on Tyne Polytechnic, 1977), pp. 141–2.
44. Prestige, *op cit,* pp. 275, 277, 335; R. H. Tawney, 'The establishment of minimum rates in the chain-making industry under the Trade Boards Act of 1909', *Studies in the Minimum Wage,* No 1, 1914, Ratan Tata Foundation.
45. W. Cunningham, *The Causes of Labour Unrest and the Remedies for it* (Murray, 1912).
46. James Carpenter, *Gore: a study in Liberal Catholic Thought* (Faith Press, 1960) pp. 148 ff., 178 ff., 211–2; C. Gore, *Belief in God* (Murray, 1926, new edn.) pp. 63, 112 ff., 146, 155.
47. Gore, *Belief in God, op cit,* p. 60.
48. C. Gore, *Belief in Christ* (Murray, 1926, new edn.) pp. 613–14.
49. C. Gore, 'Strikes and Locks-out: the Way out', *Present Day Pamphlets,* No 1, 1926.
50. C. Gore, 'Christianity and Socialism', *Pan Anglican Papers* (London, 1908).
51. Gore, 'Strikes and Locks-out', *op cit,* p. 12.
52. Gore, Belief in Christ, *op cit,* p. 555.
53. Craig, *op cit,* p. 41.
54. A. E. Taylor, '*Mens Creatrix* by William Temple', *Mind,* Jan 1918; W. Temple, *Mens Creatrix* (Macmillan, 1917).
55. W. Temple, *The Faith and Modern Thought* (Macmillan, 1913) p. 142.
56. *Ibid,* p. 18.
57. E.g. W. Temple, *Christus Veritas* (Macmillan, 1924).
58. Collini, *op cit,* pp. 164–5; C. L. Morgan, *Emergent Evolution* Gifford Lectures, 1922, published as *Life, Mind and Spirit* (Williams and Norgate, 1925); S. Alexander, *Space, Time and Deity* (Macmillan, 1920).
59. Temple, *Mens Creatrix, op cit,* p. 174.
60. W. Temple, *The Nature of Personality* (Macmillan, 1911).
61. Temple, *Christus Veritas, op cit,* pp. 65 ff.
62. Temple, *Mens Creatrix, op cit,* pp. 187–8.
63. Alexander, *op cit,* p. 320.

64. Temple, *Christus Veritas, op cit,* p. 84.
65. Scally, *op cit,* p. 347; L. Curtis, *With Milner in South Africa* (Blackwell, 1951).
66. L. Curtis (ed.), *The Commonwealth of Nations* (London, 1916) pp. 8, 850. Cited in *Mens Creatrix, op cit,* pp. 211, 250.
67. H. C. G. Matthew, *The Liberal Imperialists* (OUP, 1973) pp. 288, 295.
68. Temple, *Mens Creatrix, op cit,* pp. 222–3.
69. Temple, *Christus Veritas, op cit,* pp. 204–5.
70. G. A. Studdert Kennedy, 'Playing the Game: there is only one team big enough to play for, and that is humanity', *The Torch,* Jan 1927.
71. Temple, *Mens Creatrix, op cit,* p. 224.
72. W. Temple, *Christianity and the State* (London, 1928) p. 84.
73. W. Temple, *Personal Religion and the life of Fellowship* (Longmans, 1926) p. 58.
74. Temple, *Personal Religion, op cit,* p. 52–3.
75. Iremonger, *op cit;* Joseph Fletcher, *William Temple: Twentieth Century Christian* (New York, 1963); Jack F. Padgett, *The Christian Philosophy of William Temple* (Hague, 1974).
76. W. Temple, 'The Man and his message', in Mozley (ed.), *G. A. Studdert Kennedy, op cit.*
77. Temple, *Personal Religion, op cit,* pp. 11–14; G. A. Studdert Kennedy, *The Word and the Work* (Hodder and Stoughton, 1929). Hereafter cited as *WW.*
78. Craig, *op cit,* pp. 21, 70–6, 98.
79. Owen to his mother, 1913, cited in John Silkin, *Out of Battle* (OUP, 1972) p. 198.
80. Gore, *Belief in Christ, op cit,* p. 564.
81. J. T. Merz, *A History of European Thought in the Nineteenth Century,* 4 vols (Blackwood, 1914); W. McDougall, *Body and Mind* (Methuen, 1911); C. H. S. Matthews, 'Studdert Kennedy, 1883–1929', in R. S. Forman (ed.), *Great Christians* (Nicholson and Watson, 1933) p. 315.
82. Collini, *op cit,* p. 173.
83. W. H. Mallock, *The Limits of Pure Democracy* (London, 1918) pp. 58–9, 126, 357; *L,* pp. 47, 50, 101.
84. John W. Mason, *Anti-socialist thought in Britain, 1880–1914,* Ph.D. Thesis, University of Birmingham, May 1975; D. J. Ford, 'W. H. Mallock and socialism in England', in K. D. Brown (ed.), *Essays in Anti-Labour History* (Macmillan, 1974).
85. E.g. S. Webb, 'Historic', in Bernard Shaw (ed.), *Fabian Essays* (Allen and Unwin, 3rd edn. 1920) p. 33; *Socialism in England* (Swan Sonnenschein, 1890) p. 94; 'The Basis and Policy of Socialism', *Fabian Socialist Series,* No 4, 1908, pp. 16, 25, 47.
86. Mallock, *op cit,* pp. 78–9.
87. A. A. Young, 'Mr Mallock as statistician and British income statistics', *Quarterly Journal of Economics,* Vol 25, 1911, p. 376.
88. H. B. Gray and Samuel Turner, *Eclipse or Empire?* (Nisbet, 1916).
89. *Ibid,* p. 24.
90. Macassey, *op cit,* p. 98.
91. Mason, *op cit,* p. 332.

92. W. H. Mallock, *Aristocracy and Evolution: a study of the rights, the origins and the social functions of the wealthier classes* (Black, 1898) p. 45, cited in Mason, *op cit*.
93. McDougall, *The Group Mind, op cit*.
94. L. W. Grenstead, *Psychology and God* (Longmans, 1930).
95. T. W. Pym, *Psychology and the Christian Life* (SCM, 1921); F. R. Barry, *Christianity and Psychology* (SCM, 1923).
96. C. Raven, 'Cult or Craze? Plain words on psycho-analysis', and H. Crighton-Miller, 'Canon Raven and psycho-analysis', *Diocese of Liverpool Review*, Vol 1, No 1, No 2, 1926.
97. *Church Times*, 3 Nov 1922.
98. G. A. Studdert Kennedy, *I Pronounce Them* (Hodder and Stoughton, 4 edns between 1927 and 1929). Reviewed with Sinclair Lewis' *Elmer Gantry*, in the *Church Times*, 22 Apr 1927.
99. Temple in Mozley (ed.), *op cit*, p. 206.
100. *WWC, op cit*.
101. J. A. Hobson and Morris Ginsberg, *L. T. Hobhouse: his life and work* (Allen and Unwin, 1931); M. Ginsberg, *The Psychology of Society* (Methuen, 1921); Ch 1, 'The General Nature of Instinct'.
102. Reba N. Soffer, *Ethics and Society in England: the revolution in the social sciences, 1870–1914* (University of California, 1978) Ch 10, 'Fear of the New Democracy: the setting for social psychology', Ch 11, 'Social Psychology as a solution: William McDougall, Wilfred Trotter, and the Elitist Refuge'.
103. E.g. Wilfred Trotter, *Instincts of the Herd in Peace and War* (London, 1916).
104. McDougall, *Group Mind, op cit*. p. 20.
105. *Ibid*, p. 80.
106. *Ibid*, p. 61.
107. *Ibid*, p. 64.
108. Soffer, *op cit*, p. 218.
109. Francis Mulhern, *The Moment of 'Scrutiny'* (NLB, 1979) p. 188.

CHAPTER 5. VERSE AND RHETORIC

1. *The Atheneum*, 20 June 1914.
2. I. A. Richards, 'Poem IV' and references in the text of *Practical Criticism* (Kegan Paul, 1929); Roy Fuller, ' "Woodbine Willie" Lives!', Ch 2 of *Owls and Artificers* (Deutsch, 1971), the first volume of his lectures as Professor of Poetry at Oxford.
3. C. K. Stead, *The New Poetic* (Hutchinson, 1964) p. 90.
4. Raymond Williams, *Culture and Society, 1780–1950* (Penguin, 1961) p. 245.
5. Fuller, *op cit*, p. 33.
6. Personal communication.
7. Jon Silkin (ed.), *The Penguin Book of First World War Poetry*, 1979; *Out of Battle, op cit*.
8. Fussell, *op cit*; M. Howard, Review in *The Times Literary Supplement*, 4 Dec 1976.
9. *A Choice of Kipling's Verse, made by T. S. Eliot, with an Essay on Rudyard Kipling* (Faber, 1941).
10. Stead, *op cit*, pp. 131 ff.

11. Fussell, *op cit*, p. 26.
12. Stead, *op cit*, p. 75.
13. Charles Carrington, *Rudyard Kipling* (Macmillan, 1955) p. 305.
14. E.g. W. Bainbridge-Bell, *Repentance and Perseverance* (London, 1902); J. Sinker, *Through the Grace and Gate of Death* (London, 1919); F. B. Macnutt, *From Chaos to God* (London, 1929); W. P. G. McCormick, *Be of Good Cheer* (Longmans Green, 1930).
15. Henson, *Diaries*, 3 Aug 1923.
16. *The Torch*, May 1926.
17. Lord Birkenhead, *Rudyard Kipling* (Weidenfeld and Nicolson, 1978) pp. 70, 98.
18. Silkin, *Out of Battle*, *op cit*, Ch 3 and 9.
19. *St Martin-in-the-Fields Review*, Mar, Apr, July 1920.
20. G. A. Studdert Kennedy 'The unwanted woman: should we revolutionise marriage to help her?' *The Torch*, July 1926.
21. R. K. Alspach and C. C. Alspach, *The Variorum Edition of the Plays of W. B. Yeats* (Macmillan, 1966).
22. Temple, *Mens Creatrix*, *op cit*, pp. 115–16.
23. B. Litzinger, *Time's Revenges: Browning's reputation as a thinker, 1889–1962* (University of Tennessee, 1954); Graeme Greene, *op cit*, pp. 84–6.
24. Temple, *The Nature of Personality*, *op cit*, xxxii.

CHAPTER 6.   THE CHURCH PUBLIC OF THE ICF
1. E.g. J. Oliver, *op cit*, p. 118; Norman, *Church and Society*, *op cit*, p. 316; John Barnes, *Ahead of his Age* (Collins, 1979), p. 400.
2. A. M. Scott, *Diaries*, 12 Jan 1925, University of Glasgow. It was not Scott himself, who joined the Labour Party in 1925.
3. The *Guardian*, 6 April 1923.
4. Hubert Handley, *The Fatal Opulence of Bishops* (London, 1901); *The More Fatal Opulence of Bishops* (Allen and Unwin, 1919).
5. H. M. Blalock, *Social Statistics* (McGraw Hill, 1960) p. 324.
6. H. L. Hubbard, *Social Prayer; Studies in the Lord's Prayer as the Prayer of Social Action and the expression of Social Needs* (London, 1919).
7. Archbishop C. G. Lang to Baldwin, 3 July 1923, *Lang Papers*, Borthwick Institute, York.
8. H. A. Wilson, *Reflections of a Back Bench Bishop* (London, 1948).

CHAPTER 7.   THE ICF IN ACTION
1. Birkenhead, *op cit*, p. 301.
2. Oliver, *op cit*, pp. 80 ff; Stuart Mews, 'The Church' in M. Morris (ed.), *The General Strike* (Penguin 1976).
3. *Church Times*, 14 Jan, 20 May 1921; 16 June 1922, 16 Feb; 25 May 1923; 22 Feb, 4 Apr 1924; 20 Feb, 22 May 1925; 12 Feb, 4 June 1926; 11 Feb 1927; 10 Feb 1928.
4. E.g. correspondence in the *Guardian*, 2 Dec 1921, and *The Times*, 24 Nov 1926.
5. *The Torch*, July 1927.
6. *Portsmouth and Hampshire County Times*, 23 May 1924.
7. Ruth Kenyon, 'Does the Church stand for a living wage?' *League of the*

Kingdom of God, Pamphlet No. 1, 1927.

8. Norman, *Church and Society, op cit*, p. 321.
9. Ruth Kenyon, 'Unemployment', *Major Issues of the Day, No 3*, The Christian Social Council.
10. *Guardian*, 5 Nov 1920.
11. *The Times*, 23 Feb 1923.
12. British Empire Exhibition, *Official Catalogue*, 1924.
13. *Executive Minutes*, 14 Dec 1923; 7 Mar, 13 June 1924; *Finance Committee Minutes*, 22 Feb 1924.
14. Barnes, *op cit*, p. 77.
15. Barnes to Kirk, *Sir John Barnes*, Nov 1933.
16. *Derby Daily Express*, 7 May 1921.
17. *The Times*, 19 Nov 1926.
18. *The Times*, correspondence, 27 July, 9, 11, 12, 15, 19, 21, 23 Oct, 19, 24, 29 Nov 1926; leader, 17 Nov 1926.
19. *Rugby Observer*, 6 May 1921; *Guardian*, 27 May, 7, 24 June 1921.
20. *Coventry Standard*, 15 June 1923.
21. *Coventry Herald*, 18–19 May 1923.
22. *Coventry Herald*, editorial and 'Critic on the Hearth', 15–16 June 1923.
23. *R. T. Davidson Papers*.
24. *Guardian*, 7 Dec 1920.
25. E.g. *Patriot*, Dec 1922, 19 June 1926; *Morning Post*, 13 Dec 1922; 30 May 1923; 3 Mar 1926.
26. *The Times*, leader, 17 Nov 1926.
27. *Spectator*, 10 Apr 1926. Cutting with *Davidson papers*.
28. *Spectator*, 24 July 1926.
29. *Spectator*, 11, 18 Aug 1923.
30. *Southport Visitor*, 7 Oct 1926; *Southport Guardian*, 9 Oct 1926.
31. Sermon preached at Annual Service of the ICF at St Martin-in-the-Fields, 27 Jan 1926. Copy with *Davidson papers*.
32. *Christianity and Economics*, by the Master of Balliol, being a reply to the pamphlet 'Economics and Christianity' by the Rt Rev. Arthur C. Headlam, CH, DD, Bishop of Gloucester, the Industrial Christian Fellowship, 1927.
33. *Ibid*, p. 6.
34. *Church Times*, 30 Apr 1920; 6 May 1921.
35. E.g. *The Birmingham Businessman: the official organ of the Birmingham Business Club*, W. Hill, 'Restriction of output: the problem and its solution', Oct 1918; T. C. Taylor, 'Profit sharing and Labour copartnership', Nov 1918; J. D. Stevens, 'Bridging the Gulf', July 1920.
36. *Ibid*, Nov 1921, p. 75.
37. J. W. Tuffley, *Grain from Galilee: the romance of the Brotherhood Movement* (Headley, 1935).
38. Peter Clarke, 'Whipping the Wicked', review of *The Optimists: themes and personalities in Victorian Liberalism*, by Ian Bradley (Faber, 1980), in *London Review of Books*, 17 Apr 1980.
39. C. G. Ammon, 'The Road to Jericho', in C. G. Ammon (ed.), *Christ and Labour*, Addresses under the auspices of the Oakley Place Brotherhood (London, 1912).

40. *The Brotherhood Outlook*, Oct 1920; Feb, Oct 1922; Sept 1924; Oct 1927; Dec 1928.
41. S. Baldwin, *Democracy Old and New*, John Clifford Lecture for 1930 (Brotherhood Movement, 1930); J. Stamp, *Internationalism*, John Clifford Lecture for 1931 (Brotherhood Movement, 1931).
42. *The Brotherhood Outlook*, Oct 1921, p. 141; *Derby Daily Telegraph*, 18 Apr 1921.
43. *The Brotherhood Outlook*, July 1920; Apr 1921; Oct 1927.
44. *Ibid*, Oct, Nov 1927.
45. *Trade Union Congress Report*, 1921, p. 418.
46. *Church Times*, 11 Sept 1921.
47. W. L. Hichens, 'The Principles by which Wages are determined', *The British Association Annual Meeting*, Edinburgh, Sept 1921.
48. *South Wales Journal of Commerce*, 12 Sept 1921.
49. *Church Times*, 18 Sept 1922.
50. *Hull Times*, 6 Sept 1924.
51. *Edinburgh Evening News*, 6 Sept 1927.
52. *Church Times*, 12 July 1929.
53. A. L. Lee, *Origins of the Popular Press in England, 1855–1914* (Croom Helm, 1976) pp. 133 ff.
54. H. Pelling, *Social Geography of British Elections* (Macmillan, 1967).
55. *Guardian*, 30 Oct 1919.
56. Barnes to Kirk, 22 Sept 1926. *Sir John Barnes*.
57. R. P. Hastings, 'Birmingham' in Jeffrey Skelley (ed.), *The General Strike, 1926* (Lawrence and Wishart, 1976).
58. Guy T. Rogers, *The Church and the People* (London, 1930) Ch 5, 'Lessons from the Birmingham Crusade'; *Birmingham Post*, 23 May–2 June 1930; *Birmingham Gazette*, 26, 29 May 1930.
59. *Derby Daily Telegraph*, 19 Apr 1921.
60. *Bristol Evening News*, 4 May 1925.
61. Various reports in *The Torch*.
62. *Derby Daily Telegraph*, 23 Apr 1921.
63. *Derby Daily Express*, 21 Apr 1921.
64. *Derby Daily Telegraph*, 25 Apr 1921.
65. *Derby Daily Express*, 19 Apr 1921.
66. *Ibid*, 2 May 1921.
67. W. A. Millington, 'Communism or Communion', *The Torch*, May 1922.
68. *News* and *Barrow Guardian*, 17 Sept 1921.
69. *Ibid*, 24 Sept 1921.
70. *Church Times*, 30 Sept 1921.
71. *Barrow Guardian*, 8 Oct 1921.
72. *Ibid*, 1 Oct 1921.
73. *Staffordshire Sentinel*, 18 Oct 1923.
74. Pelling, *op cit*, pp. 270 ff.; F. Bealey, J. Blondel and W. P. McCann, *Constituency Politics: a study of Newcastle-under-Lyme* (Free Press, 1965) p. 82; F. W. S. Craig, *British Parliamentary Election Statistics, 1918–1949* (Macmillan, 1977) p. 253.
75. *Staffordshire Sentinel*, 18 Oct 1923.
76. *Ibid*, 10, 12, 15, 16, 17, 18, 19, 22 Oct 1923.

77. *Croydon Advertiser and Surrey County Reporter*, 7, 14, 21 Feb 1925; *Croydon Times*, 11 Feb 1925.
78. *Weekly Argus*, 16 June 1928.
79. T. Brennan, E. W. Cooney and H. Pollins, *Social Change in South West Wales* (Watts, 1954); K. O. Morgan, *Wales in British Politics, 1862–1922* (Cardiff University, 1963); Colloquium on Welsh Labour History, *SSLH Bulletin*, No 23, Autumn, 1921.
80. *Weekly Argus*, 23 June 1928.
81. *South Wales Gazette*, 15 June 1928.
82. *Birkenhead News*, 10 Mar 1928, 'Ace of the ICF: The Rev Studdert Kennedy at Tunstall: The need for strong men'; *Hampshire Telegraph and Post*, 23 May 1924, 'Woodbine Willie talks to Dockyard men; Good men wanted'.
83. *Cornish Echo*, 13 July 1928; *Amman Valley Chronicle and East Carmarthen News*, 18 Oct 1928; *Barry and District News*, 23 Nov 1928; *Carlisle Journal*, 27 Nov 1928.
84. *Croydon Advertiser and Surrey County Reporter*, 14 Feb 1925.
85. Liverpool Echo, 24 Mar 1924, 'Woodbine Willie's Week; famous padre's lenten discourses'; 26 Mar 1924, 'Political mind and chaos: it is based upon God knows what: Woodbine Willie's address'; *Birkenhead and Cheshire Advertiser and Wallasey Guardian*, 29 Mar 1924, 'Industrial Troubles: Woodbine Willie's inspiring address: competition for service'.
86. *Weston-super-Mare Gazette*, 20 Nov 1926, 'Woodbine Willie: trenchant speech at Weston Town Hall: The Coal Dispute'; *Oxford Times*, 2 Dec 1926, 'Religion and Rationalism: man compared with the animals'; *Birkenhead News*, 16 Mar 1927, 'Sentiment and Political Economy: Woodbine Willie and lying propaganda'; *Wallasey and Wirral Times*, 18 Mar 1927, 'Sentiment in Economics: Is Woodbine Willie a Communist?'; *Pudsey Advertiser*, 6 May 1926, 'Sense and Sentiment in argument: Woodbine Willie on facing the facts'.
87. *Weston-super-Mare Gazette*, 20 Nov 1927.
88. *South Wales Gazette*, 23 Sept 1927, 'Woodbine Willie in Abertillery'.
89. *Weston-super-Mare Gazette*, 22 Oct 1927.
90. *Amman Valley Chronicle*, 22 July 1926.
91. *Pudsey Advertiser*, 9 May 1924, 'Wit and wisdom of Woodbine Willie; The Rev G. A. Studdert Kennedy at Pudsey: Democracy and Despair: How mental pictures determine actions'.
92. *Ibid*, 14 May 1926.
93. *Mansfield and Notts Advertiser*, 24 Sept 1926.
94. *Cromer Post*, 12 June 1925, 'A Modern Prophet: Woodbine Willie at Cromer'.
95. *Southport Visitor*, 23 July 1925, 'Visit of Woodbine Willie: Darwinism and Marxism condemned'; *Birmingham Gazette*, 3 Mar 1926; *Yorkshire Post*, 18 Feb 1926; 'Leeds Wesleyan Mission: Woodbine Willie on Modern Madness'; *Stockport County Borough Express*, 18 Mar 1926, 'Passion and Politics'; *Mansfield and Kirkby Chronicle*, 23 Sept 1926, 'Woodbine Willie and Common sense'; *Merthyr Express*, 31 Mar 1928.
96. *Chorley Guardian and Leyland Hundred Advertiser*, 17 Mar 1928; *South Wales*

Gazette, 23 Sept 1927; *Accrington Gazette*, 17 Oct 1925, 'Woodbine Willie on Past and Future: Cannot do without Capital'.
97. *Edinburgh Evening Dispatch*, 6 Sept 1927, 'Gasbags no good; Woodbine Willie tired of agitators'.
98. Purcell, *op cit*, Ch IX, 'That's All'.

CHAPTER 8. TOWARD THE CITY OF GOD

1. *The Times*, 16 June 1921.
2. *Church Times*, 24 June 1921.
3. *The Times*, 28 Apr 1921.
4. *Guardian*, 20 May 1921.
5. Rowland, *op cit*, p. 534.
6. E.g. *Lichfield Diocesan Magazine*, 'The Bishop's Letter' May and June 1921; 'The Bishop's Address to the Lichfield Diocesan Conference', Dec 1922.
7. W. R. Garside, *The Durham Miners, 1919–1960* (Allen and Unwin, 1971) p. 137.
8. *Ibid*, Ch III, 'The Sankey Commission and Industrial Unrest', Ch IV, 'The 1921 Lock-out'.
9. *Ibid*, Ch V, 'The origins and course of the 1926 dispute'.
10. Everard Hesketh, *J. and E. Hall Ltd, 1785–1935* (Glasgow University Press, 1935).
11. D. Carnegie, *Can Church and Industry Unite?, op cit.*
12. Rodger Charles, SJ, *The Development of Industrial Relations in Britain, 1911–1939* (Hutchinson, 1973) pp. 88–9.
13. Max Muspratt, 'Industry and Property—I'; R. H. Tawney, 'Industry and Property—II', *The Pilgrim*, Vol 5 No 1, 1924.
14. J. H. Jones, *Josiah Stamp: Public Servant* (Pitman, 1964) p. 168.
15. Allan Bullock, *The Life and Times of Ernest Bevin*, Vol. 1 (Heinemann, 1960) Ch 6.
16. A. P. Thornton, *The Habit of Authority: Paternalism in British History* (Allen and Unwin, 1966) p. 326.
17. Macassey, *Labour Policy, op cit.*
18. *Ibid*, p. 30.
19. *Ibid*, p. 19.
20. *Transport Workers—Court of Inquiry, Report of Minutes and Evidence of the Inquiry*, Cd. 936, 1920, e.g. pp. 107 ff.
21. Macassey, *op cit*, p. 79.
22. L. Hichens, 'The Gospel in Business', Address delivered to the Church Congress at Sheffield, 12 Oct 1922, *Journal of Commerce*, 13 Oct 1922.
23. J. D'E Firth, *Winchester College* (Winchester Publications, 1949) p. 190; R. Hamilton (ed.), *Budge Firth: a memoir and some sermons* (P. and G. Wells, 1960).
24. W. L. Hichens, *The Foundation Oration*, 1929, Birkbeck College.
25. *Sheffield Telegraph*, 12 Nov 1919, 'Capital and Labour: Mr Hichens discusses the duty of both'. Some occasions in the immediate post-war period when Hichens discussed the place of Christianity in modern industry are reported in the *Sussex Daily News*, 3 May 1918; *Yorkshire Herald*, 17 Dec 1918; *Sheffield Telegraph*, 16 Feb 1920; *Daily Telegraph*, 16

July 1920; *Journal of Commerce*, 22 Nov 1920; *Liverpool Post*, 7 Feb 1920; *Bournemouth Guardian*, and *Bournemouth Times and Directory*, 4 June 1921.

26. A representative selection from Hichens's output on these themes: *Journal of Commerce*, 10 Jan 1917, 'Education and Business: address delivered to the Incorporated Association of Head Masters; *Mimeo*, 'Introductory Speech at Conference of Boy's Welfare Supervisors', Ministry of Munitions, 26 Oct 1917; *Organiser*, August 1918, 'The limitations of State interference'; *Sheffield Telegraph*, 29 Sept 1918, Report on Foremen's Fraternal Dinner; 'Industrial Reconstruction Council Lecture', 30 Oct 1918; *The Royal Society of Arts*, 'The Wage Problem in Industry', 26 Feb 1919; *Mimeo*, 'State trading', address at St Martin-in-the-Fields, 4 July 1919; *Financial News*, 7 Oct 1921, interview; *Evening Standard*, 31 Oct 1919, interview; *Mimeo*, 'What principles should guide arbitrators in making awards?' Lecture to Political Economy Club, 1 Dec 1920; *Mimeo*, 'Private Enterprise or Individualism in Industry', Lecture to Department of Industrial Administration, College of Technology, Manchester, 25 Jan 1921; *Morning Post*, 7 July 1921; *Weekly Dispatch*, 23 Oct 1921, 'Joint Move to Revive Industry'; *Westminster Gazette*, 10 Dec 1921, 'World Financial Crisis'; *Observer*, 23 Oct 1921, interview; *Evening Standard*, 27 Jan 1922; *Lloyds Sunday News*, 10 Sept 1922, interview; *Liverpool Post*, 8 Nov 1922, comment in support of Sir Leslie Scott as a first-class business candidate for Parliament; *Westminister Gazette*, 6 Jan 1923, 'A trade revival'; *Industrial Welfare*, Oct 1923, 'The Partners in industry'; *Journal of Commerce*, 6 Nov 1923, speech at Birkenhead Chamber of Commerce Annual Dinner; *Financial News*, 8 Mar 1924, comment on coal; *Westminster Gazette*, 20 Sept 1924, interview on lost shipbuilding contracts; *Yorkshire Observer*, 9 May 1924, address on industrial research; *Daily Mirror*, 22 Apr 1925, interview; *Journal of the Institute of Bankers*, Dec 1925, 'The Development of our Overseas Trade'; *Mimeo*, Address at ILP Summer School on improving engineering industry, Aug 1924; *Birmingham Post*, 1 May 1926, speech to Birmingham Chartered Accountants; *Belfast Evening Telegraph*, 31 May 1927, interviews with Sir Lynden Macassey, Sir A. Mond and W. L. Hichens; *Cost Accountant*, Nov 1927, a report; *Sheffield Telegraph*, 23 Oct 1928, lecture on rationalisation; *Accountant*, 24 Nov 1928, 'How far should the policy of rationalisation be applied to British industries?'; *Journal of the Royal Sanitary Institute*, 1929, Presidential Address; *Manchester Statistical Society*, 12 Feb 1930, 'Rationalisation'; *Leicester and County Chamber of Commerce Journal*, July 1933, 'Is the pedestal on which competition has been enthroned tottering?'.

27. P. S. Bagwell, *The Railwaymen; the History of the National Union of Railwaymen* (Allen and Unwin, 1963) p. 521.

28. L. Urwick, *The Meaning of Rationalisation* (London, 1929) p. 156.

29. Wigham, *op cit*, p. 115.

30. J. C. Carr and W. Taplin, *History of the British Steel Industry* (Blackwell, 1962) p. 442.

31. J. R. Hicks, U. K. Hicks and L. Rostas, *The Taxation of War Wealth* (OUP, 1941).

32. Elizabeth Sidney, *The Industrial Society* (London, 1968).

33. Information from Mrs Hichens.
34. *Report of the Fourth Annual Lecture Conference*, Industrial Welfare Society, Sept 14–19, 1923.
35. Robert B. Patterson, 'Lord Milner and Patriotic Labour' *English Historical Review*, LXXXVII, 1972, p. 718.
36. *Clarion*, 9 May 1924; *Sunday Chronicle*, 15 Mar 1925.
37. P. S. Bagwell, 'The Triple Alliance, 1913–1922', in Asa Briggs and John Saville (eds.), *Essays in Labour History, 1886–1932* (Macmillan, 1971).
38. *Grimsby Daily Telegraph*, 14 Oct 1926.
39. Bullock, *op cit*, p. 411.
40. Hichens to Appleton, 21 Feb 1921, *Mrs Hichens*.
41. B. C. Roberts, *The Trade Union Congress, 1868–1921* (Allen and Unwin, 1958) p. 329.
42. R. Lowe, 'The failure of consensus in Britain: the National Industrial Conference, 1919–1921', *Historical Journal*, Vol 21, 3, 1978, p. 650.
43. Charles, *op cit*, p. 239.
44. *Cardiff Times and South Wales Weekly News*, 10 Sept 1921.
45. W. R. Garside, 'Management and Men: aspects of British Industrial Relations in the inter-war period', in Barry Supple (ed.), *Essays in British Business History* (OUP, 1977).
46. Lowe, *op cit*, p. 673.
47. B. A. Waites, 'The effect of the First World War on class and status in England, 1910–1920', *Journal of Contemporary History*, Vol II, 1976, p. 29.
48. F. Hughes, *By Hand and Brain: the story of the Clerical and Administrative Workers Union* (London, 1953).
49. Charles, *op cit*, pp. 147, 206.
50. Information from Mr O. J. Whitley, Miss Whitley's brother.
51. Cowling, *op cit*, pp. 180, 177.
52. Charles Ammon MP, 'The Future of Labour', *Wesleyan Methodist*, 1 Feb 1923.
53. R. F. Wearmouth, *The Social and Political Influence of Methodism in the Twentieth Century* (London, 1957) p. 170.
54. M. A. Hamilton, *op cit*. p. 215.
55. Lowe, *loc cit*; S. Armitage, *The Politics of Decontrol of Industry* (Weidenfeld and Nicolson, 1969).
56. Paul Abrams, 'The Failure of Social Reform: 1918–1920', *Past and Present*, Apr 1963, p. 58.
57. James Hinton, *The First Shop Stewards' Movement* (Allen and Unwin, 1973); J. Harris, *William Beveridge* (OUP, 1977) p. 215 ff.; E. Eldon Barry, *Nationalisation in British Politics: the historical background* (Cape, 1965) p. 211.
58. Walter Kendall, *The Revolutionary Movement in Britain, 1900–1921* (Weidenfeld and Nicolson, 1969) p. 295.
59. Barry, *op cit*, p. 186.
60. F. Brockway, *Bermondsey Story: the Life of Alfred Salter* (London, 1949) p. 31; *Wesleyan Methodist*, 7 Feb 1924.
61. Webb, *Diaries*, *op cit*, 1 Dec 1919.
62. Bullock, *op cit*, p. 9.
63. S. Koss, *Nonconformity in Modern British Politics* (Batsford, 1975) p. 172.
64. F. Hughes, *Socialism and the Human Soul* (John Bale, 1931).

65. G. D. H. Cole, *Labour in the Coal Mining Industry* (Oxford, 1923) p. 78.
66. Frank Hodges, *My Adventures as a Labour Leader* (Newnes, 1925).
67. R. Page Arnot, *South Wales Miners* (Allen and Unwin, 1967) p. 169.
68. Joyce M. Bellamy and John Saville, *Dictionary of Labour Biography*, Vol III (Macmillan, 1976).
69. Barry, *op cit*, pp. 240–1.
70. Garside, *Durham Miners*, *op cit*, p. 147.
71. Armitage, *op cit*, p. 71.
72. Bagwell in Briggs (ed.), *loc cit*.
73. A. M. Scott, *Diaries*, 13 May 1922; Webb, *Diaries*, 28 July 1927.
74. Frank Hodges, *Nationalisation of the Mines* (London, 1920).
75. Richard Lyman, *The First Labour Government, 1924* (Chapman and Hall, 1957) p. 149.
76. Cowling, *op cit*, pp. 67 ff.
77. Lord Henry Bentinck, *Tory Democracy* (Methuen, 1918).
78. J. F. C. Harrison, *A History of the Working Men's College, 1854–1954* (Routledge and Kegan Paul, 1954) p. 160.
79. *The Working Men's College Journal*, XV–XX, 1917–28.
80. Charles, *op cit*, p. 272, and Part Four *passim*.
81. Garside in Supple (ed.), *loc cit*, p. 259.
82. G. W. McDonald and Howard F. Gospel, 'The Mond–Turner Talks, 1927–1933: a study in industrial co-operation', *Historical Journal*, XVL, 4, 1973, 807–29.
83. *Derby Daily Express*, 25 Jan 1929; *British Association*, *loc cit*, 1921.
84. G. H. Frodsham, 'The Church and Nationalism', sermon at University of Cambridge, *Guardian*, 19 June 1919; 'The King and the Empire', sermon, *Guardian*, 28 May 1920.
85. Lyman, *op cit*, pp. 174 ff.
86. E.g. W. L. Hichens, 'Hours and Wages in relation to Employment', Address at ILO Conference, Mar 1924, under auspices of League of Nations Union; *Towards Industrial Peace*, Report of League of Nations Union Conference, at the LSE, 1–14 Feb 1927, on Systems of Fixing Minimum Wages and Methods of Conciliation and Arbitration.
87. Martin Gilbert and Richard Gott, *The Appeasers* (Weidenfeld and Nicolson, 1963); Martin Gilbert, *The Roots of Appeasement* (Weidenfeld and Nicolson, 1966); Neville Thompson, *The anti-appeasers: conservative opposition to appeasement in the 1930s* (OUP, 1971).
88. *The Wesleyan Methodist*, 17 Apr 1924, on Studdert Kennedy's COPEC speech.
89. Letter from Hichens to Mrs Alfred Lyttleton, discussing international arbitration, 28 Mar 1934; J. E. Wrench, *Geoffrey Dawson and our Times* (London, 1955) p. 75; A. L. Rowse, *All Souls and Appeasement* (Macmillan, 1961).
90. Sir Frederick Maurice, 'International disarmament', in *Essays in Liberalism*, papers delivered at Liberal Summer School, 1922 (Collins, 1922).
91. M. Cowling, *The Impact of Hitler* (CUP, 1975) p. 199.
92. Gilbert and Gott, *op cit*, p. 160; Graham Wootton, *The Official History of the British Legion* (Macdonald and Evans, 1956) Ch XXIX.

93. *Pilgrim*, Oct 1920.

CHAPTER 9. CONCLUSION

  1. Max Weber, *The Protestant Ethic and the Spirit of Capitalism*, Foreword by R. H. Tawney (Allen and Unwin, 1927); R. H. Tawney, *Religion and the Rise of Capitalism*, *op cit*.
  2. Ernest Gellner, 'Concepts and Society', in *Cause and Meaning in the Social Sciences* (Routledge and Kegan Paul, 1973) p. 19.
  3. Oliver, *op cit*, p. v.
  4. Albert O. Hirschman, *The Passions and the Interests; Political arguments for capitalism before its triumph* (Princeton, 1977), p. 129.
  5. *The Torch*, Jan 1929, p. 16.
  6. A. W. Wright, *G. D. H. Cole and Socialist Democracy* (OUP, 1979) p. 143.
  7. *Ibid*, p. 97.
  8. *Ibid*, p. 51: S. Beer, *Modern British Politics* (London, 1969).
  9. Gianfranco Poggi, *The Development of the Modern State* (Hutchinson, 1978) Ch VI, 'State and Society under Liberalism and after'.
 10. Kenneth Young, *Stanley Baldwin* (Weidenfeld and Nicolson, 1976) p. 45 and *passim*: Middlemas and Barnes, *op cit*, pp. 170, 609–11; *Manchester Guardian*, 28 July 1923.

Selective Bibliography of Publications by leading supporters of the Industrial Christian Fellowship

A. BOOKS BY THE REV. G. A. STUDDERT KENNEDY

All were published by Hodder and Stoughton. (Abbreviations employed in the text are given in brackets.)

PROSE
Rough Talks by a Padre, delivered to Officers and Men of the BEF, 1918. (*RT*)
The Hardest Part, 1918. (*HP*)
Lies, 1919. (*L*)
Democracy and the Dog Collar, 1921. (*DDC*)
Food for the Fed Up, 1921. (*FFU*)
The Wicket Gate, 1923. (*WG*)
The Word and the Work, 1925. (*WW*)
I Pronounce Them, 1927.(novel).
The Warrior, the Woman and The Christ, 1928. (*WWC*)
The New Man in Christ, 1932. Mainly Retreat addresses, hitherto unpublished. W. Moore Ede (ed.).
The Best of G. A. Studdert Kennedy, 1947. Anthology of Prose and Verse.

VERSE
Rough Rhymes of a Padre, 1918.
More Rough Rhymes of a Padre, 1919.
Peace Rhymes of a Padre, 1920.
The Sorrows of God, 1921. Collected verse,
Songs of Faith and Doubt, 1922.
Lighten our Darkness, some less rough rhymes of a padre, 1925.
The Unutterable Beauty, 1927. Collected Verse. Reissued as *Rhymes* (7 edns 1929–34).
The Rhymes of G. A. Studdert Kennedy, 1940.

B. PUBLICATIONS BY OTHER CLERICS

J. G. Adderley, *In Slums and Society* (London, 1916).
W. Bainbridge-Bell, *Repentance and Perseverance* (London, 1902).

F. R. Barry, *Christianity and Psychology* (SCM, 1923).

L. E. Binns, *The Evangelical Movement in the English Church* (Methuen, 1928).

——, *Mr Wells' Invisible King* (SPCK, 1919).

F. L. Boyd (ed.), *Tasks and Visions* (Mowbray, 1917).

——, *Law and Love* (London, 1909).

E. A. Burroughs, *A Faith for the Firing Line*, two addresses to officers of the BEF at Rouen, together with a sermon preached in the chapel of the British Headquarters there (Nisbet, 1915).

——, *The Patience of God*, some thoughts in preparation for the National Mission of Repentance and Hope (Longmans, 1916).

——, 'Evangelicalism and Personality' in T. G. Rogers (ed.), *Liberal Evangelicalism* (Hodder and Stoughton, 1923).

——, 'The Church in the World' in *The Inner Life: Essays in Liberal Evangelicalism*, 2nd Series, 1925.

A. J. Carlyle, 'Religion and Wages', *Pan Anglican Papers* (London, 1908).

W. H. Carnegie, *Churchmanship and Character* (Murray, 1909).

——, *Democracy and Christian Doctrine* (Macmillan, 1914).

——, *Democracy and Personal Leadership* (Macmillan, 1916).

——, *Personal Religion and Politics* (Murray, 1920).

——, *Anglicanism, an introduction to its history and philosophy* (Putnam, 1925).

S. C. Carpenter, *Let God arise: the challenge of the National Mission to Catholic Churchmen* (Longmans, 1916).

——, *Supernatural Religion in its relation to Democracy* (London, 1932).

F. Lewis Donaldson, 'The Unemployed', *Pan Anglican Papers* (London, 1908).

A. J. Talbot Easter, *Sermons* (Sheffield, 1931).

W. Moore Ede, *The attitude of the Church to some of the social problems of town life* (CUP, 1896).

C. F. Garbett, *The Church and Modern Problems* (London, 1911).

——, 'The seed ground of the revolutionary', Bishop's Letter, *Southwark Diocesan Gazette*, Nov 1925.

C. Gore, 'Christianity and Socialism', *Pan Anglican Papers* (London, 1908).

——, *The Sermon on the Mount* (Murray, 1910).

——, 'Strikes and Locks-out' *Present Day Papers*, no 1, 1926.

——, *Christ and Society* (Allen and Unwin, 1928).

——, *The Reconstruction of Belief* (Murray, 1926).

B. M. Hancock, *My Vote*, privately published.

M. M. Firth and A. W. Hopkinson, *The Tolpuddle Martyrs* (Martin Hopkinson, 1934).

A. W. Hopkinson, *Pastor's Progress* (London, 1958).

——, *Hope; reflections of an optimist on the psychology of holiness, happiness and health* (London, 1923).

J. A. Kempthorne, *Pastoral Life and Work Today* (Longmans, 1919).

W. P. G. McCormick, *Be of Good Cheer* (Longmans Green, 1930).

F. B. Macnutt (ed.), *The Church in the Furnace* (Macmillan, 1917).

——, *From Chaos to God* (London, 1929).

J. Merrin, *Pressing Problems* (SPCK, 1915).

S. Nowell-Rostron, *The Church*, pamphlet, 1944.

T. W. Pym, *Psychology and the Christian Life* (SCM, 1921).

C. E. Raven, *Christian Socialism, 1848–54* (Macmillan, 1920).

Dog-collar Democracy

T. G. Rogers (ed.), *Liberal Evangelicalism* (Hodder and Stoughton, 1923).
———, *The Church and the People* (London, 1930).
H. R. L. Sheppard, *The Impatience of a Parson* (Hodder and Stoughton, 1927).
W. Temple, *The Nature of Personality* (Macmillan, 1911).
———, (ed), *The Industrial Unrest and the Living Wage*, (London, 1913).
———, *The Faith and Modern Thought* (Macmillan, 1913).
———, *Studies in the Spirit and Truth of Christianity* (Macmillan, 1914).
———, *Mens Creatrix* (Macmillan, 1917).
———, *Christus Veritas* (Macmillan, 1924).
———, *Personal Religion and the life of Fellowship* (Longmans, 1926).
———, *Essays in Christian Politics and kindred subjects* (Longmans, 1927).
———, *Christianity and the State* (Macmillan, 1928).
H. A. Wilson, 'Problems and opportunities in church life today', Preliminary Charge as Bishop of Chelmsford (London, 1930).
T. F. Woods, *A new Fellowship in Industry* (SPCK, 1918).
———, *The Great Fellowship; last message as Bishop of Peterborough* (Hodder and Stoughton, 1924).
E. S. Woods and F. B. Macnutt, *Theodore Bishop of Winchester* (SPCK, 1933).

C. Publications by laymen

E. N. Bennett, *Problems of Village Life* (Home University Library, 1914).
Lord Henry Bentinck, *Tory Democracy* (Methuen, 1918).
David Carnegie, *Can Church and Industry Unite?* (London, 1920).
D. Eyre, 'Christianity and Socialism: What is now practicable?' *Pan Anglican Papers* (London, 1908).
E. Hesketh, *J. and A. Hall Ltd* (Glasgow University Press, 1935).
L. Hichens, 'Some Problems of Modern Industry', *Papers of the Greenock Philosophical Society* (London, 1918).
Frank Hodges, *Nationalisation of the Mines* (London, 1920).
———, *My adventures as a Labour Leader* (London, 1925).
F. Hughes, *Socialism and the Human Soul* (Bale, 1931).
Sheila Kay-Smith, *Anglo-Catholicism* (Chapman and Hall, 1925).
R. Kenyon, 'Does the Church stand for a living wage?' *League of the Kingdom of God*, Pamphlet No 1, 1927.
———, 'Unemployment', *Major Issues of the Day No 3*, Christian Social Council, n.d.
———, 'Fascism and Christianity', *ICF Pamphlet*. n.d.
E. C. P. Lascelles and S. S. Bullock, *Dock Labour and Decasualisation* (London, 1924).
A. D. Lindsay, *Christianity and Economics* (London, 1927).
———, *The State, the Church and the Community* (King, 1927).
Lynden Macassey, Cd 8136, 'Report on the Clyde Munitions Workers by the Rt Hon Lord Balfour of Burleigh and Mr Lynden Macassey', *Reports from Commissioners, Inspectors and others, 1914–16*, Vol 25.
———, 'The National Wage Position', *The Nineteenth Century*, Nov 1920.
———, *Labour Policy—False and True* (Butterworth, 1922).

Sir Frederick Maurice, 'International disarmament', in *Essays in Liberalism* (Collins, 1922).

——, *Haldane 1857–1955*, 2 vols (Faber and Faber, 1937).

E. Picton-Turbervill, *Christ and International Life* (Morgan and Scott, 1921).

——, *Musings of a Laywoman on the Life of the Churches* (Murray, 1919).

——, *Christ and Woman's Power* (Morgan Scott, 1919).

H. Slesser, *A History of the Liberal Party* (Hutchinson, 1944).

——, *The Law in Relation to Trade Unions* (Nisbet, 1921).

——, (with A. Henderson Jr), *Industrial Law* (London, 1924).

Constance Smith, *The Case for Wage Boards* (London, 1908).

——, *Children as Wage Earners* (SPCK, 1908).

C. Smith and G. Tuckwell, *The Workers Handbook* (Duckworth, 1908).

G. Tuckwell, 'The human interest in industry', *Fortnightly Review*, 19 July 1919.

——, *The State and its Children* (Methuen, 1894).

——, 'The regulation of women's work', in *Women in Industry; from seven points of view* (Duckworth, 1908).

Index

Scott, A. M., 182, 203, 210
Scott Holland, H., 4, 5, 8, 10–11, 46,
    64, 77, 78, 131
Scott Lidgett, J., 152
Scott-Moncrieff, General Sir G. K.,
    18
Searle, P. R., 198
Scrutiny, 108
Seeley, J. R., 60, 198
Selwyn, E. G., 197
Selwyn College, 57
Semmell, B., 26, 194, 198
Shaftesbury Society, 138
Shakespeare, J. M., 53
Shannon, R. T., 198
Shaw, B., 79, 201
Shaw Inquiry, *see* Industry
Sheffield, ix, 20, 44, 139, 151, 172
Sheppard, H. R. L., 58, 147, 185
Sidney, E., 208
Silkin, J., 111, 201, 202, 203
Sinker, J., 203
Sitwell, O., 199
Skelley, J., 205
Slesser, Sir Henry, 29–31, 156, 194
Smillie, R., 181
Smith, A. L., 76
Smith, C., 198
Smith, Constance, 37, 184, 195, 198
Smith, D. ('Navvy'), ix, 17, 18, 19,
    104, 145, 152
Smith, H., 135, 181
Smith, M. L., 157
Smith, O. H., 29
Snowden, P., 12, 146–7, 173, 182
Social Credit, 136
Socialism, 5, 10–15, 19, 25–6, 29, 32,
    39, 46, 88, 99, 102, 103, 124,
    139–41, 151–63, 173, 177–82,
    189–91
Socialist National Defence
    Committee, 175
Soffer, R., 202
South Africa, 24–6, 38, 64, 90, 113,
    140
Southport, 162
Spectator, 141
Spencer, H., 97, 101
Spoor, B., 147, 149, 154, 179

Stacy, P., 29
Stamp, Sir Josiah, 146, 168, 173, 205
Stanton, A., 10
Stead, C. K., 109, 202, 203
Stockport, 151–2, 171
Stokes, D., 192
Strachey, John St Loe, 141
Strikes, *see* Industry
Stuart-Smith, C., 40
Stoke-on-Lyme, 156
Studdert Kennedy, G. A., ix, 6–9, 10,
    109–22, 195, 196, 197, 198, 201,
    202, 203; economics, politics,
    13–14, 19, 36, 63, 69–72, 81–6,
    96–108, 116–19, 139–40, 148,
    157–63, 171, 179–81, 189; Great
    War, 14, 43–74, 93–6, 109–20, 136,
    171, 185; ICF Messenger,
    preacher, 3, 13–15, 40–3, 55–62,
    75, 109, 131, 136, 138, 139–43, 149,
    152–3, 155, 157–63, 171, 179–81;
    psychology, 89, 103–8;
    sacramental theology, 52–3,
    62–74, 81–6, 95–6, 112, 115–16,
    141, 149, 163, 172; sources, 62, 65,
    75–108, 122; verse, publications,
    49, 52, 55–7, 62, 69, 73, 92, 98, 104,
    106, 109–21, 179, 212; *see also*
    Bevin, Davidson, Industrial
    Christian Fellowship, Industry
Studdert Kennedy, W. A., 151
Supple, B., 209, 210
Swinburne, A. C., 110
Symonds, J. A., 76, 141
Syndicalism, 181

Talbot, E. S., 60, 165
Talbot, N., 50, 196
Tanner, E. V., 197
Taplin, W., 174, 208
Tawney, R. H., 75–80, 82, 86, 169,
    172, 186–7, 199, 200, 207, 211
Taylor, A. E., 88, 200
Taylor, Brother, 17, 19
Temple, W., ix, 3, 7, 9, 10, 13, 14, 36,
    40, 52, 66, 75–9, 86–96, 107, 122,
    135, 141–3, 160–1, 168, 175, 185,
    191, 200, 201, 202, 203, 211
Teeside, 151